D1265788

AN INTRODUCTION TO
The Theatre

BY FRANK M. WHITING
PROFESSOR OF SPEECH AND THEATRE ARTS, UNIVERSITY OF MINNESOTA

Harper & Brothers PUBLISHERS, NEW YORK

AN INTRODUCTION TO THE THEATRE

Copyright, 1954, by Harper & Brothers

Printed in the United States of America. All rights in this book are re-
served. No part of the book may be used or reproduced in any manner
whatsoever without written permission except in the case of brief quota-
tions embodied in critical articles and reviews. For information address
Harper & Brothers, 49 East 33rd Street, New York 16, N.Y.

G-D

73133

792
W598i

Library of Congress catalog card number: 54–8592

CONTENTS

LIST OF ILLUSTRATIONS

These illustrations follow page 80

List of Illustrations

List of Illustrations

List of Illustrations

List of Illustrations

List of Illustrations

PREFACE

HIS BOOK ATTEMPTS TO COMPRESS BETWEEN THE COVERS OF A SINGLE volume a brief but comprehensive view of the theatre in the belief that it is wise for the beginning student of the theatre to examine the whole before plunging into a detailed study of any one of the numerous arts and crafts that comprise the complex fabric of stage art.

Part one is concerned with plays and playwrights, for the play is the theatre's central and enduring core. Live acting is recorded only in the memories of those who experience it. Scenery, lights, and props are struck after the final performance; playhouses fall into decay, but the script remains to provide an enduring link with the past. Part Two considers acting and directing: acting because the actor is even older and more indispensable to theatre than the playwright, and directing because the director, especially in the modern theatre, is the central and unifying force in transforming the play from the script into a living production. Part Three considers the architects, artists, and craftsmen who provide the environment in which the actors perform, while Part Four is a short chapter on the theatre as a profession.

Needless to say, however, the hope is that any division into parts will not prevent the reader from gaining an overall view of the theatre as a complex but organic whole. Divisions whether based on subject matter, geography, or chronology, are a matter of arbitrary convenience, and all have their inherent advantages and disadvantages. So vast is the subject of theatre that even a lifetime of study cannot hope to exhaust possibilities for further discovery. Consequently, in writing *An Introduction to the Theatre* the problem has not been one of finding things to say, but rather of deciding what to leave unsaid. Therefore it was arbitrarily decided that the book should concentrate on the legitimate theatre of Western civilization, ignoring the Oriental theatre and the related arts of opera, dance, variety, motion picture, radio, and television. For the sake of condensation, it has been necessary to employ generalizations and some didacticism, while the exceptions that such sweeping statements frequently arouse have had to be ignored. The temptation to be original rather than fundamental, to advance new ideas and theories at the expense of those that are well established and basic, has also been avoided. Yet in spite of such limitations it is hoped that the conscientious reader will upon finishing the book have gained a fundamental knowledge of theatre that will need no serious revision as he progresses to a more detailed consideration of any one of the arts and crafts that through combined effort make up the whole.

As to acknowledgments I am at a loss to know where to begin. Consciously or unconsciously one borrows practically everything from somebody. A special word of gratitude is probably due to Constantin Stanislavski, Allardyce Nicoll, John Dolman Jr., John Gassner, Sheldon Cheney, and George Freedley, whose books I have used as texts for so many years that I am often quite unaware whether an idea originated with one of them or with me. I am indebted to George Freedley and his staff at the Theatre Collection of the New York Public Library for their extraordinary courtesy in assisting with the problem of illustrations. Gratitude is likewise due to many of my former teachers, especially Maud May Babcock, Frank M. Rarig, and C. Lowell Lees. More particularly I am indebted to Lousene Rousseau for having been my guide through the new world of publication. I am also indebted to Robert E. Moore, David W. Thompson, and Arthur H. Ballet, for having read and criticized the manuscript. Above all I am grateful to my wife Josinette, for without her energy and encouragement the manuscript would never have been completed.

Minneapolis, 1954

F. M. W.

PART ONE

Plays and Playwrights

CHAPTER I

Introduction: Why Theatre?

ONIGHT IN AMERICA OVER 8,000,000 PEOPLE WILL ATTEND MOTION picture theatres, over 80,000,000 will listen to radio, over 45,000,-000 will view television, while fewer than 65,000 will attend the legitimate professional theatre.[1] In the face of such figures one well may ask, "Why write a book about theatre? Is it not like writing a book about the covered wagon in this age of the atom and jet propulsion?"

Were the theatre a mere matter of entertainment, such a question would be difficult to answer, but good theatre is much more than entertainment. In its periods of greatness its playwrights, actors, directors, and designers have sought for the meaning and beauty of existence with the same passion and sincerity that has characterized the work of great scientists, philosophers, and theologians, for in its essence the art of the theatre rests on a common foundation with all learning: on man's capacity to explore, wonder, and reflect. Most of our lives drift by in a hubbub of the trivial, the confused, and the habitual, our vision numbed by the blind staggers of conformity, but occasionally alone on some hilltop under the stars, on the timbered shore of a lake under the northern lights, at the bedside of a sick child, or simply at a glimpse of April's crisp water cress in a hillside spring the trivial, confused, and habitual disappear and an awareness of meaning and beauty sweeps over us. It is with moments such as these that great art deals, and it is primarily with the place of the theatre as an art that this book is concerned.

On the other hand, it would be dishonest to pretend that theatre functions on the level of great art only. In fact, it seems necessary to digress from our main question long enough to point out that few words in the English language have a wider range of connotation than the word "theatre." As an imitation of life it eventually embraces almost everything that

[1] These estimates are of April, 1953, by courtesy of Abel Green, editor of *Variety*.

~ 3 ~

life embraces, including much of life's chaos and confusion. Consider, for example, some of the contradictory attitudes toward it.

To the Greeks the theatre was a religious ritual commanding the devotion of the best minds in the community; to the Romans on the other hand, it eventually became little more than a degraded pleasure, a project by slaves for the titillation of their masters. To the early church the theatre was an evil to be crushed, along with thievery and prostitution; to the same church a few centuries later some of the great mystery and miracle plays became almost holy rites. To many entertainers, from strolling players to television comedians, the theatre has usually been regarded as a means of earning a living through a few jokes and antics designed to catch the momentary fancy of the general public. To great playwrights, on the other hand, it has, as already suggested, provided a means of probing honestly and fearlessly for the meaning of life and mystery of existence. To some parents the theatre is regarded as a disease bound to wreck the personality and character of any child who succumbs to its lures; to many teachers and some psychiatrists it is practically a panacea for all personality and character ills. So the contradictions go, and so they might be extended almost indefinitely.

The amazing scope of the word "theatre" may also be seen by examining the variety of interests that impel college students to register for courses in the subject. Some are English majors concerned primarily with the theatre's literary core. Some are engineers interested in lighting and sound. Some are recreation majors interested in theatre as a source of group entertainment. Some are art majors interested in scenic design. Quite a number have dreams of an acting career in radio or television, and a few are always secretly determined someday to crash one of the Meccas of American success, Broadway or Hollywood.

It is only natural that anything so controversial should be the object of many misconceptions. Among these is the persistent belief, now centuries old, that the theatre is dying. On the surface however, and especially as far as the commercial theatre is concerned, this belief is no longer a misconception, for the second quarter of the twentieth century saw the legitimate theatre dwindle from a business that filled thousands of playhouses into one occupying a mere handful. If we include motion pictures, radio, and television under the term theatre, then the theatre was never so alive, but if we consider legitimate professional productions alone, then its present state of health, from a business standpoint at least, is feeble indeed.

Yet in spite of all this there are still many excellent answers to the ques-

Introduction: Why Theatre?

tion, "Why theatre?" To begin with, the legitimate theatre, unlike its amazing twentieth-century offsprings, has been a powerful influence on human civilization for over 2500 years. To some who distrust anything not of their own generation the theatre's age may brand it as old-fashioned, but to those with true insight the theatre's heritage commands deep respect. Civilization is not a result of the accomplishments of any one generation; it represents the cumulative accomplishments of all ages. Left naked and alone at birth, man would be helpless and ignorant. It is his tremendous inheritance from the past that provides the knowledge and skills that have made him the lord of creation. Each of us owes a staggering debt to those who have gone before, and so it is with the theatre, for although movies, radio, and television have added much that is new, they rely on much more that is old. The things that excite, that move, that cause laughter and tears have changed but little. In spite of the cleverness of modern man most of the greatest plays were written centuries ago. Stability, humility, and wisdom may be gained by a knowledge of the past, and such qualities are needed by those who wish to work in any of the theatre arts. Too many young actors, flushed with their first success, become victims of the cruel delusion that nothing like them was ever seen before. One who knows the long story of the theatre is far more likely to take both public adulation and condemnation in a much calmer frame of mind. No matter, therefore, whether one's interest lies in motion pictures, radio, television, or the legitimate theatre, it is wise to begin by gaining some of the stability and wisdom that lie in a knowledge of the theatre's heritage from the past.

But the theatre not only has age and tradition. In its finer moments it has reached peaks of excellence that stand as some of the finest achievements of mankind. The importance of such achievements by those in theatre as well as by those in the other arts is frequently forgotten. Booth Tarkington once wrote: "A country could be perfectly governed, immensely powerful and without poverty; yet if it produced nothing of its own in architecture, sculpture, music, painting or in books, it would some day pass into the twilight of history, leaving only the traces of a creditable political record."[2] America today faces such a challenge. In wealth, energy, military might, and material power she is magnificent, but in the realm of culture and great ideas she has yet to prove herself. Rome also excelled in most of the ways that America has done: her engineers were without equal; her armed might was supreme; her financiers amassed untold wealth; her politicians

[2] Reprinted from a brochure, *The Indiana University Auditorium,* published in commemoration of the completion of Indiana University's auditorium and theatre in 1941.

wrangled with undignified fervor; her swimming pools and banquets were quite as lavish as those of Hollywood. And yet after approximately five centuries in control of the entire western world Rome left little to excite the mind and admiration of men comparable in lasting glory to the contributions of the little city of Athens, which controlled but a fraction of the earth's surface and held world leadership for less than a century. One Greek play, *King Oedipus,* probably outweighs all the words and deeds of the entire Roman Senate. Were it not for the achievements of her architects, sculptors, and a few of her early Latin poets and philosophers, Rome's reputation today would be sorry indeed.

The theatre or any of the other arts, therefore, is not like the covered wagon or other material things. The wagon once discarded, the banquet once consumed, the automobile once burned out, lose their value, but great art is essentially eternal. "A thing of beauty is a joy forever." Art reaches across the barriers of time and space. It penetrates the barriers of creed, race, and nationality. Through its magic we share experience with Sophocles, Shakespeare, Goethe, Strindberg. *The Trojan Women* and *Lysistrata* have as much significance for belligerent nations today as they had for Athens and Sparta 2500 years ago. *Electra* and *King Lear* have left modern audiences more genuinely and deeply moved than anything our own age has to offer. Present day productions of *The Taming of the Shrew* and *The Merry Wives of Windsor* have provoked gales of laughter that have literally stopped the shows for almost minutes at a time. Styles in the material things of life may change and grow old-fashioned but the fundamental experiences of human nature—the exuberance of youth, the thrill of young love, the sting of ingratitude—these are the heritage and common property of all people and all ages. These are the type of thing with which great art deals. These do not grow old-fashioned.

Without quibbling over which is the greatest of the arts, let us remember that the theatre makes its appeal on two levels, the aesthetic and the intellectual. On the aesthetic level the theatre, like music, painting, and dancing, makes its contribution to the emotional needs of man and to his hunger for the beautiful. On the intellectual level a tremendous proportion of the greatest ideas ever expressed by man have been expressed in dramatic form. We need only remember that students of philosophy study Aeschylus, Goethe, Ibsen, and Shaw as well as Plato, Schopenhauer, Nietzsche, and Dewey. No other branch of human learning can point with pride to a more impressive list of great names. No other field of literature can quite equal the drama in the total extent of its contributions.

Introduction: Why Theatre?

It is odd that in spite of such a heritage, parents should often try to discourage any desire on the part of their children to study the theatre. It is odd that some excellent students who are attracted by theatre should resist their impulse to associate with it because they feel that for some mysterious reason it is not quite respectable. The father of an outstanding theatre major at a large university made life almost unbearable through his insistence that his daughter give up her work on the stage and devote herself to something sensible and "worth while." Finally the director of the theatre was driven out of curiosity to ask, "What does your father do for a living?" The answer was, "He works in a pickle factory." Unfortunately the majority of American parents would probably agree that the production of pickles is a worthy and sensible profession, whereas the art of bringing the greatest masterpieces of our literature to life on the stage somehow borders on the unworthy and the impractical. Human beings are indeed curious creatures.

But the legitimate theatre not only has a long and glorious heritage, it is still important today. Although its quantity is not great in comparison with motion pictures, radio, and television, its quality is still superior. Professor Barnard Hewitt writing in 1952 observes that:

Paradoxically, the prestige of the professional living stage remains largely undiminished. It may in fact be higher than it was in 1900 or even in 1929, for with the decline in the number of plays, the quality on the average has risen. At any rate, the stage wields an influence on the rest of theatre in America out of all proportion to its size and scope. . . . If size, scope, and dollar investment are the criteria, obviously the real professional theatre today is not that of the living actor but of radio, moving pictures, and television. Here is the audience of millions, here is large-scale industry. . . . Nevertheless, the theatre of the mass media does not have the prestige of the professional stage. It is regarded as commercial through and through. The professional stage somehow manages to be regarded as more than commercial—as business but also as art."[3]

One reason for the comparatively high quality of legitimate drama may lie in the quality of its audience. To its sorrow financially but to its credit artistically it has lost most of its audience of tired business men, twelve-year-old intelligences, thrill seekers, and others who regard any form of theatre as a matter of entertainment only. By and large the taste and intelligence of the average Broadway audience today is well above the taste and intelligence of the average audience at a first-rate movie and far above the taste and intelligence of the audience at a second-rate movie. It may be significant that playwrights like Eugene O'Neill arrived on the American

[3] Barnard Hewitt, "Theatre U.S.A.: Actual and Potential," *The Quarterly Journal of Speech,* December, 1952, pp. 385–386.

scene after the movies had begun to drain away the theatre's popular audience.

If this assumption that the quality of the audience has an influence on the quality of the playwriting is correct, then one of the brightest hopes for the future of legitimate drama lies in the outstanding quality of the audience now attending college and university theatres throughout the country. In educational background, in taste and intelligence, and in freedom from undue prejudice the average university and college audience is probably equal or superior to any audience that ever existed. It is an audience that enjoys and understands a good production of Sophocles, Shakespeare, or Strindberg. It is an audience that is not shocked by *Lysistrata, Volpone,* or *Desire Under the Elms.* It is an audience that should challenge and stimulate the best in any serious playwright, and it is an audience large enough to provide a modest income for such a playwright. We can at least hope that these university audiences, plus the high quality of legitimate theatre audiences in general, will eventually stimulate some exciting achievements in playwriting and production.

The final and most inherent advantage that legitimate drama holds over its more prosperous rivals lies in its intimacy. In the theatre the process of stimulation and appreciation functions in two directions at once—from actor to audience and from audience to actor. As a result, something resembling a chain reaction of stimulus and response may reach proportions that can result in an "inspired" performance. With the living actor and an intimate theatre this sharing of experience, which is the essence of art, is heightened to a degree that is difficult to achieve in any mechanical media. In Greece, for example, the production of plays was a matter in which almost the entire community participated. I have always imagined that the great holiday spirit in which the plays were performed was somehow related to the spirit with which my own home town celebrated the Fourth of July in the days before automobiles, oiled roads, and radios made such celebrations too troublesome and old-fashioned. I realize that my memory has surrounded the whole experience with a halo, for it now seems that the weather was always perfect, and that the valley with its river and background of mountains assumed a special beauty in honor of the occasion. There were weeks of planning and preparation. Then came the great day itself, which began officially at sunrise with the parade. First came the grand marshal riding with such dignity that it was hard to believe that he (like everyone else) was one of our neighbors. Then came the mounted color guard followed by the band—not a hired band or a truck wired to play phonograph records—but a band led by the school principal and made up of farmers, ranchers, local merchants, and others who somehow, in addition to all their regular work, had found time to practice at tooting a brass horn or thumping a drum. There were clowns also, and, of course, the numerous patriotic floats—mostly hay wagons transformed by eager energy into tableaux of various patriotic themes.

So the day began and so it continued through the orations, songs, and band music that made up the morning outdoor program, through the afternoon sports climaxed by the annual baseball game between single and married men, and finally into the evening dance—the highlight of the day for the young couples, but an anticlimax to tired, sticky children now beginning to sag to sleep on benches or on the laps of weary mothers. The day stretched from dawn to midnight. Everyone came and stayed to the end—almost everyone, that is. I remember my feeling of pity and wonder regarding one man who never came. I remember one morning when we passed his fields on our way to the celebration and saw him already starting his lonely rounds on the mowing machine. My father muttered something to the effect, "When will he ever learn that money isn't everything?" I doubt that money was the reason that he avoided his neighbors, but to me there was a touch of both mystery and sadness in the fact that anyone could miss the Fourth of July.

I have never convinced myself that the halo that surrounds these boyhood memories of Independence Day is entirely a matter of sentiment and illusion. Modern civilization with its wealth of material things has contributed great values, but in the process other values have been lost. Certainly there is something admirable about sharing together in a creative cause. Certainly there is something admirable about people who can create their own celebrations, their own sports, and their own art.

All this is one of the main reasons why I am devoted to the legitimate theatre, for the theatre is one of the few places where something of the old Fourth of July spirit still survives. Weeks of hard, imaginative work go into a production. Directors, stage crews, actors, and business staff are drawn together around a common goal. Finally comes the realization of the goal as the result of the work is shared with the audience. Laughter, silence, excitement, applause, the warm feeling of respect and mutual admiration for a job well done, the happy crowds backstage—these are things that movies, radio, or television can never quite duplicate.

It is strange that, although intimacy is the one certain element that gives the legitimate theatre an advantage over its rivals, almost nothing has been done to capitalize on this element during the period of the theatre's decline. The general tendency has been to move in the opposite direction toward a more formal and austere actor-audience relationship. Thus the twentieth-century theatre revolted against the old declamatory style of acting; it avoided the asides and soliloquies of old melodrama; many theatres abandoned curtain calls and undue applause; textbooks stressed the importance of aesthetic distance until students were filled with the fear that they might be too convincing rather than with the much more essential fear that they might not be convincing at all; and worst of all, the playhouses tended to grow larger and larger until the distant actor became more impersonal to those in the back half of the house than did the shadows on the movie screen. Ironically almost every major reform tended to drive further apart actor and audience, the chief partners in the theatrical experience.

There have been exceptions, of course. Some community theatres, most summer theatres, and several new educational theatres are fortunate enough to have small, intimate auditoriums. Many community groups have tried to make theatre-going a more friendly and sociable activity by serving tea or coffee during intermissions or after the show. The one really positive step toward intimacy, however, has been the appearance of theatre-in-the-round, and the success of this new form, in spite of its many inherent disadvantages, is perhaps the most convincing evidence we have of the need for a strong bond between actor and audience.

There are many other answers to the question, "Why theatre?" For example, almost everyone agrees that the legitimate theatre offers the best possible training ground for actors. Nothing can teach an actor the finer points of his art so effectively as the spontaneous response of a living audience. Legitimate theatre on a resident basis also offers an opportunity to select and adjust the play to the tastes and needs of a particular audience. Thus a production of Strindberg done for a university with a strong Scandinavian department may provide one of the most exciting evenings of the season, while the same play produced for the average movie-goer would be a total failure. Again *Lysistrata* played for an audience that understands the devastating satire of Aristophanes' attack upon war may be highly moral as well as brilliantly entertaining, whereas the same production viewed by the general public would be censored as shockingly indecent.

Related to this is the fact that legitimate theatre can be far more daring and experimental than its rivals. The comparative cost of producing a play, especially on the noncommercial level, is trivial compared with the cost of producing a movie. Those creative enough to do so can experiment with the production of new scripts, new staging techniques, new acting and directing styles, without encountering the overwhelming hazards, restrictions, and rules of censorship that neutralize so many creative ideas in the realms of motion pictures, radio, and television.

To summarize, the legitimate theatre, because of its long and outstanding history, because of its contribution both to the aesthetic and intellectual needs of man, because of the quality of its audience, because of its strong bond between audience and performer, and finally because of other values such as its effectiveness as a potential area for new experiment, seems destined to live on—especially on the noncommercial level—for another few thousand years. Even should the professional theatre fulfill the ancient predictions of the pessimists by dying, the educational theatre would still be the logical training ground and starting point for the student of any or all theatre arts, for it is the root, the parent, from which all others have sprung.

CHAPTER II

The Classic

UST WHEN THE FIRST PLAY WAS WRITTEN NO ONE KNOWS. THE THE-
atre's origin has been traced as far back as Egypt in the year 4000
B.C.,[1] and it undoubtedly extends much further. For our purposes,
however, the real beginning is comparatively definite: it centers in
Greece during the fifth century B.C. The first important date seems to be
534 B.C., when Thespis, a man justly or unjustly hailed as the "world's first
actor" won the "first tragic contest." Such an item becomes insignificant,
however, when placed beside the overwhelming fact that during a single
century, from 500 B.C. to 400 B.C., the little city of Athens gave the world
four of its greatest playwrights: Aeschylus, Sophocles, Euripides, and
Aristophanes.

The factors responsible for this amazing burst of creative energy—and it
expressed itself in all the arts and sciences, not just in theatre—have never
been entirely explained, even though volumes have been written on the
subject. Certainly religion had something to do with it, for the Greeks had
developed a friendly, personal, human attitude toward their gods—an attitude that emphasized the here rather than the hereafter—an attitude that
called for expression, not repression. Politics played a part: democratic in
spirit if not always in practice, Athens produced a generation of citizens
bursting with pride, curiosity, and independence. Finally the very pattern
of historical events in the early years of the period set off a surge of national exuberance seldom if ever equaled. At Marathon, Thermopylae,
Salamis, and Platea the Greeks, fighting against overwhelming odds, had
covered themselves with undying military glory. It requires no strain of the
imagination to realize the emotional and intellectual potentials that such
events must have engendered. In all probability life has never held more

[1] George Freedley and John A. Reeves, *A History of the Theatre*, Crown Publishers,
1941, p. 2.

promise for the future; the privilege of living has never seemed more exciting; nor has the thirst to share and enjoy experience ever infected mankind to a healthier degree than during these few short years commonly referred to as "The Golden Age."

In a sense the theatre provided an almost perfect medium of expression for this surging spirit of Greece. Its purpose and nature must not be confused, however, with the more common forms of dramatic entertainment today. It was not primarily a form of romantic escape. It was not primarily an art for the select few. It was not primarily an avenue of self-expression for the stage-struck. It was rather a vital, living experience that was shared by the entire community. It probed into some of life's most basic problems with courage, honesty, and virility.

Its origin lay in religious ceremonials, not to a god of vengeance but to a very jolly little fellow with a red face, grapes in his hair, and the joy of living in his soul, the god of fertility, Dionysus. Most of the plays were presented in his honor during a great spring festival, The City Dionysia, intellectual counterpart of the great physical festival, The Olympic Games. The excitement and anticipation that preceded The City Dionysia—rehearsals, ceremonials, torchlight parades—finds its nearest analogy today in the lavish buildup accorded to a university's annual homecoming game, or to the local high school's athletic rally as its team departs for the state tournament, for The City Dionysia was a great annual event to practically everyone in Athens. Business, politics, and even war came to a standstill; the play was the thing. Consequently, it should not be surprising to learn that the men responsible for the plays were not narrow specialists; they were leaders in thought and often in action.

GREEK TRAGEDY

Aeschylus (525–c. 456 B.C.), first of the great playwrights, had been outstanding at both Marathon and Salamis; it is likely that every Athenian knew and respected him. Consequently, when he wrote his concern was not with petty things nor with mere entertainment. He had ideas and experiences to share, and as a result his plays have scope and surging power. They feature heroes, kings, and gods caught up in volcanic crises. Since he was a "founding father" in the city as well as in the theatre, his faith in his country was firm; his belief in the gods unshakable; and his hope for the future of man unlimited.

Of the ninety plays he is supposed to have written, only seven complete scripts remain: *The Suppliants, The Persians, Prometheus Bound, The*

Seven Against Thebes, and *The Oresteia,* which is actually a group of three plays (*Agamemnon, The Choephori,* and *The Eumenides*), that form one of the world's most famous trilogies.

The first play of the group, *Agamemnon,* begins at dawn as signal fires bring news to the queen, Clytemnestra, that Troy has fallen and that Agamemnon, the king, will soon be home. The dramatic intensity of this news is apparent when we learn that Clytemnestra hates Agamemnon because ten years before he had sacrificed her daughter, Iphigenia, in order that the Greek fleet might sail against Troy. Moreover, in his absence the queen has taken a lover, Agamemnon's mortal enemy, Aegisthus. The play moves swiftly. Clytemnestra and her paramour plot the king's death. We see Agamemnon return, accompanied by his mad and visionary mistress, Cassandra. We see him greeted by a cordial but false show of affection, and finally see him walk up the purple carpet into his palace and death. The first play ends as his murderers appear before the chorus, boldly justifying their deed because of crimes Agamemnon had committed against them.

The second play, *The Choephori,* begins many years later. The murder of Agamemnon has gone unavenged. Aegisthus and Clytemnestra have firmly established themselves as king and queen; but they have underestimated the drive for revenge on the part of Agamemnon's children, Electra and Orestes. In this second play these children, goaded by Apollo, are reunited after years of forced separation. The trap is soon laid, and Clytemnestra and Aegisthus meet death at the hand of Orestes. Instead of peace, however, this act of revenge launches a pack of Furies upon Orestes, for he is now guilty of the blood of his own mother.

The third play of the Trilogy, *The Eumenides,* again centers in Orestes, who after years of torture finally appeals for a trial in the Athenian court of justice. After much debate the goddess Athena herself intervenes to acquit him, and thus the long, terrible blood feud comes to an end.

This account can of course serve only as the barest suggestion as to what a Greek tragedy is about. It indicates none of the poetic richness, the penetrating ideas, or the dramatic energy that make Aeschylus great. Nor does it reveal such defects as his carelessness regarding details and motivation. Yet this very disregard for detail points toward his strength, which lies in the boundless energy and unrestricted scope of his imagination, thought, and expression.

The Classic

Not so colorful as a man but greater as a playwright is Sophocles (c. 497–405 B.C.). Both his personal life and his writing seem to have verged on perfection. His craftsmanship has been held up as a standard for twenty-five centuries. No other playwright who thought so deeply has ever expressed himself with such technical perfection. Motivation, suspense, dramatic irony, poetry, and balanced judgment are among the things of which he was master. Like Aeschylus, seven of his plays, *King Oedipus, Electra, Oedipus at Colonus, Ajax, Antigone, The Trachiniae,* and *Philoctetes,* have been preserved, and at least one of them, probably *King Oedipus, Electra,* or *Antigone,* should be required reading for every student in theatre. Anyone with sufficient imaginative ability to respond to the dramatic intensity that surges through these plays should find no difficulty in understanding why Sophocles is universally accorded a place as one of the greatest writers of all time.

King Oedipus is regarded by many as the most perfect tragedy ever written. In the century following its first production Aristotle used this play to illustrate many points in his great critical work, *The Poetics.* In particular, he praises its involved plot, where every incident is somehow so involved in a cause or effect relationship with other incidents that not only motivation, but a supreme effect of dramatic irony, is achieved. As the tragedy begins, the city of Thebes is being racked by plague; death, sorrow, and suffering are everywhere. Then into the crisis steps the young King Oedipus. He stands before his people in morning sunlight, strong, proud, and confident; his words ring with conviction as he pledges every ounce of strength in lifting the plague.

The action that follows is swift and terrible. At the end of the play Oedipus again stands before his people, but the contrast is one that shakes and humbles us; even his eyes, blinded and bleeding from self-inflicted wounds, are not so terrible as the suffering within. In the space of an hour this proud and almost perfect man has been broken and humbled, humbled beyond the misery of the meanest slave in his kingdom. As he leaves his children and his city to begin a life of self-exile the chorus speaks:

> Make way for Oedipus. All people said,
> "That is a fortunate man";
> And now what storms are beating on his head!
> Call no man fortunate that is not dead.
> The dead are free from pain.[2]

[2] Reprinted from *King Oedipus* by W. B. Yeats by permission of The Macmillan Company. Copyright 1928 by The Macmillan Company.

Read the story the next time overbearing pride and self-sufficiency threaten to take possession of you. It may help to humble you before these evils blind and destroy you. Perhaps Sophocles wrote it for his own city of Athens, which at that time stood strong and confident, even as Oedipus had done when the play began, but which, again like Oedipus, was destined soon to lie bleeding and broken. The play has profound and universal meaning for all men, all groups, and all nations that attain power and success. It has meaning for twentieth-century America.

It would be misleading to imply that only one universal idea, the danger of overbearing pride, is found in *King Oedipus*. Sophocles is concerned with many ideas, among them the ironic truth that men with eyes often see less than those who are blind. We are also challenged by the nobility and strength with which Oedipus searches out the truth no matter who suffers or how great the cost. Beyond this there is rich imagery and beauty in the language, and finally there is the terrible fascination of the struggle itself, for every move that Oedipus makes only serves, by some ironic twist of fate, to draw the meshes of doom more securely about him.

Last of the great Greek tragic writers was Euripides (c. 485–406 B.C.). Expressions such as "I laud Aeschylus, I read Euripides," and "Aeschylus wrote of the gods, Sophocles of heroes, and Euripides of men" suggest some of the basic differences between Euripides and the older masters.

The relationship of the playwright to his environment is nowhere more apparent than in the examples of Aeschylus and Euripides. The first, born of a wealthy and fairly privileged family, lived at the time of Marathon when Athens was young and full of unlimited hope. Euripides, although only 45 years younger, found himself in a world that had already started to decline. Doubt, suffering, and skepticism appear to have become his early companions. Not that he was a malcontent or hopeless pessimist, for almost any thinking man born without a film over his eyes would have felt the same. He was simply a free thinker and humanitarian thrust into a world where war, profit, blind obedience, and intolerance were rapidly gaining the upper hand. His plays clearly reflect the environment in which he lived. In 416 B.C. for example, the Athenians sent a brutal military expedition against the island of Melos. Successful in battle, they slaughtered the men and took the women prisoners. The following year Euripides in *The Trojan Women* depicted an almost identical crime with a burning pathos generally regarded as the most powerful attack ever hurled against war. While this is the outstanding example, many other plays of Euripides show close and unmistakable relationship between what he saw and what he wrote.

Throughout most of his plays runs a thinly veiled skepticism of the gods, a disregard for the supernatural or the accidental, and a fascination with the human and psychological motives behind men's acts. In *Medea,* for example, we do not study a struggle of man against fate so much as the inner struggle of a woman torn between the devouring passions of love and revenge. On the other hand, this tendency toward "realism" does not destroy the bursts of penetrating insight and poetic beauty that may be found in all his plays.

It must be admitted that the plays of Euripides are spotty and uneven in comparison with those of Sophocles. Perhaps his discouragement and disillusionment with life in general resulted in the disregard for dramatic technique that frequently mars his work. He died in exile, having known little of the success and fame that ironically were to be heaped upon him almost as soon as he was gone, for in the century that followed, Euripides became the most popular of the three tragic playwrights. This probably accounts for the fact that eighteen of his plays have been preserved, among the best known being *Electra, Medea, The Trojan Women, Hippolytus,* and *Iphigenia in Aulis.*

Before we leave the discussion of Greek tragedy there are several general characteristics that deserve further amplification:

1. Greek tragedy does not always end in the death of the main characters or the protagonist. The subject matter, as Aristotle points out, is always serious and of magnitude, but as in *The Eumenides,* for example, the leading character is sometimes left alive and free, redeemed and to a certain extent ennobled through suffering.

2. A single Greek tragedy lasts only slightly more than one hour. The entire *Orestia* trilogy of three plays requires approximately the same playing time as either *Hamlet* or *King Lear.* This fact throws some light upon the much-discussed problem of the three classic unities: *time,* which required that the action take place within a single day; *place,* which required that the action be confined to a single locality; and *action,* which required that there be but one plot. The individual plays within a Greek trilogy quite naturally obeyed these unities, but the entire trilogy did not. Moreover a rigid insistence upon the unities is found neither in the Greek plays nor in the writings of Aristotle. This originated centuries later through misinterpretation of Aristotle by overzealous French and Italian critics.

3. Immediately apparent to anyone reading a Greek tragedy is the importance of the chorus. Much of the finest poetry, some of the dramatic action, and many of the ideas are left to the chorus. To understand this we should remember the religious origin of drama. At first the chorus with its leader was the whole show. Then Thespis added one actor, Aeschylus a second, and Sophocles a third, but even with three actors the chorus still remained a very important part of Attic drama.

4. To the Greeks, tragedy was designed to serve a definite purpose. That purpose, according to Aristotle, was to effect a catharsis, the purgation of the soul through pity and fear. While no one today seems certain of exactly what this means, it was probably nothing as mysterious as one is often led to believe. Almost everyone has experienced something not unlike it when, obsessed with petty troubles and worries, studies, tea parties, or public performances, he has been forced to pause for an experience that for a moment at least has swept life's pettiness away. I remember attending a performance of *Uncle Vanya* at a time when I was discouraged and near the breaking point. As I sat in a tiny auditorium and watched excellent young actors, often with quiet tears in their eyes, suffer with Sonya, Vanya, and the others, while life, always unfulfilled, rusted away, my own feeling of depression vanished to insignificance. I had shared deep experience; I was no longer alone, for Chekhov, the young actors, their director, and all those beside me in the audience understood the thing I understood. It was probably to provide experiences not greatly unlike this that Aeschylus, Sophocles, and Euripides wrote their tragedies.

GREEK COMEDY

Turning to comedy we find that it too served a definite function. At first the function seems to have been closely interwoven with the religious rites of fertility and reproduction. This accounts for so much that today is considered shocking and obscene. By the time of Aristophanes, however, a more direct function is apparent, for in the hands of this master, comedy became a powerful lash with which to attack social and political follies. The function was not unlike that of the modern gridiron show or even the freshman take-off on the faculty. The amazing thing was the complete freedom of speech that Aristophanes seems to have enjoyed. At a time when Athens was fighting for survival in a war even more stupid and tragic than most wars, Aristophanes produced plays that unmercifully flayed Athenian leaders and Athenian institutions. In fact the audience seems to have enjoyed the ridicule of anyone or anything important, whether the ridicule was funny or not. In a surprising number of instances real people were impersonated without so much as changing their names. Even mild-mannered Socrates suffered the indignity of finding himself caricatured as little more than a muddle-headed buffoon suspended between earth and heaven in a basket. Tradition has it that with characteristic good humor the great philosopher rose from the audience to take a bow and show that he too enjoyed the fun.

Aristophanes (c. 448–c. 385 B.C.) was by no means the only comic writer of the period, but everyone agrees that he was the greatest. Moreover, he is the only one to have had several of his comedies preserved in their entirety. After reading them one comes to view Aristophanes as a man of unlimited brilliance and devastating wit. Absolutely fearless, he seems to have held nothing sacred. He ridiculed whomever and whatever his fancy dictated. Curiously enough he was a conservative, constantly crusading for a return to the good old days, always opposing the new or the progressive —which included both Socrates and Euripides. From the standpoint of technique and dramatic structure his plays are frequently defective. Obviously he could have done better had he tried, but it is altogether characteristic that such a hell-raising old genius would not want to try. As a matter of fact, conscientious care regarding details would probably have destroyed the audacious, breath-taking mixture of ribaldry, satire, and poetic fancy that are the essence of his fascination. One moment we have a passage that is a gem of tender, unexcelled lyricism, the next moment we are plunged into a scene so lusty and bawdy that even the modern twentieth-century sophisticate may be thoroughly shocked.

Most of his plays, *The Frogs, The Wasps, The Clouds,* for example, take their titles from his chorus, whose antics undoubtedly provided much of the merriment. A brief sketch of *The Frogs* may serve to give some inkling of the mad brilliance and originality with which his mind worked. Both Sophocles and Euripides appear to have died in the same year, 405 B.C.,[3] and Athens suddenly found itself without a major tragic poet. To any ordinary mind this would have occasioned nothing more than a stuffy tribute and a moment of regret. Not so with Aristophanes. This was material for his next comedy! It begins as Dionysus, alarmed by the absence of a first-

[3] The death date has never been definitely established for either Sophocles or Euripides.

rate tragic poet, decides to visit Hades and demand the return of Euripides. Accompanied by his servant Xantias, he sets out disguised as Hercules, the only person successfully to have made the dangerous journey. The slap-stick possibilities afforded by equipping roly-poly Dionysus with the club and lion skin of Hercules are obvious, but this is only the beginning. Ar-riving at the door of Aeacus, judge of the dead, Dionysus announces him-self as Hercules and receives such a vicious tongue lashing that he falls to the ground overcome with fear. (Hercules on his previous journey had strangled the old man's dog, Cerberus, who guarded the gates of Hades.) Finally recovering his wits, Dionysus changes places with Xantius on the theory that it is safer to be the servant than the master. Again the door opens, but this time a beautiful maid of Persephone appears to welcome him. Before Xantius can join the waiting dancing girls, however, Dionysus again forces him to change places, just in time to be caught by a raging landlady. Finally the two are apprehended by guards of Aeacus. To escape torture, Dionysus protests that he is a god. To make sure, they torture him and Xantias anyhow, on the theory that if either is a god he can feel no pain. God or not, Dionysus does feel it, and a hilarious endurance contest follows.

After a half hour of such buffoonery—antics that would do credit to any vaudeville house—Dionysus and Xantius arrive at the realm of Pluto, where they find not only Euripides but also Aeschylus and Sophocles. Soon a great trial is under way to decide which of the three playwrights deserves to return. Sophocles, quite in character, graciously withdraws, but the battle rages between Aeschylus and Euripides. Finally it is settled by literally weighing the verse of each, which of course makes Aeschylus the winner. Played as the Greeks must have played it, the comic possi-bilities are practically unlimited.

The plays of Aristophanes and his contemporaries are classified as "Old Comedy." Some hundred years later another form, "New Comedy," had evolved. We know about this genre primarily through two sources: por-tions of some of the plays by the New Comedy's greatest playwright, Menander, have been preserved; and, secondly, Roman comic playwrights based their own work almost entirely on that of these New Comedy play-wrights. The characteristics of New Comedy are many, but perhaps the most important are: (1) its loss of all personal satire, (2) its preoccupation with the stock situation of a young man and his amours, (3) its use of general stock characters rather than highly individual ones, and (4) the disappearance of the chorus.

If the plays of other Greek playwrights had survived and we knew the whole story of the Greek theatre, our attitudes might change, but as it is, the fame of Greek comedy rests almost entirely on the able shoulders of one man, Aristophanes. But this one, together with his tragic contemporaries, Aeschylus, Sophocles, and Euripides gave the world a wealth of dramatic literature that would be hard to overestimate.

ROMAN DRAMA

Perhaps the main point that needs explaining about Roman drama is the lack of it. True, the Romans could boast of three important playwrights, Plautus, Terence, and Seneca, but Plautus and Terence wrote early when the empire was young, and even then did little more than adapt and translate from the Greek; while Seneca—well, Seneca is an isolated phenomenon, a sort of accident. Reasons for Rome's sterility in drama—especially after the great empire matured—are not hard to deduce. A native drama of some promise had begun to develop; then Rome became a conqueror, and early among its victims was Greece. Now what does a conqueror do after defeating a nation whose art is infinitely superior to its own? Obviously, one solution is to dismiss such art as unimportant, the work of an inferior race. Consequently, Romans might condescend to enjoy theatre, but the work—writing, acting, technical effects and all the rest—was left to slaves—Greek slaves if possible, often rather brilliant and nice fellows, but of course an inferior race. Because of this it is not surprising to learn that Terence began his career as a slave, that Seneca was a foreigner, a Spaniard, and that Plautus, though not a slave, was a rough Italian jack-of-all-trades in the early days before Romans had learned to have proper regard for racial dignity. Contrast all this with the social and religious prestige of the playwright at the time of Aeschylus, and you have at least one reason for Rome's inferiority.

So much for the great Roman plays that were not written; now a few words about the good ones that were. The first to have any of his plays preserved was Plautus (Titus Maccius Plautus, c. 254–184 B.C.). According to tradition, his colorful life included adventures as an actor, soldier, merchant, and grinder of meal. Then finally, past middle age, he turned to playwriting and seems to have scored immediate success. The rough and rowdy vigor of his life carried over into the spirit of his comedies in a way that engendered enthusiastic response from the noisy crowds that appear to have made up the early Roman audience. He knew this audience; he knew theatre; and he wrote to please, with no thought of literary immortality. It is ironic that more of his plays (twenty-one) have been preserved than of any other classic playwright.

There is a sameness about his plots; in fact all evidence points towards the conclusion that there was a sameness about the plots of all Roman comedy. The basic theme ordinarily centers around a young lover and his amours. To gain the object of his affection he is almost always assisted by a clever rogue of a slave. Mistaken identity or deliberate deception are almost invariably involved. The plot of *The Haunted House* (*Mostellaria*) is typical. In the absence of his father, Philolaches purchases the freedom of a beautiful slave girl, then runs through his father's wealth in riotous living. At the height of one of his wild parties, news arrives of the father's return. In desperation the young man turns to his clever slave, Tranio. The slave's first frantic act is one of sheer inspiration; he frightens the old man away from the house with a story that it is haunted. The ruse has barely succeeded when a moneylender descends upon Tranio, demanding the return of a large sum of money Philolaches had borrowed. This arouses the father's suspicion, but Tranio saves the situation by a hastily inspired announcement that the boy borrowed money to buy a new house. Things relax for a moment as the old man pays the moneylender; then the bottom drops out of everything as he suggests to Tranio that they inspect the new house. But the ever-resourceful slave is equal to the situation. He goes to a neighbor's house, explains to the kindly owner that the father is suffering from a delusion that the house is his. Would the neighbor humor the old man by allowing him to inspect the dwelling? Permission is granted, and an inspection tour full of hilarious misunderstanding results. Finally the entire deception collapses, and Tranio barely escapes the mortal wrath of the enraged father by taking refuge on an altar. In the meantime Philolaches and his lawyer friend have had time to sober up and plead forgiveness, but neither the situation nor Tranio are really saved until it is discovered that the slave girl purchased by Philolaches is none other than the long lost daughter of the father's best friend!

In many ways Terence (Plublius Terentius Afer, c. 195–159 B.C.) was a direct opposite of Plautus. Whereas Plautus wrote for the common man in his audience, Terence catered to the élite. Refinement, scholarship, and polish were among the virtues he tried to cultivate. He had been brought to Rome as a slave, but his master, quickly recognizing the boy's intellectual potentials, set him free, and it appears that Terence resolved to prove his gratitude by humbly being as perfect as possible in the eyes of the Roman upper class. Consequently, while his plots and characters are drawn from the same sources as those of Plautus, he adds nothing of the boisterous originality of his predecessor. Literary merit appears to have been his objective. According to George E. Duckworth, "Terence writes with a lightness and grace that are almost Greek and which reflect the linguistic interest of his friends of the Scipionic circle; Plautus writes with an exuberance and freedom that reveal his knowledge of the theatre and his audience."[4]

The care with which Terence wrote is indicated by the fact that although he finished his first play, *Andria,* at the age of nineteen, he managed to write only five more before he was drowned at sea about sixteen years later. All six of his plays have survived, however, and together with those of Plautus have had tremendous influence on the history of comedy. It was Plautus and Terence rather than Aristophanes who were held up as models during the Renaissance, and among those who borrowed from them are Molière and Shakespeare.

The one important writer of Roman tragedy was Seneca (Lucius Annaeus Seneca, c. 4 B.C.–65 A.D.). A Spaniard by birth, he is outstanding in Roman history not only as a playwright but also as one of Rome's leading stoics and as Nero's tutor who, incidentally, met death at the hand of his pupil. Among Seneca's literary works are nine, possibly ten, tragedies. With but one exception all are based on extant Greek tragedies. While no one can be certain, it seems probable that they were not written to be acted on the stage but simply to be read or declaimed. They tend to be exercises in rhetoric and stoic philosophy rather than imaginative dramatic poetry. Speeches are frequently of excessive length, while entrances and exits are often unmotivated.

It is not surprising that Seneca had difficulty in writing tragedy, for its basic ingredients, pity and terror, are taboo to the stoic. Seneca seems to have compensated for the lack of them by introducing ghosts, deeds of violence, and gory descriptions. Yet while his plays are not nearly so bad as some have tried to make out, they are studied more because of their enormous influence than because of their own merits. Renaissance critics

[4] George E. Duckworth, *The Complete Roman Drama*, Vol. I, Random House, 1942, p. xxxii.

and playwrights in France and Italy came near making Seneca the theoretical model of tragedy for all time, and while this veneration did much harm it also resulted in much good. Even in England, Shakespeare and the other Elizabethans borrowed Seneca's five-act form, his ghosts, his blood and thunder, and other items too numerous to mention. Certainly a man of such influence cannot be ignored.

CHAPTER III

Renaissance to Modern

PROLOGUE: THE MEDIEVAL

THE YEAR 476 SAW THE FINAL COLLAPSE OF ROME AND ITS WESTERN Empire. As far as theatre is concerned, however, Rome's fall is a fact of slight importance, since theatre of any artistic merit had already been dead for centuries. Seneca, the last writer of importance, died in A.D. 65, and even he had not written for public presentation. Stage shows continued to be given but soon degenerated into entertainments that featured obscenity and vulgarity. Consequently, when the Christian church came into power one of its first acts was to abolish all theatrical activity and to classify actors with thieves, prostitutes, and other undesirables.

Rome fell, but not the church. The latter assumed a power over the life of Europe that was to exert a fundamental guiding influence for the next 1000 years. Certain aspects of this medieval church were highly commendable. For example, almost the only kindness, learning, art, and beauty of this dark period were centered within the church. From another point of view, however, its influence was less fortunate. Many of its attitudes and practices originated not from the example or teaching of Christ, but as a reaction against anything Roman or Greek. Thus while the Greeks had emphasized the here rather than the hereafter and the Romans had extended this to a philosophy of eat-drink-and-be-merry-for-tomorrow-you-die, the early church pronounced the present a vale of tears, a trial to test us as we passed from the eternity of preëxistence to the eternity of the hereafter; the greater the suffering now the greater the reward in heaven. The Greeks had admired and cultivated the human body; the church covered it with robes as a thing of shame, if not evil. The Greeks had looked upon the expression of beauty through art as one of man's highest functions; the church frowned upon this as pleasure and vanity. The Greeks had sought for the answers to the great mysteries of life and death; the church insisted on faith in the established answers.

Whatever the causes, the fact remains that from the death of Seneca until the beginning of the so-called middle ages the art of playwriting was practically nonexistent. There were exceptions of course. We know that the mimes and strolling players never entirely disappeared. We also know that in the tenth century, Roswitha, a nun in Saxony, wrote several pious comedies after the manner of Terence. But on the whole the dark ages, as far as playwriting was concerned, were dark indeed.

Curiously enough the rebirth of drama is traced not to the strolling players nor to Roswitha, but to the very church that had been so influential in the theatre's destruction. At some time during the tenth century a tiny four-line playlet was introduced into the Easter service. It dramatized the Resurrection in the simplest possible terms, and yet it must have scored a success, for soon Christmas and other holy days were also being embellished with dramatizations. Finally these short biblical plays were moved outside the church and organized into groups known as mystery cycles. Based always on the holy scriptures, their function remained fundamentally religious, yet in spite of religious and other restrictions we begin to see the playwright's creative faculties once more at work. Thus the story of Adam picks up new insight into human nature as Lucifer shrewdly plays upon Eve's vanity; the sacrifice of Isaac becomes more touching because of the boy's tender regard for his mother; while the story of Noah gains a delightful quality from the character of Noah's shrewish wife who refuses to board the ark unless permitted to bring her local club of town gossips.

In England famous mystery cycles were developed at York, Wakefield, Coventry, and Chester. In Germany one may still see the Passion play at Oberammergau, which dates back to 1662, and is essentially a medieval mystery play that has survived to the present day.

Only a short step from the mystery play, which dealt with biblical themes, is the miracle play, which depicted the lives of the saints. Apparently hundreds of these plays were written, although few have survived. They usually gave the playwright greater freedom than the mystery plays had done. Some depict exciting scenes of torture and martyrdom, others verge on secular romance. The religious purpose is sometimes preserved only by the device of introducing a saint or the Virgin at some point in the otherwise romantic adventure to perform a miracle and resolve the tangled situation, thus preserving the spiritual and moral function of the production.

A third type of drama that developed during the medieval period was the morality play, the familiar *Everyman* being the outstanding example. We see Everyman, summoned by Death, appeal in vain to Fellowship, Cousin, Kindred, and Goods. Even Strength, Discretion, Five Wits, Beauty, and Knowledge desert him as he reaches the grave. Only Good Deeds, frail but true, is willing to accompany him and plead for him before the judgment seat of God. On the surface such an allegorical form—the personification of virtues, vices, and other abstract qualities—seems stiff and unpromising, yet closer examination reveals that these morality plays are a step nearer to true drama than either the mysteries or miracles had been. The challenge to the imagination of the playwright was much greater and his freedom in dealing with his material comparatively unrestricted.

One other type of drama developed during the middle ages, or perhaps it had never entirely died out. This was the farcical interlude. Perhaps these interludes grew from the moralities, perhaps from the strolling players, but in any event they represent an important step in the history of playwriting, for in these the theatre once again emerges as entirely secular, once more devoted to the primary purpose of entertainment. Many excellent examples have survived. From France comes the famous *Pierre Pathelin*. Modern audiences can still view with delight this story of the clever shyster, Pierre, who among other adventures manages to secure the acquittal of a sheep stealer through the audacious prank of having his client answer "Baa" to every question of judge and prosecutor, only to be trapped by his own cleverness as the not-so-dumb client, in answer to Pierre's request for his fee, produces a final and lusty "Baa."

Perhaps the best farces of all came from Germany where Hans Sachs (1494–1576), the beloved poet-shoemaker of Old Nuremburg, turned out dozens of homely but cheerful examples of the genre. In *Der todte Mann* we see a harassed little husband, no longer sure of his wife's affection, decide to test her by the naive device of lying down and pretending to be dead. We can be sure that he never attempts such deception again, for the shrewd little wife, immediately seeing through his hoax, proceeds to torture him by rejoicing over the prospects of widowhood until he rises from the dead in consternation and anguish. Even though the wife finally confesses that she was only teasing, we sense that the distraught husband can never be quite sure. He has saddled himself with greater tortures of uncertainty than before. Never try to play tricks on a woman.

England, too, had her farcical interludes, those by John Heywood being the most celebrated. In fact it is but the slightest step from a play like John Heywood's *Johan Johan* to plays like *Ralph Roister Doister* and *Gammer Gurton's Needle*, which mark the beginning of Renaissance playwriting in England, a beginning that was to culminate in the genius of Shakespeare.

ITALY: THE RENAISSANCE

Early in the fourteenth century Dante, possibly sensing the coming of a dangerous new age, summed up the essence of medieval thought and fear of punishment with gigantic scope of imagination in *The Divine Comedy*. Already the old faith was beginning to crumble. Men were beginning to question, to reëxamine life and death. Whether the new age started with the invention of gunpowder or the printing press, with the establishment of universities, with the fall of Constantinople which drove scholars and classic literature into western Europe, or whether it grew from a combination of these and other influences matters little. What does matter is that man once more became interested in man and in living. Once more he dared to believe, as the Greeks had believed long before him, that a healthy body was better than an unhealthy one, that a happy life was more desirable than an unhappy one, and that the improvement of man's lot in this life was not a vanity but a virtue. This freedom to examine for one's self, to question authority, to struggle with the restless energy of a Faust—these qualities and others were all a part of the spirit known as humanism, and are associated with the term Renaissance.

More specifically, of course, the Renaissance refers to the rebirth of interest in the civilization of Greece and Rome. Almost at once Renaissance man sensed that in classic ages the emphasis had been upon living rather than preparation for death. He began to rediscover, through books and ruins, the arts and sciences that classic man had cultivated to improve his lot.

Like all great movements, the Renaissance was infinitely complex and variegated. Evil frequently balanced or overbalanced the good. The new-found freedom to live was all too frequently interpreted as the freedom to exploit, rape, murder, or oppress. In a sense the Renaissance is still in progress, and whether it will eventually end in the destruction or exaltation of man seems at this midway point of the twentieth century to hang in precarious balance.

But whether good or evil, the life of western civilization since the dawn of the Renaissance has seldom been dull. Contrast it with the pace of life in civilizations that have crystallized under religious faith—Egyptian, Hindu, or Medieval—and one will see the speed and chaos with which Renaissance man has moved.

While the above discussion has viewed the Renaissance in its large and general sense, as a spirit still very much alive, it is also customary to restrict the term to a much narrower span of years, and especially to Italy during the fourteenth, fifteenth, and sixteenth centuries, for it was here that the movement first developed. During this period Italy's accomplishments in painting, architecture, sculpture, and the sciences were outstanding. By comparison the results in theatre were disappointing. Much was achieved, but it does not compare with what had been accomplished in Greece and Rome or was soon to be accomplished in England, Spain, and France.

Largely responsible for Italy's weak showing in drama was the political state of the area. There was no national unity and very little stability. Individual city states were under the control of powerful and frequently despotic families. These were the privileged few; the art and learning of the Renaissance was sponsored by them, but in most cases there were not enough of them in any given city to make much of a playgoing audience. When a nation has centered its court and life in one city as France centered hers in Paris at the time of Molière, then a theatre of the élite may have vigor. Otherwise the drama has seemed to flourish best where the spirit has been far more democratic than it was in Renaissance Italy.

This failure to produce great plays may also have been due to a contradiction between life and theory. Italian scholars in their enthusiasm had unearthed Aristotle, as well as most of the extant Greek and Roman plays. With overzealous eagerness they proclaimed such principles as the three unities and applied them with a rigidity that practically outdid the medieval church in intolerance. Consequently, a rigid and highly restricted form was forced upon the would-be playwrights of an age that was bursting with color, energy, and imagination. This contradiction between life and theory was felt primarily in the field of tragedy. Scholars have always had a tendency to deal ponderously with tragedy, to fetter it with rules and restrictions until free and honest expression becomes next to impossible; this happened during the Italian Renaissance.

But having admitted that it produced no tragedies of great merit, the Italian Renaissance is still of vast importance in any history of the theatre. It reëstablished the art of playwriting on somewhat the same plane as the

Greeks and Romans had left it. It also saw the birth of opera, pastoral drama, and *commedia dell' arte.*

The *commedia* will be treated more fully in a later chapter on acting, since it was a theatre that centered in the actor, not the playwright. With only a scenario to guide them, these talented performers improvised some of the most enjoyable entertainments ever seen. This was the popular theatre, the theatre of the people. The scenarios, many of which have been preserved, are usually quite trivial, and ordinarily feature some variation of cuckoldry or the eternal triangle. The artistry and skill came from the players.

Opera, the most notable contribution of the period, was to some extent an accident, the result of a misinterpretation of Greek acting by a group of enthusiastic scholars who believed that Greek tragedies had been intoned and sung. It was not long until the enthusiasm of two of the group, Peri and Rinuccini, produced *Dafne* (1597), which is commonly regarded as the world's first opera. Not bound by the classic restrictions that had hampered and were to hamper tragedy, opera gained ground rapidly. The musical genius of Monteverdi had much to do with this. There was also the influence of scenic embellishment, which quickly associated itself with opera, and through its appeal to a Renaissance taste, aided opera in becoming the characteristic theatrical expression of Renaissance Italy.

As for the pastoral drama of Italy during the sixteenth century, it cannot be entirely ignored, primarily because of the writings of one man, Torquato Tasso (1544–1595). His plays are too idyllic and sentimental to be of first rank, yet there is a sincerity and nostalgic beauty about them that has created wide appeal. They are important because of both their merit and their influence.

But Italy's major contribution to the dramatic literature of the period lies in the field of comedy. For some reason scholars and critics concentrated their attention on tragedy, leaving comedy free; or perhaps there is something in the very nature of the comic playwright that refuses to bow to rules and restrictions.

Of the many skillful, though rather licentious, comedies that were written, the best example is Niccolo Macchiavelli's *La Mandragola* (*The Mandrake*) (c. 1520). The plot concerns Callimaco, a young man whose love has been inflamed by the beauty of Lucrezia, wife of the middle-aged and gullible Messer Nicia Calfucci. In order to be with her the young man has his assistant convince the husband that he, Callimaco, is a wonder-working doctor from Paris who can cure Lucrezia of her apparent sterility by having her take a potion of Mandragora. The only problem is that the next man to lie with her must surely die. To avoid making himself the victim of such a catastrophe, the stupid husband decides to kidnap some worthless young drunk from the streets and place him with Lucrezia to absorb the fatal effects of the medicine. Lucrezia offers stout resistance to this evil plan, but when the arguments of her husband are reinforced by those of her mother, and even by those of her priest, she is finally forced to consent. Callimaco, of course, has arranged that he shall be the one who is kidnapped. Alone with Lucrezia he wins her affection by revealing his own love and her husband's stupidity. The play ends the next morning with the cuckolded husband showering praises upon Callimaco, who has now returned as the doctor. The unsuspecting cuckold even insists that Callimaco accept the key to the back door in order that he may come and go at will.

As the above plot indicates, Italian Renaissance comedy resembles Roman comedy, except that it is even more licentious. It is usually preoccupied with a young man and his love affairs, which consequently leads to comedy of disguise, mistaken identity, and misrepresentation. The object of the young man's affection is almost always a married and essentially virtuous woman, one capable of putting up a good fight. Although immoral, these comedies are important because of their wit, their brilliance, and the insight they afford into their times.

SPAIN: THE GOLDEN AGE

The coming of the Renaissance found Spain in control of most of Italy and much of Europe. Discovery and plunder of the New World had resulted in power and riches that established Spain (in her own estimation, at least) as the leading nation of the world. Her achievements in art and learning, however, are of a somewhat hollow and disappointing quality. The fault probably lies in the fact that in Spain the Renaissance spirit encountered two stumbling blocks, the Inquisition and the defeat of the Armada. If any one characteristic of the Renaissance was important it was freedom of thought—freedom to question, to probe, to reëxamine life and life's values. While this freedom of thought met with natural opposition everywhere—and still does—it has never met with anything to equal the Spanish Inquisition. Freedom of thought in religion was effectively discouraged by means of the iron maiden, the rack, and the flaming stake.

Freedom of political thought fared little better, and thus the Spanish nobility maintained its position of superiority through a highly artificial code of conduct and an insistence that this code be rigidly obeyed.

The effect upon playwriting is quite obvious. Religious plays, exciting romances, melodramas, and clever comedies could be written, but true greatness in literature comes only from those who dare to probe deeply and honestly into life and then report fearlessly what the mind discovers by such soul-searching. It may not be so serious if an author is required to conform only to a few general codes that harmonize with logic and common sense, but unfortunately many Spanish codes did not do this. As a result we can have a play like Calderón's famous *Physician of His Own Honour,* where a husband who murders his wife because he suspects that she has stained his honor, is exonorated by the king and given another woman as a bride, even though we know that the first wife was entirely innocent. Adherence to a code of honor that condones such "justice" is not characteristic of great writers. Fortunately it is not characteristic of Spanish writing at its best, but unfortunately it is characteristic of most Spanish playwriting during the period.

This partial failure of the Renaissance in Spain had at least one advantage. If the Spanish playwright failed to gain freedom from his state and church, he at least gained freedom from the restrictive rules of the literary critics who had stifled the life of serious drama in Italy. In general, while the major playwrights of Spain knew of the "rules," they made little attempt to follow them.

The defeat of the Armada also encouraged the avoidance of deep thinking. It was easier and far more pleasant to use drama as an escape—to build castles in Spain—than to face the reality of defeat. It was this Spanish tendency to live in a world of dreams, romance, and chivalry that Cervantes so effectively debunked in his great satirical novel, *Don Quixote.*

There were many important playwrights during the period. Cervantes himself wrote a number of plays. There was also Juan Ruiz de Alarcón who was born not in Spain but in Mexico. For the beginner, however, it seems best to concentrate on two playwrights who tower above their fellows: Lope de Vega and Calderón. Lope de Vega (1562–1635) is the more colorful and interesting. In fact, it seems doubtful whether any other playwright in history can match Lope in this regard. His personal life was sensational. He survived the sinking of the Armada, was exiled, was rescued, became a tempestuous lover, and finally as a playwright turned out a volume of work that staggers the imagination—somewhere between 1600 and 2200 plays, in addition to other literary works. No one in the pages of history seems to have written with such speed and facility (Shakespeare, writing in England during the same years, turned out a total of thirty-seven plays.) With such an overwhelming quantity to his credit it should not be surprising to learn that Lope's plays tend to have shortcomings. On the contrary one is amazed to discover how much merit they do possess. At times their poetry picks up a lyrical quality that is excellent; so far as scholars can determine, his characters and plots were usually original; finally there is a sense of action and excitement that shows a keen awareness of how to hold an audience. Lope's influence on playwriting has been important not just in Spain but throughout the world. If nothing else he deserves a reward of some sort for having cheerfully ignored the classic rules that had proved so stifling in Italy.

His plays are not easy to classify. There is no cleancut division into tragedy and comedy as in classic drama. Although the proportions vary, almost all the plays have elements of both serious and comic. Much of his best work fits somewhere under a classification known as "cape and sword drama," a phrase that is highly descriptive of Lope's dashing, flamboyant style. Romantic interest in love, especially the clash between love and honor, is usually the core of the excitement; in many respects Lope fulfilled the same function in his age that Hollywood does in our own.

But while he usually concerned himself with entertainment rather than with depth and experience, there are moments that surprise us—moments when a genuine spirit of freedom, justice, and independent thinking breaks through in opposition to the ruling codes of church and state. One such play is *Fuente Ovejuna* (*The Sheep Well*), which deals with the rebellion of the peasants of the little village, Fuente Ovejuna, against their aristocratic and corrupt Commander. The play rises to genuine greatness in many scenes, for example, when Laurencia, a young girl who has just been ravished by the Commander, stirs the timid Town Board into action:

My face is bruised and bloody in this court of honest men. Some of you are fathers, some have daughters. Do your hearts sink within you. . . . You are sheep, sheep! Oh well-named village of Fuente Ovejuna, The Sheep Well! Sheep, sheep, sheep![1]

Even greater in dramatic potentials is the scene where the judge, sent by the king to investigate the murder of the Commander, meets a united village. Boys of ten, old men, and women are put to torture in a brutally

[1] *Fuente Ovejuna*, Act 3, in Lope de Vega, *Four Plays*, Charles Scribner's Sons, 1936.

determined effort to discover who killed the Commander, but although all know the answer not one will confess. The reply wrung from the tortured victims is always the same, "Fuente Ovejuna!"; in other words, the entire village killed him. Finally the king, filled with admiration for the courage and strength of the people, pardons their crime and takes Fuente Ovejuna under his own protection.

It seems strange that a man capable of such genuine power should have written hundreds of plays where entertainment is the only objective. Also it is strange that this man could have stood by and watched a monk burned at the stake for heresy. But perhaps inconsistency is as inherent a characteristic of his life and works as color and energy.

The other highly regarded playwright of the age is Calderón—Pedro Calderón de la Barca (1600–1681). While his output is feeble in comparison with Lope's, it nevertheless included 70 religious plays and 111 dramas. Considering that his time was largely occupied with duties as an important figure of state and church, we can scarcely dismiss him as lazy.

In contrast to Lope, Calderón's life, like that of Sophocles, appears to have been serene and exemplary. He was a Spanish gentleman in the finest sense of the word. His plays excel Lope's in only one respect: the poetry is generally regarded as superior, or at least more polished. This does not mean that he was a painstaking craftsman. Some of his errors and anachronisms growing from hasty writing are quite as startling as those of his great predecessor. He has Herodias describe America, he places Jerusalem on the sea coast, and locates the Danube between Russia and Sweden!

Calderón's best plays are probably *The Mayor of Zalamea* and *Life Is a Dream*. The first resembles *Fuente Ovejuna* in that the rugged honor of the Spanish peasant is once more pitted against the corruption of the nobility. The central figure is Crespo, the mayor of Zalamea, who, finding that his daughter has been ravished by the Captain, defies custom and authority by bringing the offender to trial and execution. *Life Is a Dream* is usually regarded as Calderón's masterpiece. King Basilio of Poland, having been warned by prophecy that his son Segismundo will do great evil if ever allowed to rule, is forced to imprison the child for life. With the approach of old age and death the King relents and determines to allow his son a trial of one day in his rightful place. Accordingly the young prince is given a sleeping potion, dressed in royal robes, and brought to the palace. But his character proves to be so brutal and ungovernable that the old King is forced to order another sleeping potion, and Segismundo returns to prison. On waking, Segismundo is convinced that the royalty of yesterday was but a dream—or is the present a dream?—a problem that foreshadows Pirandello.

Aside from the two plays outlined above, Calderón's work, like Lope's, was largely concerned with the conventional themes of love and honor and the popular excitement of the cape and sword. Surrounded by less circumscribed codes of thought and behavior, he might, like Shakespeare and Sophocles, have become one of the world's outstanding playwrights. As it is, we admire him as a man, but his work seldom reaches the depth characteristic of truly great literature.

ENGLAND: SHAKESPEARE AND THE ELIZABETHANS

While the dramatic output of Renaissance Italy was somewhat disappointing, that of Renaissance England exceeds all expectations. Even without Shakespeare the period would have been an important one, but including his genius it may be claimed that London from about 1580 to 1642 contributed more great plays than any other city during a comparable period before or since, the only exception being Athens during the fifth century B.C.

There are certain parallels in the backgrounds of both London and Athens. Both were young in spirit, boisterous, eager, and filled with zest for living. Commerce and trade flourished; activity and excitement were in the air. Both cities experienced the exhilaration of finding themselves in positions of world power, London through the defeat of the Spanish Armada in 1588, Athens through the defeat of Persia during the early years of the fifth century B.C. Both, in other words, provided the stimulation and widening horizons that great playwrights require.

Other forces were at work, of course. Some scholars trace much of the greatness of Shakespeare to a happy blending of two views of life, medieval and Renaissance. Happily, when these two met and merged, neither completely dominated the other. The medieval contributed scope, imagination, homely realism, and hearty laughter, while the Renaissance contributed the classic form with its sense of order, skillful plots, deft solutions, brilliant word play, and Senecan verse. Thus the best features of each tended to combine to produce the age of Elizabeth, one of the truly dazzling literary periods of all time.

Renaissance influence on playwriting was first felt in the colleges. As early as 1553 or 1554 Nicholas Udall, headmaster of Eton, using Plautus as his model, wrote *Ralph Roister Doister.* This is a fairly robust comedy and one which substituted English for Latin types. It was soon followed by *Gammer Gurton's Needle,* of uncertain authorship, a rousing farce-comedy that is still performed.

In serious drama the Renaissance influence made its first appearance in *Gorboduc* (1562), by Thomas Sackville and Thomas Norton. This was a Senecan tragedy of blood and revenge that employed blank verse, the verse form later perfected and used with such success by both Marlowe and Shakespeare. Like *Ralph Roister Doister* and *Gammer Gurton's Needle,* however, it substituted English characters and an English setting for the Latin originals. From these beginnings Elizabethan drama grew, until by 1564, the year in which both Shakespeare and Marlowe were born, fully developed plays could already be seen.

Shakespeare's immediate predecessors were for the most part brilliant young college graduates who had been caught up in the reckless, dangerous spirit of the age. In evaluating these men, not so much on their own merit as in terms of their influences, it is logical to begin with John Lyly, an Oxford graduate, poet, and playwright of high favor in the court of Queen Elizabeth. While unpopular today, Lyly, through his comedies and poetry, may have done more than any other early Elizabethan to add refinement, eloquence, and taste to the prevailing ruggedness of the English style. In fact the term euphuism, commonly associated with high-flown diction and excessive elegance of style, is derived from Lyly's famous *Euphues,* or *The Anatomy of Wit.*

In vivid contrast to Lyly stands Thomas Kyd (c. 1557–1595). Seldom have two names been more delightfully descriptive. The appropriateness of "Lyly" is apparent. As for Kyd, both his life and his plays had much of the dashing danger that we might now associate with some two-gun "Thomas the Kyd" of a western melodrama. He fired drama with native Elizabethan qualities of vigor, power, and imagination. Only one surviving play, *The Spanish Tragedy,* can be traced with certainty to his hand. This play, enormously popular during his day, still has qualities that merit its occasional revival. The plot is sensational. Hieronimo, the elderly Marshal of Spain, awakened one night by cries from his arbor, hurries outside to find that his only son has been brutally murdered. The main action of the play follows the old man, at times on the brink of madness and always an object of pity, as he charts his way through intrigues and counterintrigues until he at last achieves revenge by the destruction of those responsible for the terrible crime. The play shows unmistakable Senecan influence in its ghosts, its theme of revenge, and its bloody deeds. Unlike Seneca, however, the scenes of blood and violence, instead of being related by a messenger, take place on stage in the best medieval tradition. The murder of the son, the father's discovery of the body, the play within the play where the guilty ones instead of meeting only a make-believe death are actually killed, and the final scene where the old man, having been captured, bites out his tongue to avoid confession, are all scenes of violence that Kyd dared to portray to the last drop of blood.

Between the extremes of Lyly and Kyd is Robert Greene, who, in *Friar Bacon and Friar Bungay*, told a delightful love story and told it well. He also gave the English theatre its first really effective and charming heroines, for up to his time romantic love seems to have been considered either embarrassing or forbidden.

In this brief account we must skip the contributions of the other "University Wits," with the exception of Christopher Marlowe (1564–1593), who, save only for Shakespeare, ranks as the greatest tragic playwright England has produced. Both his life and his plays reflect his stormy, revolutionary spirit. The son of a shoemaker, he worked his way to an M.A. from Cambridge. One great poem, four great tragedies, and some lesser works had come from his pen by the time of his death in a tavern brawl at the age of 29.

Marlowe's contribution to the theatre rests largely upon four plays: *Tamburlaine, Dr. Faustus, The Jew of Malta,* and *Edward II. Tamburlaine* is a heroic tragedy of such colossal proportions that it sometimes escapes the ridiculous only because of the originality, poetic skill, and impassioned sincerity of its author. *Dr. Faustus* brings a new kind of dignity to tragedy, not the dignity of a king or titled hero, but that of a common man, the restless medieval scholar, Faustus. It also combines what is essentially a medieval morality play with the spirit and form of the Renaissance. Barabas in *The Jew of Malta* is frequently compared to both Shylock and Iago, while *Edward II,* Marlowe's masterpiece of playwriting, ranks as England's first great chronicle play.

Marlowe's general contribution to Elizabethan literature has been well expressed by the words passion, poetry, and power. He created plays in the white heat of inspiration. Like Kyd he served notice that he would not have his imagination bound by petty academic rules or unities. Above all else stands his contribution as a poet, for it was in this quality that he outdistanced Kyd and the others.

> Was this the face that launch'd a thousand ships,
> And burnt the topless towers of Ilium?[2]

Lines like these indicate that blank verse in the hands of Marlowe had come of age.

Scholars love to speculate on what might have been achieved had Marlowe lived to maturity as Shakespeare did. Certainly his early death robbed the world of much tragic greatness. That he could ever have matched his great contemporary, however, seems most unlikely. He had none of Shakespeare's sense of humor or humanity, none of his whimsical sensitivity, and none of his humility or sense of order. But even so, Marlowe's contribution, particularly as a dramatic poet, makes him a striking figure at the dawn of the great age.

It seems safe to assume that any student sufficiently interested in the theatre to read this far will already have acquired considerable knowledge of William Shakespeare (1564–1616). Accordingly, we could almost omit him from this account, yet a few general comments seem necessary. There are probably few who would not agree that Shakespeare is the greatest writer who ever lived, yet one of his most appealing qualities seems to be that he was essentially unconscious of this greatness. Lacking the college degrees of so many of his contemporaries, he seems to have applied himself humbly to the task of writing as best he could for his fellow actors and his audiences. He made no attempt to collect or publish these plays. He does not even mention them in his will, though he does mention his "second best bed." A country boy lacking a college education, it probably never seriously occurred to him that he had outdistanced his contemporaries in lasting literary value.

In common with almost all the great playwrights, Shakespeare knew his theatre, loved his theatre, and lived with his theatre; as a result his plays play even better than they read. Nor are they limited in appeal to the select few. High school audiences have been known to laugh and applaud with more genuine enthusiasm for *Taming of the Shrew, Midsummer Night's Dream,* and *Much Ado About Nothing* than for anything the modern theatre has to offer. I have never seen a modern audience so deeply moved as during a performance of *King Lear.* Even in the movies, which

[2] *Dr. Faustus,* scene 13.

have traditionally scorned Shakespeare as "highbrow," Sir Laurence Olivier's *Hamlet* and his *Henry V* have both established box office records.

The sources of Shakespeare's effectiveness have been variously analyzed. All would agree, however, that he tells a dramatic story with tremendous theatrical effectiveness. He also displays an insight into character that is truly remarkable. Even when intellectually unsympathetic toward a character, as in the case of Shylock, Shakespeare still is able to see life from the character's point of view and, almost in spite of himself, gives his Shylock motivation that makes him human—tragic as well as comic. Because of his skill in drawing character, Lady Macbeth is certainly more real to the average adult than Queen Elizabeth. The "real" historical figures of Antony, Cleopatra, Enobarbus, and Octavius Caesar remain distant and blurred to most of us who read only history, but to those who have worked closely with Shakespeare's *Antony and Cleopatra* these characters suddenly acquire life, vividness, and conviction. One who reads, one who sees, and especially one who acts Shakespeare gains in wisdom and experience, for it is almost as though he had lived many lives, had passed through many great crises, in company with many great people—as though he had been there with Lear, Falstaff, Macbeth, Cleopatra, and so many others. While the excellence of Shakespeare's major characters is universally recognized, his genius is nowhere more apparent than in his vivid delineation of hundreds of so-called minor characters. In *King Lear* a captain is summoned by Edmond and handed a warrant for the death of Lear and Cordelia. He has one speech: "I cannot eat oats or draw a cart, but if it's a man's work I'll do it." Here is characterization in a single line. The captain stands before us more vividly than do characters of lesser writers, though they may hold the stage for a full two and one half hours.

Finally we must glance at Shakespeare the poet. Who else has ever expressed so many things so well? Take the music of Oberon's: "I know a bank whereon the wild thyme blows. . . ."; of Antony's, "Sometime we see a cloud that's dragonish. . . ."; of his final refrain, "I am dying, Egypt, dying. . . ."; the heart-breaking simplicity of Lear's, "Pray, do not mock me: I am a very foolish fond old man. . . ." Take the tragic mixture of weariness and bitterness in Macbeth's, "To-morrow, and to-morrow, and to-morrow, creeps in this petty pace from day to day. . . ." Even such tiny snatches indicate a poet of extraordinary quality.

There are flaws in his work. He was often careless of details. His descriptions of offstage events sometimes verge on ridiculous bombast; his subplots sometimes clutter rather than help; some critics lament his lack of social criticism and satire; he is guilty of *Titus Andronicus* and a few other plays of questionable merit, but perhaps his very lack of perfection, along with his unconsciousness of greatness, increases our affection for him. For both Shakespeare and his characters are of this imperfect world—they are a part of each of us.

The final marvel is that he excelled in so many areas. A man selecting the world's greatest writers of tragedy might name Shakespeare, Sophocles, and Goethe. The greatest comedy writers might be Shakespeare, Molière, Aristophanes, and Shaw. The greatest writers of chronicle plays might be Shakespeare, Schiller, and Strindberg. Even in the field of romantic tragicomedy there is nothing by Beaumont and Fletcher or anyone else to equal *The Tempest.* Nor is Shakespeare's fame solely a matter of English pride. His plays have been translated into almost every language. They are performed wherever a stage is to be found, and they have made living a richer experience for millions.

As Christopher Marlowe with his tragedies is outstanding among those who preceded Shakespeare, so Ben Jonson (1572–1637) with his comedies is outstanding among those who followed. A big man, colorful, daring, Elizabethan, he fought duels with both the pen and the sword. His most colorful exploit with the latter weapon is reported to have occurred while fighting with the English volunteers. In the best theatrical tradition Jonson challenged the enemy to send forth a champion. Then as both armies looked on Ben slew his man and carried the armor home in triumph. His belligerent duels with the pen were almost as spectacular, and yet in spite of his blustering nature a certain good humor shines through. It is significant that he later collaborated in writing plays with some of the men with whom he had quarreled. It is also significant that he ended his days surrounded by a group of young admirers who called themselves "The Sons of Ben."

As to his plays, he wrote—or attempted to write—both tragedies and comedies. His tragedies, while highly regarded by Ben Jonson, find few admirers today. Perhaps they smell of Jonson's self-conscious attempt to write in the correct classic style, or perhaps Jonson, in spite of such lovely lyrics as "Drink to Me Only With Thine Eyes," simply did not have sufficient gift as a poet. In any event even his best tragedy, *Sejanus,* makes one appreciate the old remark, "Shakespeare came from heaven, Jonson from college."

In comedy, on the other hand, Ben Jonson stands out as Shakespeare's only contemporary rival; in fact in the area of satire Jonson is clearly superior. In characteristic academic fashion Jonson had reasons and theories for almost everything he did. Consequently, he becomes an interesting and important figure in the history of dramatic criticism. The theory for which he is famous, both as playwright and critic, is that of the "comedy of humours." The concept of "the humours" is an outgrowth of medieval physiology which held that four elements, moist, dry, hot, and cold, according to their balance and proportion, determined man's disposition. By the time of Jonson the term "humour" was in common usage much the same as the term "complex" was between World Wars I and II. Jonson conceived the idea that if all these "humours" were evenly balanced a normal and non-comic personality would be the result, but that if unbalanced—if the personality had too much of any one element—an eccentric and potentially comic personality would emerge. Jonson, of course, did not limit himself only to four basic "humours," but he did try to find some quality or trait in almost every character that if sharply accentuated would render the character comic. While we today may smile at the physiological concept that was the root of the Jonsonian theory, we cannot deny that he came close to the discovery of a basic truth. Every satirist from the professional cartoonist to the high school author of take-offs on the faculty knows the comic potentials of exaggerating traits or features already too prominent in his victim.

Jonson's first important comedy was entitled *Everyman in His Humour,* his second, *Everyman Out of His Humour.* Yet, while these are vigorous and interesting, they cannot compare with his four masterpieces: *Volpone, The Alchemist, Epicoene,* and *Bartholomew Fair.* Jonson's skill in plot construction is well illustrated by *Epicoene; or The Silent Woman.*[3] It concerns Morose, a testy old gentleman whose "humour" consists of a violent allergy to noise. The least sound, other than that of his own voice, throws him into a fit of rage. Being at odds with a young nephew, his only relative and consequently his heir, Morose determines to thwart the young rascal by marrying—provided that he can find a silent woman. Luck smiles upon him. He soon discovers a beautiful, and extremely soft-spoken young lady; he proposes; she accepts; he marries her, but the moment the ceremony

[3] Dryden, in the *Essay on Dramatic Poesy,* discusses *Epicoene* as an example of this particular excellence of Jonson's.

is performed she finds her tongue! Soon the house is full of wedding guests, including an assortment of young suitors bent on turning Morose into a cuckold at the earliest possible opportunity. The act reaches a climax of discord as Captain Otter, one of the wedding guests, joins in the bedlam with his troupe of trained bulls and bears!

In desperation Morose appeals to the lawyers to have the marriage annulled, but the learned gentlemen of the bar only distress him further with their endless discourses on legal technicalities. Although he submits to gross personal humiliation he cannot escape from his bride or from the pandemonium she has created. At this point the erring nephew, Dauphine, arrives on the scene. He pretends to be shocked by his uncle's distress and promises to clear up the whole mess provided that Morose will sign over his fortune. At his wits' end, the old man consents, whereupon Dauphine reveals that the wife is a boy, Dauphine's own page, in disguise, a revelation which leaves the seductive suitors quite as disconcerted as the avaricious old man.

While *Epicoene* is perhaps Jonson's funniest play, his masterpiece is undoubtedly *Volpone; or The Fox.* This was not written just to be amusing; it is an indictment of the viciousness of the human race. Written during the same period that Shakespeare was writing his great tragedies, its bitter theme suggests that both men may have been motivated by the decay and growing evil in life about them. Shakespeare lashed out with tragedy, Jonson with comedy. Euripides and Aristophanes had complemented each other in the same way 2000 years earlier.

Jonson centers the action of his masterpiece around a vicious, cynical, avaricious old man, Volpone, who with the help of his servant Mosca (the fly) conceives a brilliant swindle by pretending to be on his deathbed in order that money-mad self-seekers may be drawn into the trap of offering everything from gifts to the use of their wives in the hope of being named sole heir to Volpone's fortune. In this mad merry-go-round of corruption Volpone finally overreaches himself, and everyone suffers his just deserts. In this comedy, at least, Ben Jonson proves himself worthy to stand beside Aristophanes, Molière, and Shaw in satiric comedy's hall of fame.

There were many other important playwrights in the period, but rather than briefly list all of them our discussion will be limited only to those few who were leaders in some particular trend of the later Elizabethan or Jacobean Period.

One such trend that came early and influenced Shakespeare's later plays grew from the work of Beaumont and Fletcher in the field of tragicomedy.

This genre tended toward the romantic. It verged on the tragic but usually avoided death. Both Beaumont and Fletcher were cultured, well-bred gentlemen, and while both wrote some independent works, their most important contributions were made in collaboration. *Philaster* is perhaps their best play in the standard tragicomic style. In it they take over one of Shakespeare's favorite devices by disguising their heroine as a page-boy. It is interesting to note, however, that Beaumont also gave the period its only important example of burlesque with his well-known *The Knight of the Burning Pestle.*[4]

A few plays of the period deserve mention because they provide insight into the lives of common men. Next to Shakespeare's *Merry Wives of Windsor,* the best comedy in this respect is *The Shoemaker's Holiday,* by Thomas Dekker. Here the delightful and very human adventures of a group of London shoemakers are mixed with the proud success story of their master, who rises to the exalted station of Lord Mayor.

As far as tragedy about the common man is concerned, there is Thomas Heywood's *A Woman Killed With Kindness,* where a wife unfaithful to her husband is given no punishment save separation from the gentle spouse and from their children. Under such generous treatment she soon wastes away from remorse, finally to be forgiven on her deathbed, amid many tears and much pathos. While not a great play, it does, along with two others, *Arden of Feversham* and *The Yorkshire Tragedy,* foreshadow the coming of bourgeois tragedy.

The final characteristic of the period that merits attention is the trend toward tragedies of horror, suspense, and death. Most of the best writing in the late years of the period belongs to this genre. Much of it contains great poetry; much of it is fascinating even if unpleasant. It is the sign perhaps of a dying age. Two examples of the trend are *The Changeling* by Thomas Middleton and *The Duchess of Malfi* by John Webster. The first is a gripping case study of a young woman who hires a middle-aged man to murder an undesirable suitor. We see her go from the first shock when the murderer claims her virtue as his reward, through a strange mixture of fascination and loathing for his love, until at the end both she and the murderer are destroyed.

Webster's study of evil in *The Duchess of Malfi* is made slightly less somber than in *The Changeling* by the fact that the two leading characters are sympathetic. Having lost her husband, the Duchess is forbidden to marry

[4] Fletcher may have also collaborated with Beaumont in writing *The Knight of the Burning Pestle.*

by her brothers, the Cardinal and the Duke, who hope thereby to inherit her fortune. In spite of their threats she secretly marries her steward, a man of excellent character but lowly rank. Learning that their sister has deceived them, the Cardinal and the Duke hunt her down in the most relentless manner. At times the suspense and horror grow almost unbearable. Finally after many brilliantly conceived and macabre scenes, the Duchess, her husband, her children, the Duke, and the Cardinal are all killed. According to T. S. Eliot, Webster could always see the skull beneath the face.

Plays continued to be written until 1642, but few bearing a date later than 1630 are of importance. The decline of the great age was nearing its final stage. Consequently, there is little need to bemoan the fact that one of the first official acts of the Puritans, as they rose to power under Cromwell in 1642, was to close the theatres. Perhaps the very act of closure gave the English theatre a much needed rest in preparation for its resurrection under the reign of the Merry Monarch, Charles II.

FRANCE: MOLIÈRE AND NEOCLASSICISM

One characteristic of the French mind has always been its passion for reducing life to a system of rules, regulations, and logic. As early as 1402 the *Confrèrie de la Passion,* a brotherhood of tradesmen-actors, secured a monopoly on theatrical production in the Paris area, a privilege that enabled them to dictate, control, and frequently hamper the free growth of the theatre. As the Renaissance influence began to grow strong another group, the *Pléiàde,* began exercising a dictatorial power over playwriting, enforcing the classic rules as they understood them.

The first important play to show this classic influence was *Cléopâtre Captive* (1552) by Étienne Jodelle, written in rhyme and adhering to the unities. The neoclassic form of playwriting finally reached greatness in the tragedies of Racine. However, it did not entirely dominate the period, for the most famous playwright during the early years of Renaissance influence was Alexandre Hardy (c. 1575–1631), who resembled his Spanish contemporaries both in the prolific volume and the dashing romantic style of his work.

The first truly great French playwright, however, was Pierre Corneille (1606–1684), whose first play, *Mélite,* quietly ignored "the rules," probably because the author was quite ignorant of them. His next plays were more "correct." Then came his masterpiece, *Le Cid,* in which heroism, excitement, and beauty of verse were blended in a way that won him tremendous success with his audience, although much to the annoyance of the literary élite, including Cardinal Richelieu, it disregarded the unities. The plot follows two young lovers, Chimène and Rodrigue, whose romance is shattered when a quarrel develops between their fathers. A duel results, in which the girl's father is slain by Rodrigue, and Chimène finds herself bound by the rigid Spanish code of honor to avenge her father's death. Rodrigue responds to all this by resolving to die in the service of his country. He hurls himself into the war against the Moors, but instead of being killed he vanquishes the enemy and becomes a national hero. Torn between love and honor, Chimène continues to seek his death. She selects her champion and a duel is arranged. Once again Rodrigue is victorious and at last, with the help of the king, plus some involved rationalization, love triumphs over honor, and Rodrigue is united with his Chimène.

Even though Corneille had not openly defied the unities, it is easy to see why Richelieu considered it "improbable" that all this could happen in a single day! Corneille was censured for his violation of the rules and temporarily retired from playwriting. Later he resumed his work but never quite returned to the level of *Le Cid,* possibly because he seems a bit self-conscious about restricting himself. One cannot help wondering what Corneille might have accomplished had he enjoyed the freedom of Lope de Vega or Shakespeare.

But if Corneille was inhibited by neoclassic restrictions this was not the case with Jean Racine (1639–1699). In general Racine possessed a natural sense of order and good taste that made the classic form not a matter of restriction but an expression of his natural style. Nor are his plays lacking in emotional depth, which in spite of his thorough education and well-disciplined restraint, is a powerful factor. Almost without exception his plays deal with classic themes. *Phèdre,* based on the *Hippolytus* of Euripides, is usually regarded as his masterpiece. Sarah Bernhardt and other great emotional actresses have considered this story of a tragic queen enamored of her stepson one of the greatest challenges in all dramatic literature.

While Corneille and Racine reached noble heights in the serious and the tragic, it was in comedy that the age of Louis XIV excelled, and credit for this belongs largely to one man, Molière (Jean-Baptiste Poquelin, 1622–1673). Full of imagination and independence, Molière gained his first experience with theatre when as a young student of law he became active in an amateur theatrical group in Paris. Like many such groups today, the company met with financial difficulties, but its members refused to give up easily. In spite of debts, which even resulted in short terms in prison, the best actors of the troupe stayed together and under Molière's leadership set out to conquer the provinces. Competition and hardships were numerous, but they learned from these and after twelve years emerged as the outstanding troupe in France. Then, on October 24, 1658, came the great night when they appeared before Louis XIV and his court. Unfortunately they decided to rise to the dignity of the occasion by performing one of Corneille's tragedies. The performance was a failure, but Molière, skilled as a showman and speaker, stepped before the curtain to beg that the company be permitted to present one of his own slight farces, *Le docteur amoureux* (*The Love-Sick Doctor*). In the tradition of the best Hollywood romance, the little farce scored a brilliant success and Molière found himself and his company established in royal favor.

During his years of trouping the provinces, Molière had written several clever pieces, but his first important contribution to the world of dramatic literature, *Les précieuses ridicules* (*The Affected Young Ladies*), came after his dramatic debut before the king. The plot is simple but delightful: two gentlemen rejected by two affected young ladies take revenge by disguising their clever servants as supergentlemen, who spend a mad half hour completely unmasking the insincerity and shallowness of the silly girls and their whole affected cult. Like Aristophanes, Molière had used material immediately at hand. While he had not designated them by name, everyone knew that the barbs were aimed at a certain Madame de Rambouillet and her group. The *précieuse* ladies were outraged, but since Molière enjoyed royal protection they could do nothing except eventually modify their ways. Here is comedy once more returning to its highest function: rich in wit and entertainment, while serving as a satirical lash against social follies.

Some of the plays that followed were written for entertainment only, but most of them had purpose behind the fun. In his two most serious plays, *Tartuffe* and *Le misanthrope,* Molière's purpose is driven home with an intensity that almost, but never quite, loses its comic value. *Tartuffe* was such a stinging attack upon religious hypocrisy that not even Louis XIV dared protect it, and the play was withdrawn from public presentation. *Le misanthrope,* like so many of Molière's plays, reveals his philosophy that extremes are bad, that wisdom and goodness are to be found in the neighborhood of the golden mean, that honest acceptance of the facts and follies of life is the only sane course a man can follow if he would escape being ridiculous.

Probably nothing in the life and works of Molière does more to humanize the man and win our admiration than his last comedy. Knowing that death was not far away, he rose gloriously and ironically to the occasion and penned *Le malade imaginaire* (*The Imaginary Invalid*). His old antagonism toward the hypocrisy and pseudoscience of the medical profession is given free rein, and learned doctors receive a thorough beating, along with frugality and other human weaknesses. It is one of the most entertaining and popular of all his plays. Game and theatrical to the last, Molière himself played the leading role. During the fourth performance he collapsed. Four hours later he was dead.

While Molière, Racine, and Corneille are the giants of French theatre, even an introduction to plays and playwrights cannot entirely ignore three figures of the next century, Voltaire, Diderot, and Beaumarchais. Voltaire claims attention because the great philosopher was keenly interested in theatre and wrote some fairly successful, if somewhat bizarre, plays. Denis Diderot, the famous encyclopedist, made an attempt to break the stranglehold of pseudoclassicism by acclaiming a new type of drama—the drama of the common man. He wrote two plays, *Le pere de famille* and *Le fils naturel*, to illustrate his principles. While not particularly moving plays, they do contain elements that foreshadow Ibsen and modern drama.

Beaumarchais' claim to greatness rests on two lively, uninhibited comedies, *Le barbier de Seville* (*The Barber of Seville*) and *Le mariage de Figaro* (*The Marriage of Figaro*). Some of their fame, of course, belongs to Rossini and Mozart, who transformed them into delightful operas. While primarily enjoyable for their entertainment value, they also contain much satirical criticism of life, particularly in the character of Figaro, who appears in both plays. Had not most of Beaumarchais' life and energy been devoted to the French Revolution he might have become a formidable rival to Molière himself.

ENGLAND: RESTORATION AND
EIGHTEENTH CENTURY

Wearied by the stern, colorless quality of life under Cromwell and the Puritans, England finally invited Charles II, "The Merry Monarch," to return from France and ascend the throne left vacant by the execution of his father eleven years earlier. With the crowning of Charles II (1660) came the return of the English Court, made up largely of a nobility which, like Charles himself, had spent most of the years of the Commonwealth in France. Consequently it should surprise no one to learn that playwriting, along with other arts and pleasures, was also restored, but that it took its style and standards from French rather than from English tradition. Though there was of course some blending of the two, the style for the most part resembled Molière and Racine far more closely than it did Shakespeare or Jonson.

Contrasts between the Elizabethan and Restoration theatres are numerous and striking. The Elizabethan theatre had been a theatre of the people and of all classes from the lowest groundlings to Elizabeth herself. The Restoration theatre on the other hand was a pleasure of the Court alone. At the height of the Elizabethan era numerous playhouses had been in profitable operation at the same time. During the Restoration only two small theatres were licensed, and even these had difficulty in attracting patrons. Consequently, it should be remembered that Restoration playwrights, instead of writing for or about the English people, were concerned only with representing and pleasing a tiny handful of the highly select and highly sophisticated upper class. This Restoration audience was perhaps the most thoroughly aristocratic audience the theatre has ever known. Professor Allardyce Nicoll[5] points out that even in the court of Louis XIV, Molière had been able to mix bourgeois with aristocratic elements, whereas to the comedy writers of the English Restoration the common man simply did not exist, or at least did not matter.

All this is beautifully mirrored by the comedies themselves, which are chiefly concerned with love and intrigue. Dorimant, a character in *The Man of Mode,* sets the keynote: he says, "Next to the coming to a good understanding with a new mistress, I love a quarrel with an old one." The ideal was to be witty and clever; the only sins, to be dull, sincere, or to be found out. The country with its commoners was regarded as boring; the clergy and professional men were treated with indifference or condescension. Wit, brilliance, and pleasure were the ideals; morality, sincerity, and "goodness" were taboo.

It is not surprising that such a society should have failed miserably in its attempt to write tragedy. In comedy, however, the results, while not to be compared with the accomplishments of a Molière or a Shaw, were sur-

[5] Allardyce Nicoll, *World Drama,* Harcourt, Brace and Company, Inc., p. 339.

prisingly excellent. Some of the success may have been due to the fact that the playwrights, who were also leaders in affairs of state, were men of ample intellectual capacity. Sir George Etherege (c. 1634–1691), the first important playwright, is an excellent example of this, for he was a favorite of Charles II, handsome, dashing, an able diplomat, and a skillful lover. Playwriting to him was not a profession, but an amusement. He bothered to write only three plays, the best being his last, *The Man of Mode; or, Sir Foppling Flutter.* The title itself gives an indication of the tone of the play.

The foregoing comments about Etherege also apply, with slight modifications, to William Wycherley, whose *The Country Wife* has been enormously enjoyed by audiences of our own day and whose *The Plain Dealer,* based on Molière's *Le misanthrope,* is greatly admired by the critics. However, it was with William Congreve (1670–1729) that Restoration comedy reached its polished perfection. His greatest play, *The Way of the World,* appeared at the exact turn of the century, 1700, and clearly marks a climax in high comedy. The plot, though clever and complicated, is not the item of chief importance. To understand anything of Restoration Comedy one must turn to the dialogue. Note the skill with which the beautiful Mrs. Millamant combats one of Mirabell's rare attempts to become serious and perhaps a bit sentimental:

Mrs. M.: Ha! ha! ha! What would you give, that you could help loving me?
Mirabell: I would give something that you did not know I could not help it.
Mrs. M.: Come, don't look grave, then. . . . Prithee, don't look with that violent and inflexible wise face, like Solomon at the dividing of the child in an old tapestry hanging.
Mirabell: You are merry, madam, but I would persuade you for a moment to be serious.
Mrs. M.: What, with that face? No, if you keep your countenance, 'tis impossible I should hold mine. . . .[6]

Although *The Way of the World* marked the climax of high comedy, forces were already working toward its destruction. Excesses of the aristocrats of the Restoration had resulted in the Bill of Rights in 1689. Money and the power that went with it were shifting into the hands of the sturdy and industrious merchant class. The problems of the common man, viewed by earlier writers as objects for laughter, were beginning to be taken seriously. As early as 1698 high comedy had come under bitter attack when Jeremy Collier, a church official, shook the theatrical world with his publi-

[6] Act II, scene 2.

cation of *A Short View of the Immorality and Profaneness of the English Stage.*

But the greatest opposition to high comedy came from the theatre itself, where a new genre, sentimental comedy, began to take over. Perhaps the most vivid foretaste of things to come occurred in 1696 with the production of Colley Cibber's new play entitled *Love's Last Shift.* The plot begins like the typical Restoration comedy. Loveless, a Restoration rake, marries a beautiful and virtuous young girl, Amanda, only to tire of her and desert her in favor of a wild life in France. As the play begins he has returned to England, dissipated, penniless, and asking only for one last fling. In trying to arrange a meeting with some lady of easy virtue his servant quite by accident makes contact with Amanda, the faithful wife. Seeing a chance to reclaim her erring husband, Amanda consents to a meeting. So Loveless meets her, does not recognize her, vows he has never known such love, such beauty, such ecstasy. At this point Amanda reveals her identity.

So far the plot might be that of any true Restoration comedy; had it continued in the high comedy vein the worthless rake of a husband would probably have been mortified to find the divine creature his lawful wife. He would probably have stormed from the house, making a fool of himself as well as of the virtuous Amanda who had thought she could reclaim him. But, instead of this, Amanda's revelation of her identity catches the soul of Loveless up in an orgy of repentance; Amanda weeps tears of joy, Loveless practically weeps tears of joy, and most astonishing of all, audiences wept tears of joy! Here was sentimental comedy, the happy tearful ending—"life as it should be."

So common are such endings today that it may be difficult for one accustomed only to modern plays to believe that an audience could ever have been surprised by such an unexpected and unnatural turn of events, but in 1696 the play was a new and a revolutionary experience.

For a while the writers of high comedy fought back. Sir John Vanbrugh wrote a brilliant answer to Cibber's sentimental ending with a play, *The Relapse,* which pictures Amanda trying to live with her "reformed" husband, who is once more on the prowl only six months after his "conversion," but in spite of Vanbrugh's efforts, and the efforts of others like him, sentimental comedy quickly became and still remains the predominant form, at least so far as quantity is concerned.

While Colley Cibber may claim credit for having written the first outstanding sentimental comedy, he is not really one of the leaders in the movement. His sentimental ending was probably nothing but a happy, unpremeditated accident. With Sir Richard Steele (1672–1729) this was not the case. This famous and beloved essayist became the ardent champion of the sentimental genre in theory as well as in practice. His own comedies, *The Conscious Lovers* and *The Tender Husband,* are among the best of their type. They advance the belief that man is fundamentally good at heart. Unlike the satirical comedies of Aristophanes, Jonson, Molière, and Congreve, which had sought to reform society by making vice ridiculous, Steele's comedies sought to reform it by making virtue attractive. They aimed to arouse not scornful laughter but kindly laughter and tears. Relationships between parent and child, nature and man, church and goodness were pictured as ideal. Above all, virtue was always rewarded, vice detected, and happiness eventually triumphant.

A complete account of the eighteenth-century sentimental movement is far more complicated and extensive than the above discussion would indicate. It may be traced in the theatre of other lands as well as in other phases of the life and literature of England. The conflict between the sentimental and the satirical view of life is still with us. Moreover the problem is complicated by the fact that sentimental comedy and satirical comedy have had a tendency to merge. This is apparent toward the end of the century in the work of Oliver Goldsmith (1728–1774), one of the two great playwrights of his day. By nature and emotion he was sentimental (Irish, lovable, and tender hearted) but by intellect and in theory he was the champion of satirical comedy. Maintaining that laughter had been all but banished from the stage, he set about the task of restoring the comic muse by writing *The Good Natured Man* and *She Stoops to Conquer.* The latter play, while imperfect, is one of the most popular English comedies between Shakespeare and Shaw, enjoying a long and successful history both with the reading public and on the stage.

Closer to true satirical comedy are the plays of Richard Brinsley Sheridan (1751–1816). His first comedy, *The Rivals,* gives us such famous characters as Lydia Languish, Sir Lucius O'Trigger, the blundering Bob Acres, and Mrs. Malaprop, whose passion for the use of polite language saturates her speeches with such famous "malapropisms" as: "the pine-apple of politeness," and "like an allegory on the banks of the Nile."

Sheridan's second play, *The School for Scandal,* is clearly an English masterpiece. It is a comedy of manners, a satire on the follies of the fashionable social circle of Sheridan's day. Against a background of scandal, gossip, and intrigue Sheridans spins a complicated plot, which among other things involves the affairs of a vivacious young wife, Lady Teazle, who has married an old husband, Sir Peter. There is nothing unusual about such a situation, but there is about the brilliance of the wit with which they quarrel.

SIR PETER T.   Very well, ma'am, very well; so a husband is to have no influence, no authority?

LADY T.   Authority! No, to be sure; if you wanted authority over me, you should have adopted me, and not married me: I am sure you were old enough.

. . . .

SIR PETER T.   Oons! madam; if you had been born to this, I shouldn't wonder at your talking thus; but you forget what your situation was when I married you.

LADY T.   No, no, I don't; 't was a very disagreeable one, or I should never have married you.

. . .

SIR PETER T.   This, madam, was your situation; and what have I done for you? I have made you a woman of fashion, of fortune, of rank; in short, I have made you my wife.

LADY T.   Well, then, and there is but one thing more you can make me to add to the obligation, and that is—

SIR PETER T.   My widow, I suppose?

LADY T.   Hem! hem!

. . .

LADY T.   For my part, I should think you would like to have your wife thought a woman of taste.

SIR PETER T.   Ay, there again; taste; Zounds! madam, you had no taste when you married me!

LADY T.   That's very true indeed, Sir Peter. . . .[7]

Perhaps people do not talk like this in real life, although we may be certain that many a woman has wished she could.

But Sir Peter and Lady Teazle are only part of the fun. There is the scene where the happy-go-lucky young Charles sells his family gallery of portraits, with most unsentimental and uncomplimentary regard for the biological accident that had made the models of the portraits his ancestors, without realizing that the buyer is really his own wealthy and scandalized uncle in disguise. There is also the screen scene, the most famous scene in the play, and one of the most famous comic scenes in all literature. Lady Teazle, about to sacrifice her honor to Charles' hypocritical older brother, Joseph, is surprised by the unexpected arrival of Sir Peter and takes hasty refuge behind a screen. Sir Peter and Joseph are in turn interrupted by Charles, and the old husband is forced to hide in the closet. In the scene that follows the possibilities for suspense and for the revelation of Joseph's

[7] Richard Brinsley Sheridan, *The School for Scandal*, Act II, scene 1.

true nature are excellent. Sheridan exploits both to the limit, until the screen is down, the eyes of Sir Peter and Lady Teazle completely opened, and even the oily-tongued hypocrite, Joseph, momentarily at a loss for words.

Among Sheridan's other plays, *The Critic*, a brilliant burlesque of heroic tragedy, is the only one that is still well known, and while it may not equal *The School For Scandal* or *The Rivals* in popularity it has long been highly regarded by those who best know the theatre. It is ironic to learn that in spite of his early success as a playwright, Sheridan, before he was thirty, withdrew from the "impractical" world of playwriting to devote himself to the practical world of politics. One may note with some bitterness and regret that only a handful of historians know of his work as a member of Parliament, while hardly anyone with so much as a secondary school education has failed to hear of *The School For Scandal* or *The Rivals*.

Having traced the major course of comedy through the Restoration to the close of the eighteenth century, we should now note that the period was also famous for having originated, or at least developed, a number of new comic forms. Most notable perhaps was ballad opera, where lyrics were interspersed with dialogue much as they are in modern musical comedy, but where, unlike musical comedy, they were sung to old tunes. *The Beggar's Opera* (1728) by John Gay is the outstanding example of the genre. It is a devastating satire on politics, morals, and Italian opera. It set a new record in London for length of run, but because of its satire it helped to stimulate the passage of the famous licensing act of 1737, which opened the way for rigid censorship of all plays.

Another genre worthy of notice is burlesque, of which there are at least three examples of importance. *The Rehearsal* (1671) by the Duke of Buckingham, *Tom Thumb* (1730) by Henry Fielding, and *The Critic* (1779) by Sheridan. Of the three, *Tom Thumb* (published in 1731 as *The Tragedy of Tragedies*) is the most fantastic and had the most telling results. It dealt a death blow to heroic tragedy, as tiny Tom conquered giants in battle and the passionate princess Huncamunca in love. This is one play where reading the script is probably more enjoyable than seeing it performed on the stage, for the copious footnotes are half the fun. For example after Tom has cried, "Oh happy, happy, happy, happy, Thumb!" a footnote solemnly informs us that Tom is exactly one-fourth happier than Masinissa, a well-known tragic character in the tragedy, *Sophonisba,* who was only "happy, happy, happy!"[8]

In addition to ballad opera and burlesque, farce enjoyed a vogue during the period. Most of these farces were short and were used as "curtain raisers" or "after-pieces." They are not of world-shaking importance, unless we wish to include *She Stoops to Conquer* in this genre, but they did serve to keep the spirit of laughter alive and healthy at a time when comedy was becoming more and more lacrimose. Some of the best of these short farces were written by the great actor, David Garrick.

Turning from the comic to the tragic muse, we find both parallels and contrasts. The greatest contrast lies in the fact that whereas comedy reached a high degree of excellence during the Restoration, tragedy reached a preposterous degree of bombast. Heroic tragedy, as it is now labeled, exhibits most of the worst qualities of Seneca. Extravagant situations, unbelievable heroes, and impossible deeds were mixed with a rigid adherence to classic rules, a strict sense of decorum, and a verse form of rhymed couplets, which had been borrowed from the French. One of the best of the heroic tragedies, *The Conquest of Granada,* was written by the great John Dryden (1631–1700), who later sensed the error of his ways by returning to blank verse and the spirit of Shakespeare (to a partial extent) in his most important work, *All For Love.* A comparison of *All For Love* with Shakespeare's *Antony and Cleopatra* on which it was based is interesting. Whereas Shakespeare had wrestled with the fate of empires in forty-two scenes that ranged over the world of the Roman Empire, Dryden compressed everything into a single place, a single day, and a single theme of love versus honor. In poetry and imaginative scope Dryden falls far short of his Elizabethan master; still, in spite of its limitations, *All For Love* stands high above the other tragedies of its day. On its own terms it is a serious, effective, and genuine example of tragic writing.

From this point on the general development of tragedy parallels the development of comedy. Like comedy it became increasingly sentimental and bourgeois. The general weakening of fiber may be noted in the plays of Thomas Otway (1652–1685). Though Otway is one of the most gifted serious writers of his day, the very title of his tragedy, *The Orphan,* suggests its overly pathetic material, while his *Venice Preserved,* in many ways

[8] Henry Fielding, *The Tragedy of Tragedies,* Act I, scene 3.

strong and vigorous, featured a very weak hero, Jaffeir, and a heroine appropriately referred to as "blubbering Belvedera." Other tragic playwrights, including Nicholas Rowe (1674–1718), the first important editor of Shakespeare, began writing what are now referred to as "she-tragedies" because they featured women in the title roles, for example *The Tragedy of Jane Shore,* and *The Ambitious Stepmother.*

But just as *Love's Last Shift* tended to establish or at least to crystallize the genre of sentimental comedy, so *George Barnwell; or, The London Merchant* established the genre of bourgeois tragedy. Written by George Lillo and produced in 1731, the plot, based on an old ballad, features an innocent young boy, only eighteen, who falls under the spell of an evil woman, Millwood. Under her influence this young apprentice plays false to his noble old employer Thorowgood, his loyal friend, Trueman, and his innocent sweetheart, Maria. Finally he is driven to the murder of his kind and thoughtful uncle. The last act shows his pitiful repentance and march to the gallows.

Several qualities establish the thoroughly bourgeois character of this tragedy. It is written in prose, it exalts the merchant class, and it presents no character of genteel or noble birth. The central character is weak and pathetic, but not tragic. George Barnwell has no strength of character. If Millwood says "come hither," George comes; if she asks him to steal from his employer he steals; if she suggests that he murder his uncle he murders his uncle. Contrast George with a King Lear or an Oedipus and one sees why the play is not tragic. To be tragic an element of strength, significance, and greatness of character must blend with the pity and terror.

Although bourgeois tragedy was definitely established by *The London Merchant,* it did not immediately sweep high tragedy from the stage. For the most part tragedy, whether high or bourgeois, tended to be pretty weak. As in the case of sentimental comedy, the trend toward bourgeois tragedy was not confined to England alone. In France, as we have already noted, both Voltaire and Diderot were identified with the movement, and it was in Germany that the bourgeois genre first gained the strength to command genuine respect.

GERMANY: THE ROMANTIC SPIRIT

The shifting tide from the aristocratic and classic toward the bourgeois and sentimental in both life and literature had during the early and middle years of the eighteenth century progressed smoothly, but as the period drew toward a close, signs of turbulence and unrest became evident. In

America the new spirit of liberty and equality broke the hold of King George III. In France a few years later it burst out in the storming of the Bastille. But even where revolution and physical violence were held in check, the minds and hearts of men were stirred with a new excitement, a new hope for an "age of reason," a new belief in the perfectability and equality of man.

In literature this new spirit of liberty and equality led to a movement known as romanticism. Inspiration not rules, variety not unity, and freedom not restriction were among its characteristics. There was also a love of nature, a worship of the noble savage, and a strange quality of nostalgic sadness that found its way into much of the literary work of the day.

In the theatre, Germany, through the work of Lessing, Goethe, and Schiller, carried the romantic spirit to its greatest heights. Germany had been slow in its theatrical development. A good beginning had been made during the sixteenth century by Hans Sachs, but then came the devastation of the Thirty Years War, and a century of progress was lost. During the years when England with Shakespeare, Spain with Lope de Vega, and France with Molière were giving the world plays rivaled only by those of ancient Athens, the best Germany had to offer was a crude, vulgar farce featuring such characters as Hans Wurst and Pickleherring.

The awakening began with the efforts of Johann Gottsched and Karoline Neuber. Working sometimes as partners and sometimes as enemies, they waged a war against the crude vulgarity of the popular German stage. Unfortunately the remedy that both proposed was almost worse than the disease itself, since both crusaded for the dull and lifeless decorum of French pseudoclassicism. But in spite of such shortcomings they did manage to rid the stage of Hans Wurst, and they did pave the way for the great period that was to follow.

Working in Karoline Neuber's company during its last years was a young man named Gotthold Ephraim Lessing (1729–1781), who was destined to become the first great playwright in Germany. His influence and contributions as a critic probably overshadow his work as a playwright. With a clearness of insight that had been lacking in both Neuber and Gottsched, Lessing saw that while the classic form had been excellent for the Greeks, it could not be applied to the restless spirit of eighteenth-century Germany. Dramatic effectiveness, not rules, became his basis of judgment; nor were Seneca or his French imitators to be the recommended models, but rather Shakespeare with his freedom and imagination. Lessing also saw merit in the attempt of George Lillo and his followers to relate drama to the life of the common man. Such views were skillfully stated in his *Hamburgische Dramaturgie,* a periodical, which though published for less than two years, ranks second only to Aristotle's *Poetics* as a landmark of dramatic criticism. Almost single-handed he turned the German theatre from the sterile path of pseudoclassicism to the stimulating freedom of Shakespeare.

Lessing's plays, *Emilia Galotti* and *Miss Sarah Sampson,* are bourgeois tragedies far superior to anything either France or England had yet contributed in that genre. *Minna von Barnhelm* still remains one of the finest German comedies, while *Nathan der Weise* (*Nathan the Wise*), although not one of the world's greatest plays, is probably one of the world's greatest pleas for religious tolerance. If Lessing's poetry and dramatic skill had equalled his thesis the last play would rank as one of the masterpieces of all time. Partly through the device of having a Christian, a Mohammedan, and a Jew discover that they are blood relations, but largely through the character and wisdom of Nathan, Lessing drives home his message.

The old Jew represents the best in all religions. While technically adhering to the faith of his Hebrew fathers he has equal respect for all other faiths. According to his famous parable of the ring, only by the test of years, only by observing which one brings the greatest good to mankind, can we determine which if any is the "true" religion.

Lessing's tendency to allow ideas to overshadow his skill as a playwright is also apparent in the works of his great contemporary, Johann Wolfgang von Goethe (1749–1832). Few names in history command greater respect, for Goethe, like Leonardo da Vinci, very nearly mastered the whole of contemporary knowledge in both art and science. The theatre may well be proud of the fact that such an intellectual giant chose to cast so much of his work in the dramatic form, even though the result does not always meet the demands of practical stage production.

His masterpiece is of course *Faust.* Into it went much of a lifetime's search for truth, for the essence of good and evil, for the meaning of man's restless striving for knowledge. Imagine Goethe's chagrin could he see what modern audiences extract from his masterpiece, usually identified in the popular mind by the Soldier's Chorus from Gounod's opera, which in common with most stage productions limits itself to the pathetic story of Gretchen. Taken alone, this first half of *Faust* is practically meaningless, if not downright immoral. The film, *Faust and the Devil,* for example, featured beautiful romantic scenery, and beautiful singing of Gounod's music, but the intellectual essence of the story seemed to be the childishly simple tale of a man who, having sold his soul to the devil, seduces a beautiful girl, kills her brother, deserts her, and returns in time to see her tried for infanticide and burned at the stake. Now what is the meaning of such a story? Do not sell your soul to the devil? Is one really likely to face the problem in quite such a direct and obvious way? And what of Gretchen? The moral is apparently beware of strange handsome men; but with the cards so stacked against her, Gretchen could not possibly have resisted. Her piety and resistance were admirable; had they been any stronger she could scarcely have avoided being frigidly unattractive. We are at a loss to find any meaning in seeing beauty and innocence tortured inhumanly for no reason at all. Or is the moral one of social protest against the fantastic cruelty and lust for punishment on the part of the medieval church and medieval townspeople? In that case Mephistopheles becomes the only admirable character, for he persecutes these innately evil, ignorant, and superstitious beings whenever possible. So much for the popularized versions of *Faust*.

Obviously Goethe had other ideas when he wrote his great dramatic poem. It would be futile to attempt here an analysis of this complex masterpiece, but it is at least possible to state the main outline, for Faust has much of Goethe in him, much of Renaissance man, much of every man who ever sought honestly and deeply for the meaning of life. Like that of all youth, Faust's first major search for happiness lies in the realm of sensual pleasure. This brings tragedy and suffering both to himself and Gretchen. His next search leads him into the realm of the aesthetic, but even this finally vanishes into nothingness. Finally his quest leads him to the service of his fellow men, and, in draining the swamps to bring happiness to others, he himself finds happiness and salvation—salvation because of the very struggle, the endless, restless quest for knowledge that had brought so much of both good and evil into the world.

We can admire the scope and greatness of Goethe's theme whether our own philosophies of life agree entirely or not. The meaning of *Faust* when viewed in its entirety is a far cry from the impression one receives when the pathetic story of Gretchen is considered alone.

While no match for Goethe as a thinker, the third outstanding playwright of the period, Johann Christoph Friedrich von Schiller (1759–1805), excelled him as a man of the theatre. Schiller's plays have dramatic fire, excitement, and lyric qualities that have never ceased to win favor with both actors and audiences. A true son of the romantic spirit, his first play, *The Robbers,* written when he was only twenty-two, breathes a passionate spirit of freedom as it traces the tragic adventures of Charles von

Moor, who under the sting of treachery becomes leader of a band of robbers. He and his band fight valliantly against injustice, but in the end his lawlessness brings death to his noble and respectable father as well as to the girl he loves. Entangled in meshes from which there is no escape, he leaves the band and gives himself up to certain death.

Schiller's *Love and Intrigue* is a more mature and much better play. It is a bourgeois tragedy that concerns a tyrannical father's attempt to prevent his son from marrying below his station. But Schiller's greatest plays are generally considered to be his historical tragedies. Not since Shakespeare had any one made the material of history so effective on the stage. Such plays as *Wilhelm Tell* and *Maria Stuart* probably gained much of their popularity from the fact that the title roles offered excellent histrionic opportunities to great stars of the nineteenth century. His greatest work from a literary standpoint, however, is *Wallenstein,* a trilogy of three complete plays greatly admired by critics, but infrequently seen on the stage.

There were many writers who followed Schiller but none are of major literary importance. To the student of literary trends the oustanding name is August Friedrich Ferdinand von Kotzebue, who along with the French playwright, Guilbert de Pixérécourt, shares the dubious honor of creating melodrama. Whether for better or for worse, melodrama dominated the playhouses of the nineteenth century. Melodrama, of course, tends not toward experience but toward mere entertainment. Its characters are usually black or white, its plots contrived, its happy endings inevitable, while anything that might stimulate controversy or thought is avoided. These qualities tend to place melodrama close to the bottom of the literary heap in the eyes of most critics. On the other hand, melodrama did and does fit the stage and the audience for which it was and is written. After all, sheer entertainment, while not the highest of human experiences, is rare enough that it should not be entirely scorned.

CHAPTER IV

The Modern

PROLOGUE: THE NINETEENTH CENTURY TO IBSEN

THE GREAT THEATRICAL EVENTS OF THE NINETEENTH CENTURY CAME during its last quarter when Ibsen, Shaw, Strindberg, and their contemporaries ushered in the dramatic movement commonly studied in college classes under the title of "Modern Drama." Prior to this the century had little to offer in the realm of dramatic literature. As already noted, melodrama tended to dominate the scene. If a great actor wanted to star in something more dignified he turned to Shakespeare and the classics.

We have already mentioned Kotzebue and Pixérécourt in Germany and France. The greatest of the melodrama writers in England was probably Edward Bulwer-Lytton (1803–1873). His *Richelieu* and *The Lady of Lyons* held the stages of England and America for over half a century, and there are still old-timers who will testify that drama never reached more sublime heights. But while Victorian audiences, filled as they were with unwavering faith, staunch codes of ethics, and abundant propriety, must have found his plays moving and true to their ideals of life, modern audiences find them unconvincing, overly sensational, and embarrassingly flowery in their expression of sentiments.

Unlike most other ages, the great writers of the Victorian period avoided the dramatic form. Perhaps the English stage had not recovered its moral respectability since the attack by Jeremy Collier; perhaps the essential cheapness of melodrama drove them away; perhaps the commercial purpose of the stage, which by judging success only in terms of the box office inevitably encouraged sensation rather than merit, was responsible, but in any event the art of playwriting was not held in high esteem. That the difficulty lay in the cheapness of the stage is evidenced by the fact that Shelley, Byron, Tennyson, and Browning were all attracted to the theatre and unable entirely to resist the temptation to write plays, but they wrote for the reading public only; their plays are called "closet dramas," for they were never seriously intended for performance.

If writers of melodrama went too far to entertain their audiences, these writers of closet drama went too far in the opposite direction. Their plays remain dramatic poems rather than pieces for production upon the stage. This avoidance of the stage is particularly regrettable in the cases of Robert Browning and Charles Dickens. Browning shows a keen sense of the dramatic. Had he been privileged to work with a real theatre and for a discriminating audience, as were Sophocles, Shakespeare, and Molière, his contribution to dramatic literature might have been outstanding. Charles Dickens is even more interesting. He loved the stage and even spent much time acting in amateur theatricals. His sharp sense of character and his flare for the dramatic all seem ideally suited for a career in the theatre, but for some reason he avoided the dramatic form.

So much for the major currents, melodrama on one hand, closet drama on the other, that characterized the English theatre from Sheridan almost to Shaw. Midway in the century another movement deserves notice. This was the beginning of a tendency toward realism, toward social or thesis drama as seen primarily in the plays of Tom Robertson. While his plays are not highly regarded today they nevertheless show an interesting attempt to deal with real problems of real people. Plays like *Caste* and *School*, with the help of a new type of realistic scenery, gave London something different to talk about, and to some extent they foreshadowed the coming of Ibsen.

When we shift our attention from England to nineteenth-century France, the first item to claim our attention is the triumph of romanticism over the psuedoclassicism that had maintained a strangle hold on French playwrights since the time of Racine. Outwardly the break was sharp and revolutionary. The groundwork had been laid with the translation of Shakespeare's plays during the 1820's. The decisive battle, however, was waged and won by Victor Hugo with his romantic tragedy, *Hernani*, which appeared in 1830. For weeks the theatre was a scene of excitement and uproar as the classicists tried to boo the play down and romanticists tried to cheer it on. It was the battle of *The Cid* all over again except in far more volcanic proportions, and this time the romanticists and Hugo scored a decisive triumph. Romanticism is not necessarily superior to classicism. No French romantic playwright ever equaled the profound and near-perfect achievements of the classic Racine. Nevertheless Hugo's victory meant new freedom and vitality to the French stage, and in 1830 both qualities were sorely needed.

A second movement to claim attention in nineteenth-century France centers in Eugène Scribe (1791–1861) and his "well-made plays." During the same years when the pseudoclassicists were laboring to protect the purity of tragedy they paid little attention to the comparatively lowbrow melodrama that was steadily growing in bourgeois popularity. Consequently, as the literary élite fought the battle of *Hernani*, Scribe, belonging essentially to the school of melodrama, was capturing the masses. Skilled in theatre and equipped with an instinct for commercial success, he set about the practical business of playmaking. Through his keen sense of audience analysis he perfected a formula for the manufacture of plays that almost placed playwriting on an assembly-line basis. Once his formula was perfected some four hundred "well-made plays" poured off the line to bring him fortune if not undisputed fame. What is wrong with such plays? Nothing, if one thinks of a play as a matter of two hours of harmless entertainment. But to one who regards playwriting as a sharing of experience, Scribe's plays are useless, for Scribe wrote practically nothing of experience into them. Characters, as in melodrama, tend toward black and white. Suspense, conflict, and plot are the essence of his effectiveness, but in Scribe's hands these contribute nothing toward an understanding of life. Still, in spite of the abuse heaped upon him, Scribe did have the sense of "theatre" that so many have lacked. It is regrettable that with all his skill he had nothing to say.

One other playwright claims brief attention, since, like Robertson, he foreshadows Ibsen and modern drama. This is Alexandre Dumas *fils* (1824–1895). His first play, *La dame aux camellias* (*Camille*), reveals the author's interest in social problems even though the approach is fundamentally romantic. Marguerite Gautier, falling in love, tries sincerely to escape from her past but fails. Reconciliation with the man she loves comes too late and she dies in his arms. From this beginning Dumas plunged deeper and more seriously into social problems. *La question d'argent* (*A Question of Money*) deals with the dangers of capitalism, *Les fils naturel* (*The Illegitimate Son*) with the problems of illegitimacy, and *Les idées de*

Madame Aubray (*Madame Aubray's Ideas*) with fundamental goodness versus moral taboos. Not profound in the sense that Ibsen, Strindberg, and Shaw are profound, Dumas did have the courage to explore problems with a degree of honesty and originality uncommon in his day. Add to this his gift of showmanship and one understands his popularity and his important position.

So much for highlights of the pre-Ibsen nineteenth century. There were hundreds of playwrights in many lands. Some of them we will meet as we discuss the theatre in America, Russia, and Italy. Much more could be said, but it all seems rather insignificant in comparison with what happened in Norway and Sweden as the century neared its close.

NORWAY: HENRIK IBSEN

The attempt to make the life of the common man the material of great drama came of age, not in the theatrical capitals of Germany, England, or France, but from the hitherto unproductive soil of Norway. The playwright was Henrik Ibsen (1828–1906). Many still regard him as both the first and the greatest figure in "modern drama."

A sensitive child, his early years were filled with struggle and disillusionment. He lived largely within himself, made few friends, and gradually developed a spirit of rebellion against society—a spirit very obvious in his earliest plays and still a motivating force in those of his maturity. Ordinarily, as with most seriously introverted types, he was unlucky, displaying a chronic tendency toward bad breaks. A glaring exception to this tendency came in 1851 when the violinist, Ole Bull, offered him a position on the staff of the new Norwegian National Theatre in Bergen, a position that Ibsen, literally on the verge of starvation, eagerly accepted.

For five years his duties as stage manager provided the same type of invaluable contact with the theatre that Shakespeare, Molière, and other great playwrights had enjoyed. In addition to this practical all-round experience his contract required that he produce one play of his own on January second of each year. While none of the early plays that he wrote as a result of this requirement achieved greatness, they did provide training of the most valuable type.

Ibsen's comparatively happy Bergen years were followed by six less fortunate years in Christiana (Oslo), but toward the end of the latter period he wrote two important plays, *The Comedy of Love* and *The Pretenders*. The first of these, with its unorthodox views on love and marriage, created such a storm of criticism that Ibsen apparently resolved to leave

Norway at the first opportunity. The second play, *The Pretenders* (1863), scored a genuine success, but it was too late. Ibsen's mind was made up, and in April, 1864, he shook the dust of Norway from his feet, to spend the rest of his life in the less austere climates of Italy and Germany.

Ibsen, like Schiller and Shakespeare, devoted much of his early energy to writing historical plays, the best ones, like *The Pretenders,* being sagas of his native land. Next came his poetic dramas, *Brand* and *Peer Gynt,* which to some critics represent Ibsen at his best. Both plays were motivated by Ibsen's indignation over the weakness of the Norwegian national character. *Brand* is the somber tragedy of a priest whose blind strength of character and uncompromising devotion to God bring more intense suffering to those about him, according to Bernard Shaw, "than the most talented sinner could possibly have done with twice his opportunities."[1] He sacrifices everything: his mother, his child, his wife, for a God and a congregation who finally drive him into the mountains, where he dies in an avalanche that thunders, "God is love!"

Peer Gynt stands in many ways in vivid contrast to the somber *Brand.* It is a wild, fantastic poem sometimes bitter, sometimes gay, sometimes skirting the tragic. Peer, in contrast to Brand, goes "round about." He always compromises—or runs away. The play rambles almost as much as *Faust,* yet the overall effect is one of greatness. The characters are unusually vivid, while scenes like the death of Aase, Peer's mother, rank among the greatest in literature.

But while many regard *Peer* as Ibsen's masterpiece, none can deny that his fame in the history of the theatre rests primarily on another group of play, his social or thesis dramas. The first of these to command world attention was *The Doll's House* (1879). During its course of action we see Nora, the central character, change from a seemingly delicate, impractical "doll" wife into a woman who walks quietly but firmly out of her house, closing the door on what contemporaries regarded as a wife's duty to her children and husband.

When the play stirred a moral protest reminiscent of *Love's Comedy,* Ibsen struck back at his critics with *Ghosts.* Mrs. Alving, the central character in *Ghosts,* unlike Nora, remains loyal to all the moral codes. Though married to Captain Alving, whose dissipation and excessive appetites make their marriage miserable, she stands by him and especially by his memory after his death. To protect her son from the father's contamination she sends the boy to Paris. She rears the husband's illegitimate daughter al-

[1] George Bernard Shaw, *The Quintessence of Ibsenism,* p. 51.

most as though the child were her own. To sustain the myth of the captain's nobility and goodness, she uses all his money to build an orphanage. But in spite of all this devotion to her "duty," the orphanage burns to the ground, the illegitimate child deserts her, and the son, having inherited syphilis from his father, turns into a babbling idiot as the play ends. These are the rewards of her loyalty to duty!

If *The Doll's House* aroused a shower of criticism, *Ghosts* created a tornado. Critics became almost incoherent in their rage. They babbled about "loathsome sores" and "reeking cesspools"; they described it as sickly, indecent, and fetid.[2]

But Ibsen still fought back. In answer to the violent attack upon *Ghosts* he wrote *An Enemy of The People,* which cries out the thesis that the majority is always wrong. A typical community has just completed the construction of new municipal baths and looks forward to a healthy and profitable tourist trade. Before the baths can be opened, however, Dr. Stockmann makes the shocking discovery that the baths are dangerously impure. With enthusiasm the idealistic young doctor reveals his discovery to the city authorities, expecting with almost childish naivete to receive thanks for his public service. Instead the news touches off a frantic drive to suppress the truth. Stockmann's determined efforts to publish the facts he has discovered earn him the title of "an enemy of the people." His home, his family, and his life are endangered by an angry mob of the city's most respectable citizens, who are far more devoted to self interests than to truth.

The next and the last of Ibsen's thesis plays, *The Wild Duck,* shows an admirable maturity of his wisdom, for he now turned against his own overly zealous followers, who had begun to cry, "Strip away falsehood at all costs; the naked truth will make us free." The play is concerned with the sincere but blundering work of Gregers Werle, one of these new disciples of truth. Coming into the Ekdal household, which is living a comfortable middle-class existence in a world of illusion, Gregers clumsily shatters the home's foundation with the revelation that the sensitive young daughter, Hedvig, is not the child of the husband but of another man. He expects thereby to establish the marriage on a foundation of truth and beauty, but instead of reconciliation the truth brings disaster. The husband plunges into an orgy of self-pity; the wife is merely annoyed by her husband's adolescent antics. They are too weak to live by anything other than their illusions, and we could simply laugh at all of them were it not that

[2] *Ibid.,* pp. 3, 4.

the sensitive young Hedvig, believing that she is somehow responsible, kills herself.

After *The Wild Duck,* Ibsen seems to have lost interest in reforming society. His plays tend to become more symbolic and more psychological. In this later period came two of his best works, *Hedda Gabler* and *Rosmersholm.* By now the storms of protest had died away. Shaw and others had come to his defense, and through his declining years Ibsen must have found a measure of respect and contentment entirely foreign to him throughout most of his life.

Ibsen's contributions are many. He gave us a host of convincing and genuine characters: not black or white like those of melodrama but challenging, complex characters, with the many-sided characteristics of real people. He handled dialogue in a realistic prose that was far advanced in its conversational quality and naturalness. Through his skill as a dramatist ideas became exciting and entertaining. Finally he is usually credited with having been the first to construct great dramas from the problems of the common man.

SWEDEN: AUGUST STRINDBERG[3]

Not so many years ago the student studying "modern drama" in an American university was likely to receive the impression that Ibsen stood like a mighty mountain on a lonely plain of Scandinavian dramatic literature. Now we are beginning to realize that August Strindberg (1849–1912), his Swedish contemporary, may have been even mightier. Until the close of the First World War Strindberg's influence was comparatively minor, but since then the position of the two writers has tended to reverse itself. Although Strindberg has never commanded a popular following, his influence among critics, playwrights, and poets has been enormous.

While Ibsen had difficulties in adjusting to life, his sufferings were minor compared with those of Strindberg. An unwanted child, nervous and hypersensitive, Strindberg grew up in a large family that could satisfy neither his hunger for food nor his greater hunger for love. Minor events and personal slights that normal children would scarcely have noticed were tortures to him. He described himself as born without an epidermis, with raw nerve ends exposed mercilessly to the brutal stimuli of life. His deep yearning for love and companionship resulted in three marriages, but his sensitivity and temperament doomed all three to failure. For a while he hovered on the brink of insanity and actually spent some time in a mental

[3] I am indebted to Professor Alrik Gustafson for many of my ideas about Strindberg.

institution. Writing was his salvation. In autobiographies, novels, poems, and plays he poured out a feverish mass of work. He stands at the opposite end of the universe from a man like Eugène Scribe, who manufactured plays as impartially as if they had been nuts and bolts, for most of Strindberg's plays are torn from his own experience; some are almost nakedly autobiographical.

Of Strindberg's historical plays several, including *Gustaf Vasa* and *The Saga of the Folkungs*, rate well above anything Ibsen produced in this area, with the possible exception of *The Pretenders*. In other plays, particularly *Miss Julia* and *The Father*, he reached peaks of naturalism that have never been excelled. The latter play, almost terrifying in intensity, deals with the struggle for dominance between a man and a woman, with the woman, less honest and less scrupulous in her choice of weapons, gradually driving the man to madness and death through the power of suggestion. Her most diabolical weapon grows from her carefully planted suspicion as to whether or not their daughter is his own.

Strindberg's greatest importance in the history of the drama, however, lies in his expressionistic plays, among them *The Dream Play*, *The Dance of Death*, and *The Spook Sonata*. The titles alone suggest his nonrealistic treatment. In *The Dream Play*, Strindberg explains that he "tried to imitate the seemingly logical form of a dream. Anything may happen; everything is possible and probable . . . On an insignificant pattern of reality, imagination designs and embroiders novel patterns: a medley of memories, experiences, free fancies, absurdities, and improvisations."[4] As the play opens we see the daughter of the god Indra falling down, down through space. Caught in the murky atmosphere and gravity of earth she cries out for help, but is told to go down and learn why man is always complaining. From this prologue the play moves with eerie unpredictability from one almost autobiographical fragment of human suffering or grotesque humor to another. Now we join The Officer inside the castle, with his painful memories of childhood; now we are outside the Opera House where a young singer has just failed in her tryouts, now we move to the Lawyer's office the air is heavy with the crimes and quarrels of humanity. As the Daughter drifts from one scene to the next we hear the refrain, "Life is evil! Men are pitiful creatures!"

It is unnecessary to explain Strindberg's greatness to a playwright, artist, or poet. To explain it to the student not accustomed to poetry or great literature is difficult if not impossible. To those who say, "Why should any-

[4] Preface to *The Dream Play* by August Strindberg.

one want to see or hear such awful plays?" the following words may help. Never has a great mind laid itself more nakedly and vividly before us. One does not read Strindberg for "entertainment" in the popular sense of the word, but for the experience of sharing in the life and ideas of one who suffered deeply, but who reflected upon and organized this suffering. Finally there is a poetic, sensitive, and imaginative quality in even his prose that raises it far above the level of the ordinary playwright. Take the following from *The Saga of the Folkungs:* The King is speaking:

MAGNUS: It is autumn!—Outside and in! (*Listens.*)

BLANCHE: What do you hear, dear?

MAGNUS: I am listening to the singing of the wind in the door-crack over there. It sounds like the moaning of sick men, or the crying of children over their lost toys—have you noticed the strange way they cry then?—And why does the wind complain in the autumn only? Isn't the air the same that blows in summer? (*Listens.*) Listen!—I should like to put words to its tones of lament.

BLANCHE: What does it sing of—that melancholy north wind?

MAGNUS: It sings of youth and vanished love; sings so that I can see it—see the blue lake, with the white castle amid oaks and lindens, suspended over roses and lilies. I see the wedding folk, cheering my youth's bride, to whom I gave my first love. . . . And one day, a long time after, she comes and lays in my arms a little creature dressed in white; and I feel as though an angel had come down from heaven; for when I gaze into his eyes I become changed from an ordinary sinful mortal to a very good one—or so it seems to me. Yet it was only my son, Erik!—Those were the days of happiness, of rejoicing. And then came the end!—He had me bound with cords. . . ."[5]

Even though the general public may never come to enjoy such lines or such plays, Strindberg's place in history is assured if for no other reason than his influence on the German expressionists, Eugene O'Neill, and so many others. Those who take drama seriously will do well to cultivate a more intimate acquaintance with this tortured, volcanic mind.

ENGLAND: SHAW AND MODERN DRAMA

Returning to England, one immediately encounters the name of Sir Arthur Wing Pinero. Not so many years ago he was regarded by many as the English Ibsen; today his plays have lost most of their appeal. Pieces like the once popular *Sweet Lavendar* are still interesting only because they are good British examples of charming and sentimental "well-made plays." As to his more serious works the best examples are probably *The Thunderbolt,* which deals quite skillfully with a greedy assortment of heirs to a fortune; *Mid-Channel,* which deals with the strain and danger that middle

[5] August Strindberg, *The Saga of the Folkungs,* Act V, translated by C. D. Lecock. In *Master Olof and Other Plays,* Jonathan Cape and Harrison Smith, 1931.

age presents to marriage; and *The Second Mrs. Tanqueray,* which created a sensation by dealing with the problem of prostitution.

But while Pinero was only partially successful in bringing convincing realism to the English stage, John Galsworthy (1867–1933) wrote some of the greatest realistic drama of all time. A lawyer, a scholar, and a gentleman, Galsworthy's personal life exhibits a balance of serenity and respectability that reminds one of Sophocles, and these personal qualities are reflected in his plays. He handles the most difficult social problems—antisemitism, strikes, crime and its punishment—with wisdom and objectivity. Like the ideal judge he is completely fair and scrupulously impartial in his presentation of all points of view. Perhaps it is a sad commentary, not upon Galsworthy but upon mankind, that his plays have not stirred the world more deeply than they have. All too often the masses have tended to follow the dogmatic Hitlers rather than the clear-thinking Galsworthys. As far as the stage is concerned however, we perhaps must admit that complete objectivity has inherent disadvantages, for a more impassioned, less scientific view is more dramatic. It also helps to have someone we can admire—a tragic hero greater than ourselves—but Galsworthy's characters are not heroes. Take Falder, in the play *Justice,* as an example; instead of a hero with courage, character, and strength hurled against the brutal cruelty of the penal system of England, William Falder is an ordinary, sensitive, but weak young man. Having fallen in love with a married woman he commits forgery in order to secure money for their escape to South America. Those who are required to deal out his punishment for the crime are not capitalistic monsters. The head of the firm whose money was embezzled, the judge who pronounces sentence, the warden, and even the guards at the prison are all understanding and sympathetic—all better than the "hero." While it is true that Galsworthy's plays have had a direct influence on society—*Justice,* for example, caused sweeping reforms of the English penal code, and *Strife* has been used to promote arbitration of strikes—the general effect of his plays tends toward sadness, resignation, and perhaps futility. Life, one senses, is shot through with evil, but there is really no one at fault. All must bear some of the blame; both sides are good and bad. Resignation and compromise seem to be the best solutions. And while to a great extent this is true of life, it does not seem to produce great drama, although in Galsworthy's hands it did produce many excellent dramas.

Among the other serious twentieth-century playwrights likely to gain permanent recognition is St. John Ervine (b. 1883) whose tragedy, *John Ferguson,* is almost a modern Book of Job. We see John Ferguson, already old and broken in health, stand firm under the loss of his home and the rape of his daughter, but when his son confesses the shooting of the daughter's assailant, even the character of John Ferguson breaks momentarily, and he begs the boy not to surrender to the police. The play closes with a broken-hearted but magnificent old man groping for strength as he struggles to read the biblical passage, "Would God I had died for thee, O Absalom, my son . . . my son."

Out of the First World War came R. C. Sheriff's *Journey's End*. It is his only important play, but its intensive psychological study of men in the face of trench warfare and death is likely to endure.

Among present-day writers whose dramas contain serious social purpose is J. B. Priestley (b. 1894). His plays are not realistic in the Ibsen or Galsworthy tradition, since almost all contain an element that is imaginative and frequently supernatural, enabling Priestley to transcend realistic time and space in order to probe for deeper values than are ordinarily apparent. Thus *Dangerous Corner* (1932) plays the same story in two ways, showing how a decision at one of life's dangerous corners can lead either to tragedy or comedy. *They Came to a City* explores reactions that range from misery to joy and contentment, as various characters from our imperfect world are placed in a magic utopian city. *An Inspector Calls* follows the work of a mysterious investigator whose quiet but relentless probing links one after another of an entire family to the suicide of a working girl whose death had at first seemed no more than a casual news item.

One other serious modern British playwright deserves attention. This is T. S. Eliot (b. 1888), the American-born English poet, whose *Murder in the Cathedral* is commonly regarded as the most important verse drama to come from twentieth-century England. Perhaps the wheel has turned its full cycle. Here is nothing whatever of the prose realism of the Ibsen thesis play. Rather we have a return to the Greek: imagination, poetry, and a chorus. To most people Eliot's later attempts, *The Cocktail Party* and *The Confidential Clerk,* are a bit disappointing when compared with *Murder in the Cathedral.* Nevertheless Eliot remains one of the most promising playwrights of the modern theatre, both because of his own potential ability and because of the influence he is almost certain to exert on others.

※

While England's contribution to serious drama has been important it is in comedy that she excels. Even without George Bernard Shaw, who seems assured of an immortal spot beside Aristophanes and Molière, the

The Modern

period has produced more than its share of comedy. To begin with there was Oscar Wilde (1856–1900), a Restoration spirit who somehow turns up in—of all places—Victorian England! While his first important play, *Lady Windermere's Fan,* flashes with such delicious epigrams as, "A man who moralizes is usually a hypocrite, and a woman who moralizes is invariably plain," the basic plot still retains the pattern of the contemporary well-made sentimental comedy. Two later plays, *A Woman of No Importance,* and *An Ideal Husband,* are much more closely related to the Restoration in both form and wit. It is in *The Importance of Being Earnest,* however, that Wilde shines in his true element. Here is brilliant farce blended with burlesque. The play is gay, rakish, and irreverent. Wilde pokes fun at society, love, morality, and the preposterous stock situations of the contemporary stage. Above all shines his dialogue, as in Lady Bracknell's interview with her prospective son-in-law:

LADY B.   Do you smoke?
JACK: Well, yes, I must admit I smoke.
LADY B.   I am glad to hear it. A man should always have an occupation of some kind. There are far too many idle men in London as it is. How old are you?
JACK: Twenty-nine.
LADY B.   A very good age to be married at. I have always been of opinion that a man who desires to get married should know either everything or nothing. Which do you know?
JACK: I know nothing, Lady Bracknell.
LADY B.   I am pleased to hear it. I do not approve of anything that tampers with natural ignorance. Ignorance is like a delicate exotic fruit; touch it and the bloom is gone. The whole theory of modern education is radically unsound. Fortunately in England, at any rate, education produces no effect whatsoever. If it did, it would prove a serious danger to the upper classes, and probably lead to acts of violence in Grosvenor Square.[6]

Most critics would agree that not only the greatest playwright but the greatest writer of the modern period was George Bernard Shaw (1856–1950), who in the English theatre ranks second only to Shakespeare. On the surface many see Shaw as a shocking disbeliever; some churches bar him as a heretic; some politicians regard him as subversive; yet if anything is consistent in him it is his deep humanitarian instinct. His boyhood years with their sting of poverty and underprivilege should not be forgotten, since they color the rest of his life. Both his long, earnest devotion to Fabian socialism and his antagonism toward poverty may well be traced to

[6] Oscar Wilde, *The Importance of Being Earnest,* Act I, scene 1.

these years. From his father he may have acquired some of his wit as well as his hatred of liquor, which had ruined his father's life and had been responsible for the family's poverty. From his mother he acquired his taste for music, a talent that he turned to great practical value as a music critic. In fact his critical works on the arts, including *The Quintessence of Ibsenism* and *The Perfect Wagnerite,* entitle him to a place as one of the most important critics since Lessing. From his mother, too, he may have gained some of the fundamental respect that he oftentimes reveals for woman as a life force.

In wit, cleverness, and brilliance of ideas Shaw is without a peer. Only Aristophanes catches something of the same impish quality: the breathtaking surprise and delightful originality. No one was ever quite comfortable in Shaw's presence. He seems to have taken irrepressible delight in doing the unexpected, often at the expense of consistency, and as a playwright, sometimes at the expense of structure and characterization. Yet had he been less contradictory, less of a paradox, he could never have been so interesting. His favorite device is to build up some pompous notion and then explode it for the joy of seeing his audience jump, like a small Puckish boy who blows up a huge balloon and then jabs it with a pin. For example in *Man and Superman* a conventionally respectable Victorian family learns that the daughter, Violet is pregnant. They react as expected with varying degrees of mortification, indignation, and shock. Finally a freethinking cousin, Tanner, whom we quickly recognize as a mouthpiece for Shaw, unable to stand their hypocrisy any longer, launches into an eloquent defence of the erring girl and especially the innocent unborn child. But now comes the surprise, for Violet explodes with moral indignation, not against those who had abused her, but against Tanner who has just defended her. She had been secretly but respectably married all the time. In fact she is one of the most narrowly respectable of the lot, much to the discomfort of Tanner and of those in the audience who had smugly assumed that they understood everything about Shaw.

He was, or so he always maintained, a great opponent of "art for art's sake." Art, according to Shaw, should have utility. To him a play was simply a more effective means of distributing ideas than either the speaker's platform or socialist pamphlets, and yet his plays promise to live on after the problems about which they were written have lost most of their interest. His first important play, *Arms and the Man,* is a good example. His basic idea that heroic notions about war are ridiculous is no longer exciting, shocking, or novel. Had he been only a common writer the play would now be dead. Instead it remains one of the most persistently popular plays in England and America. It is the skill with which he handles the theme that makes it live. Even though the art may not have been placed there for art's sake, the fact remains that it is there and there in abundance.

Shaw is frequently regarded as weak in the matter of characterization. Comparing him with Shakespeare, the criticism is certainly justified. One character in each play is usually a mouthpiece, a "raisoneur," for Shaw. Others frequently do and say the things that Shaw would have them say rather than the things they would be likely to say were they actual people; yet with Shaw this is no great crime, for a brilliant Shavian raisoneur is certainly more interesting than a dull character, however lifelike. Moreover, the charge that he does not give us great characters and character development is far from true. Candida, Caesar, Andrew Undershaft, and many others are among the most vivid characters in modern drama. It should also be noted that his fun and his message frequently rest on character development. Thus in *Arms and the Man* two romantic Bulgarians, Sergius and Raini, gasp and react throughout the play as their illusions about love and war are punctured one after another by the prosaic Swiss soldier, Bluntschli, until at last they emerge as quite mature and vastly different human beings. In the *Devil's Disciple* it is the romantic young wife of the minister who undergoes a similar transition as Dick Dudgeon punctures her illusions, while in *Caesar and Cleopatra* we see Cleopatra herself transformed through the patient disarming logic of Caesar from a silly, superstitious young girl into a rational and extremely able queen.

Another favorite Shavian device is to allow characters to discover themselves through a crisis. In *Androcles and the Lion,* Ferrovious, although determined to die as a meek, pious, Christian martyr, changes through a crisis into a warrior and a champion. Dick Dudgeon in his crisis offers his life for the sake of another, revealing to us and himself that he is more of a preacher and humanitarian than a "Devil's Disciple," while Reverend Anderson in his crisis becomes the soldier, the man of action, who raises an impromptu army to rescue his condemned benefactor from the gallows.

But while Shaw does give us characters and character development plus the other elements of good drama, it is in the conflict of ideas that he excels. No one has explored life's problems with greater sharpness and penetration; his ideas alone are enough to keep one alert and satisfied even when he stops the show in order to bombard his audience with them, as he does in the following three-page speech in *Man and Superman.* The scene is Hell; The Devil and Don Juan are engaged in discussion.

DEVIL: . . . Have you walked up and down upon the earth lately? I have; and I have examined Man's wonderful inventions. And I tell you that in the arts of life man invents nothing; but in the arts of death he outdoes Nature herself, and produces by chemistry and machinery all the slaughter of plague, pestilence and famine. The peasant I tempt to-day eats and drinks what was eaten and drunk by the peasants of ten thousand years ago; and the house he lives in has not altered as much in a thousand centuries as the fashion of a lady's bonnet in a score of weeks. But when he goes out to slay, he carries a marvel of mechanism that lets loose at the touch of his finger all the hidden molecular energies, and leaves the javelin, the arrow, the blowpipe of his fathers far behind. In the arts of peace Man is a bungler. I have seen his cotton factories and the like, with machinery that a greedy dog could have invented if it had wanted money instead of food. I know his clumsy typewriters and bungling locomotives and tedious bicycles: they are toys compared to the Maxim gun, the submarine torpedo boat. There is nothing in Man's industrial machinery but his greed and sloth: his heart is in his weapons. This marvelous force of Life of which you boast is a force of Death: Man measures his strength by his destructiveness. What is his religion? An excuse for hating me. What is his law? An excuse for hanging you. What is his morality? Gentility! An excuse for consuming without producing. What is his art? An excuse for gloating over pictures of slaughter. What are his politics? Either the worship of a despot because a despot can kill, or parliamentary cockfighting. I spent an evening lately in a certain celebrated legislature, and heard the pot lecturing the kettle for its blackness, and ministers answering questions. When I left I chalked up on the door the old nursery saying "Ask no questions and you will be told no lies." I bought a sixpenny family magazine, and found it full of pictures of young men shooting and stabbing one another. I saw a man die: he was a London bricklayer's laborer with seven children. He left seventeen pounds club money; and his wife spent it all on his funeral and went into the workhouse with the children next day. She would not have spent sevenpence on her children's schooling: the law had to force her to let them be taught gratuitously; but on death she spent all she had. Their imagination glows, their energies rise up at the idea of death, these people: they love it; and the more horrible it is the more they enjoy it. Hell is a place far above their comprehension: they derive their notion of it from two of the greatest fools that ever lived, an Italian and an Englishman. The Italian described it as a place of mud, frost, filth, fire, and venomous serpents: all torture. This ass, when he was not lying about me, was maundering about some woman whom he saw once in the street. The Englishman described me as being expelled from Heaven by cannons and gunpowder; and to this day every Briton believes that the whole of his silly story is in the Bible. What else he says I do not know; for it is all in a long poem which neither I nor anyone else ever succeeded in wading through. It is the same in everything. The highest form of literature is the tragedy, a play in which everybody is murdered at the end. In the old chronicles you read of earthquakes and pestilences, and are told that these shewed the power and majesty of God and the littleness of Man. Nowadays the chronicles describe battles. In a battle two bodies of men shoot at one another with bullets and explosive shells until one body runs away, when the others chase the fugitives on horseback and cut them to pieces as they fly. And this, the chronicle concludes, shews the greatness and majesty of empires, and the littleness of the vanquished. Over such battles the people run about the streets yelling with delight, and egg their Governments on to spend hundreds of millions of money in the slaughter, whilst the strongest Ministers dare not spend an extra penny in the pound against the poverty and pestilence through which they themselves daily walk. I could give you a thousand instances; but they all come to the same thing: the power that governs the earth is not the power of Life but of Death; and the inner need that has nerved Life to the effort of organizing itself into the human being is not the need for higher life but for a more efficient engine of destruction. The plague, the famine, the earthquake, the tempest were too spasmodic in their action; the tiger and crocodile were too easily satiated and not cruel enough: something more constantly, more ruthlessly, more ingeniously destructive was needed; and that something was Man, the inventor of the rack, the stake, the gallows, and the electrocutor; of the sword and gun; above all, of justice, duty, patriotism and all the other isms by which even those who are clever enough to be humanely disposed are persuaded to become the most destructive of all the destroyers.[7]

The above was published in 1903.

As to which of his plays is his masterpiece there is no general agreement. Many see Shaw at his best in *Saint Joan,* others prefer his monumental *Back to Methuselah,* some favor *Man and Superman,* but for myself I am partial to *Major Barbara,* which pits the ideas and ideals of Barbara and her Salvation Army against those of Barbara's father, the munitions tycoon, Andrew Undershaft. The battle of ideas is brilliant as Shaw finally convinces us that as a moral and humanitarian force his munitions manufacturer is superior to the Salvation Army, since the Army tries only to treat the symptoms and lessen the pain of evil, whereas Andrew Undershaft, through good wages and adequate housing, hits at the very tap root of evil: poverty. The play of course deals with infinitely more than this. War, munitions, religion, and life in general all find their moments of illumination. Both in philosophic content and dramatic brilliance *Major Barbara* measures up to the standards of greatness.

With the death of Shaw in 1950 the world lost one of its greatest thinkers, greatest playwrights, and greatest humanitarians. One wonders when we shall see his like again.

Twenty-five years ago there were many who considered James M. Barrie (1860–1937) to be Shaw's equal, if not his superior. While it now seems

[7] G. B. Shaw, *Man and Superman,* Act III. Quoted by permission of The Public Trustee and the Society of Authors.

clear that such an enthusiastic evaluation was unmerited, it is true that in matters of cleverness and particularly in the realm of whimsy and fantasy Barrie stands unequalled. His failure to measure up to Shaw may be due to a naturally kindhearted disposition that permitted him to see the follies of life, but never to be really unkind in attacking them. Those who admire the tough, intellectual fiber of Shaw are inclined to find too many strains of the romantic and sentimental in Barrie.

Although often sentimental and intellectually inferior if compared with Shaw, Barrie ranks high in these same qualities if compared with most modern playwrights. His *Admirable Crichton* takes many delightful jabs at the English caste system. Lord Loam and his family, while shipwrecked upon a South Sea island, soon discover that their servant, Crichton, is by knowledge, skill, and character far superior to his titled peers, and is consequently their natural leader. But with the family's rescue and return to England, all that was learned on the island is quickly forgotten. Crichton once more becomes the perfect servant and after a few nervous moments everything, including the caste system, resumes its complacent equilibrium as though nothing had ever happened. In *What Every Woman Knows* Barrie exposes a "self-made man" with the revelation that it is actually his plain little wife, Maggie, who touches up his speeches, saves him from a ruinous love affair, and quietly makes a success of him.

In *Dear Brutus* Barrie explores another theme that is close to his heart. Both theme and title come from Cassius' line in *Julius Caesar,* "The fault, dear Brutus, is not in our stars but in ourselves, that we are underlings." Through the magic of a Puckish old man and the enchantment of Midsummer Night, each of a group of characters is provided with a second chance, but in most cases the second chance brings only a repetition of the same mistakes.

Generally speaking, Barrie was sensitive to life's faults, but unlike Shaw he treats these problems with cleverness and whimsy rather than with wit and satire. Perhaps it is unfair to place Barrie against Shaw and force him to fight with the latter's weapons: penetrating wit and intellectual toughness. To enjoy Barrie at his best we should perhaps turn to *Peter Pan,* the most delightful adventure story ever written for the stage. Here is no pretense, no attempt to impress the scholars and philosophers. Here is cleverness, whimsy, flights of fancy, and the distilled essence of childhood adventure. In theatrical effectiveness it has few equals. Surely such an achievement deserves recognition.

We cannot leave England without brief recognition of Somerset

Maugham (b. 1874), Noel Coward (b. 1899), and Christopher Fry. Maugham and Coward are both highly successful writers of sophisticated comedy. In satire, skill, and intellect Maugham is the more effective. *The Circle* (1921) still rates as one of his best and is frequently presented by college theatres as one of the outstanding modern examples of sophisticated comedy.

Noel Coward would probably have been a greater playwright had he not dissipated his talents over such a wide area. He is one of the most colorful figures in the modern theatre, having enjoyed success as actor, composer, and director, as well as playwright. Like Barrie, he is probably at his best when he discards social comment and intellectual pretense and devotes himself to his own natural style—in Coward's case, sophisticated farce. The scintillating nonsense of *Blithe Spirit,* with its ghosts, séances, and sparkling dialogue may well survive after Coward's more serious efforts have been forgotten.

Of all who are engaged in the crusade to reunite poetry and drama none has been more successful than Christopher Fry (b. 1907). His experience in life and in the theatre is broad. He served as actor, teacher, director, play doctor, and soldier before winning fame as an author. His unique contribution to modern playwriting lies in the fact that he has successfully employed poetry not only when dealing with serious, tragic, and religious material but also when dealing with comic, witty, and satiric themes.

A Phoenix Too Frequent (1946), his first play to win general success, introduces us to a Roman tomb where a beautiful woman has chosen to remain until she dies beside the body of her deceased husband. Into this scene of noble devotion steps a good-looking young soldier. He is on duty outside guarding the bodies of six men who have been hanged (one had wanted to collaborate with anybody; two had refused to say anything; and one had said that the Romans hanged people for nothing). Anyhow, before morning the young wife's longing for life and love have completely overwhelmed her longing for sorrow and death. Her bliss comes to an abrupt end, however, when the young soldier discovers that during his absence someone has stolen one of the six bodies. Roman law demanded that in such an instance the guard's body must replace the body that was lost: "Section six, paragraph three in the regulations." By now however, the lady's love for life has been aroused to a pitch where she saves her soldier in the only way possible; she gives him the body of her husband to be hanged in the place of the one that was stolen.

Somewhat the same theme, love of life versus love of death, is treated with much the same ironic wit and brilliance in *The Lady's Not for Burning*. This time a man determined to die has his interest in living reawakened through his association with a fascinating girl, who has been condemned as a witch.

Perhaps the most amazing fact about Fry is the popularity of his poetic plays. In 1950 four of them were playing at the same time in London. In America both the professional and nonprofessional theatre have clamored for his works. Beyond doubt he is one of the most exciting figures in the present-day theatre.

IRELAND: YEATS TO O'CASEY

If there is such a thing as an inherent racial dramatic tendency, no nationality appears to have more of it than the Irish. Take the Irish blood from the theatres of England and America and the loss would be staggering. A quick check of the playwrights considered thus far reveals that Sheridan, Goldsmith, Wilde, Shaw, and Ervine were all of Celtic origin, while in America we will discover many others, including Dion Boucicault and Eugene O'Neill.

Evidence could be multiplied, but this is unnecessary. The interesting fact is that while Ireland has contributed more than her share to dramatic literature, most of the plays have been written in exile, so to speak, for until the twentieth century Ireland with her chronic poverty, her powerful church, and her absence of theatres offered little encouragement to playwrights.

The change in this state of affairs came about as a result of the deliberate effort and planning on the part of a small group of artists who set out to preserve Irish culture. The leaders, as far as the theatre was concerned, were William Butler Yeats and Lady Gregory, whose struggles finally led to the establishment of the now world-famous Abbey Playhouse. Both Yeats and Lady Gregory themselves made worthwhile contributions as playwrights—the former through his poetry, the latter through her keen sense of the comic. Both caught the native Irish flavor, the lilt of the language, the feel of the land, and the qualities of the common people. However, it was John Millington Synge (1871–1909) who first gave the Irish theatre plays of world-wide importance. Yeats, with his usual luck, or intuition, had discovered Synge in Paris—"an Irishman wasting his time trying to be French"—and had persuaded the young man to return to Ireland and the Irish. For the next three years Synge lived with the people of the bleak Aran Islands, in the belief that to find meaning in drama and poetry one

The Modern

should turn not to urban civilization but to people who know the meaning of harvest, springtime, life, and death. The experience would have been rewarding if nothing more had come of it than his *Riders to the Sea*. Some maintain that this short play is the greatest example of modern tragedy. Technically it is written in prose, but it is a prose far more beautiful and moving than most poetry. This tragedy of an old woman who has lost a husband and six sons could easily have become sentimental or merely pathetic; Synge has avoided both pitfalls. There is depth and honesty in lines like the following:

They're all gone now, and there isn't anything more the sea can do to me. . . . I'll have no call now to be up crying and praying when the wind breaks from the south, and you can hear the surf is in the east, and the surf is in the west, making a great stir with the two noises, and they hitting one on the other. . . . It isn't that I haven't prayed for you, Bartley, to the Almighty God. It isn't that I haven't said prayers in the dark night till you wouldn't know what I'd be saying; but it's a great rest I'll have now, and it's time surely.

Of Synge's full-length plays, *The Playboy of the Western World* is most famous. Some of its reputation may be traced to the fact that it stirred volcanic protests from certain Irish groups both in its native land and in America. To a neutral observer it is difficult to understand what was so objectionable, for this is a delightful comedy and while it sparkles with satire it is never cruel, nor is it a satire on the Irish alone. It begins as young Christy Mahon, desperate and exhausted, arrives at the public house of a small Irish village and admits that he has killed his tyrannical old father. Instead of being shocked, the inhabitants of the village, particularly Pegeen and the other young girls, react with romantic awe and admiration. Christy is soon the town hero. His confidence swells with the attention, and in a local athletic meet he wins every prize. At the height of the excitement Christy's father, his head well bandaged from the not quite mortal blow, arrives to even scores with his son. Another fight develops and Christy "kills" his father again, this time before the genuinely horrified eyes of the villagers who obviously require aesthetic distance in their killings, for they now turn on Christy as a criminal rather than a hero. They are in the very earnest process of bringing him to swift and stern justice, when the tough old father revives for a second time. But the old man has learned his lesson; a new respect for Christy has dawned; a new relationship between father and son is established, and together they walk out of the village leaving Pegeen and her friends to mourn their loss—the loss of "the only playboy of the Western World."

Synge died in 1909. The Abbey Players continued to encourage native writers, and a number of good plays, particularly several by Lennox Robinson, were written; but no real rival to Synge appeared until Sean O'Casey (b. 1884). Where Synge had captured the essence of comedy and tragedy among rural folk, O'Casey caught their essence among those in the cities. Born in the slums, he knew only too well the bitterness of poverty and underprivilege. His education was acquired by hard work, reading, and observation. He bought books even when it meant going hungry to do so. He was a fighter, a humanitarian, and is still one of the great champions of the common man.

His first play, *The Shadow of A Gunman*, was staged by the Abbey Playhouse in 1923 and showed promise of a powerful and challenging new playwright. His next play, *Juno and the Paycock*, removed all doubt about his abilities. It is one of the great plays of the twentieth century. Juno is a portrait of a woman not unlike O'Casey's own mother, whose magnificent strength of character seems to be the only hope of a disintegrating, poverty-stricken family. Juno's husband, Captain Boyle, is a romantic boaster who will do anything to escape work or responsibility; her boy Johnny is a sensitive cripple of the revolution, and her lovely daughter Mary is still young and weak. Mary becomes pregnant and is deserted by her schoolmaster lover. The furniture that Captain Boyle acquired on the strength of an expected inheritance is carted away, and finally Johnny, suspected of being an informer by his revolutionary companions, is executed. Although such events are presented with terrible realism, the play escapes being sordid or depressing because of O'Casey's rich use of language and his dramatic skill.

Following *The Plow and the Stars*, a tragedy of the Easter Rebellion, O'Casey moved toward expressionism in *The Silver Tassie* and *Within the Gates*, then far toward the left in *The Star Turns Red*. What the future holds in store for him is hard to say, but whatever the final verdict, it seems certain that few living playwrights will ever equal his power over language, his burning passion for humanity, or his deep sense of the tragic.

FRANCE: ZOLA TO SARTRE

Our last visit to the French theatre concluded with the vogue of the "well-made play" and the beginning of social criticism as seen in the works of Dumas *fils*. Any notion that the French had to wait for Ibsen to show them how to handle a social problem is quickly dispelled when we realize that Émile Zola (1840–1902) wrote an outstanding naturalistic play,

Aeschylus

Sophocles

Euripides

Aristophanes

PLATE 1. Greek Playwrights

Shakespeare

Jonson

Lope de Vega

Calderón

PLATE 2. Elizabethan and Spanish Playwrights

Corneille

Molière

Racine

Beaumarchais

Plate 3. French Playwrights

Congreve

Cibber

Sheridan

Goldsmith

PLATE 4. Restoration and 18th Century Playwrights

Hans Sachs (in his 81 year)

Lessing

Goethe

Schiller

PLATE 5. German Playwrights

Strindberg

Ibsen

Wilde

Shaw

O'Casey

Wide World Photo

Galsworthy

Barrie

Wide World Phor

Fry

PLATE 6. "Modern" Playwrights: Scandinavian, Irish, English

Culver Service

Maeterlinck

Hauptmann

Wide World Photo

Molnar

Gorki

Tolstoi

Chekhov

Schnitzler

Pirandello

Lorca

PLATE 7. "Modern" Playwrights: European

Boucicault

MacKaye

Dunlap

O'Neill

Vandamm

Anderson

Wide World Photo

Williams

Wilder

Wide World Pho

Miller

PLATE 8. American Playwrights

The Modern

Thérèse Raquin, in 1873, whereas *The Doll's House* did not appear until 1879. As a playwright Zola was no match for Ibsen. *Thérèse Raquin* is a far from a perfect play, but its importance in the movement toward a realistic study of life is significant. In the play's famous preface Zola explained clearly what he was trying to do. The stage was to become a laboratory for the study of life; a laboratory where the motives and the behavior of men could be viewed with complete objectivity, a place where case studies could be laid before an audience with the scientific detachment of the lecture hall but with greater vividness and clarity. A "bleeding slice of life" was to be held up for study and analysis.

Zola and other writers of the naturalistic school were aided in their efforts by the work of a young amateur director and producer, André Antoine, who in 1887 established his Théâtre Libre. It was a tiny playhouse but one that became world famous because of its dedication to the new naturalistic style and because of the literary quality of the plays it produced. Zola's naturalism had a tremendous influence. In France the greatest writers of the genre were probably Henri Becque (1837–1899) and Eugène Brieux (1858–1932). Among the best plays by the former is *Les corbeaux* (*The Vultures*), a bitter picture of a family left by the father's death to moneygrubbers who descend like vultures to destroy whatever is left. His comedy, *La Parisienne* (*The Woman of Paris*) might be mistaken for a sophisticated piece by Noel Coward until one discovers the author's serious and bitter purpose in painting an attractive but utterly immoral woman.

Eugène Brieux practically turned his stage into a lecture platform. *La robe rouge* (*The Red Robe*) is a stirring attack upon the corruption of the French legal system, while *Les avariès* (*Damaged Goods*), with its clinical study of venereal disease is best known, probably because of its sensational subject matter.

To some extent the naturalism of Zola, Becque, Brieux, and others was an outgrowth of the general disillusionment that followed romanticism. In turn the drab severity of naturalism was a powerful factor in causing a return to the romantic. Of course, the romantic spirit had never entirely disappeared. Even in France, where literary movements tend to be sharply defined, there are always exceptions and complexities. Thus even at the height of the realistic movement two world famous romanticists made their appearance. Edmond Rostand (1868–1918) wrote with a dash of adventure, excitement, and passion, plus a skill of craftsmanship, that made him one of the most popular playwrights of his day. *Les romanesques* (*The*

Romancers), a full-length play, the first act of which is often played as a one-act, is thoroughly delightful and lyrical, while his *Cyrano de Bergerac* is a genuine masterpiece. Seldom have comedy, tragedy, and adventure been more skillfully blended. Cyrano with his courage, intelligence, and dashing personality would fulfill all conventional concepts of the romantic hero except for one thing—Rostand has given him a grotesque flaw, an enormous nose, which opens the way for overtones, both tragic and comic, far beyond those of the usual tale of adventure. Constant Coquelin, Walter Hampden, José Ferrer are but a few of the famous actors who have portrayed the title role. Whether performed by college amateurs or the best artists of the professional stage, Cyrano seldom fails to score a success.

The second romantic writer of world importance in this period is the Belgian, Maurice Maeterlinck (1862–1949). Technically a romanticist, his plays nevertheless have little in common with those of Rostand. It is perhaps more descriptive to refer to Maeterlinck as an impressionist, for there is a vague, eerie quality in his work. Symbolism, suggestion, and mood are the things that count. His famous *Pelléas et Mélisande* drifts before us like mist and music. The gloomy, Gothic atmosphere is never lifted from the time the great warrior, Goulaud, first meets his frightened child-wife, Melisande, until she dies after he has killed her lover—his own younger brother, Pelléas.

To some Maeterlinck's best play (to others, his worst) is *L'oiseau bleu* (*The Blue Bird*). Those who object find it a pretentious, trite, and sentimental children's story. The others find it challenging and beautiful. Two children of a poor woodcutter are awakened by the fairy of light and taken on a pilgrimage in search of the blue bird (happiness). In allegorical fashion they search in dangerous faraway places only to discover at last that the blue bird is within their own home.

Maeterlinck wrote many other plays. He has greatly influenced other playwrights, even though his mysticism and symbolism are often difficult to follow, and his passion for simplicity of language is sometimes ludicrous.

Among the French playwrights between World Wars I and II we find Jean Giraudoux (1882–1944). His *Amphitryon 38* was made famous in America by the Lunts, while his *La folle de Chaillot* (*The Madwoman of Chaillot*) has also been an outstanding success both on Broadway and in the American noncommercial theatre.

Jean Cocteau (b. 1891) is one of the foremost authors of the expressionistic, or more particularly the surrealistic, style. Critics like Eric Bentley find in his writing some of the most stimulating and hopeful signs of the present-day theatre. At least his work is neither stereotyped nor imitative, for most of it spurns logic and realism, plunging toward the bizarre, the subconscious, and the impulsive. His *La machine infernal* (*The Infernal Machine*), based on the Oedipus story but viewing the tragic hero as the victim of an infernal machine of torture concocted by inhuman gods, is perhaps his best play.

During the second world war another French playwright, Jean-Paul Sartre (b. 1905), moved into the spotlight. Sartre has provoked a storm of controversy, ranging from those who utterly condemn him on moral and religious grounds to those who eulogize him as the most promising hope of the modern theatre. The philosophy of existentialism that pervades his work is vague and difficult to understand, except that, in common with the philosophy of Cocteau, it is antagonistic to the conventional and the rational. He seems to be searching with a mixture of ironic intelligence and driving passion for new meanings and values in life. His famous *Huis clos* (*No Exit*) gives us a new vision of hell. There is no river Styx, no fire and brimstone, only an ordinary comfortable drawing room, but in it is something that proves to be more terrible than physical torture. In it are three evil but recognizably real people, doomed to live in the same room forever and equally doomed to hate and torture one another. "Hell is . . . other people."

In *Les monches* (*The Flies*) he, like Cocteau, turns to the Greeks, this time to the Orestes-Electra story. But in contrast to the Greek playwrights who, in treating the same material, had regarded the gods as either neutral or good, Sartre pictures Zeus as a tyrant, and the play becomes a bitter struggle between Orestes and Zeus, between man and god, between freedom and oppression.

Whether Sartre and other gifted young writers such as Jean Anouilh will become the leaders of some great new movement in theatre, time alone will tell. But at least they have rediscovered the meaning of tragedy; they once more look at life honestly, firmly, nakedly. Such a point of view contains hope for the future.

GERMANY AND CENTRAL EUROPE: HAUPTMANN TO BRECHT

Germany's contribution to "modern drama" has been manifold. A quarter of a century before Ibsen wrote *The Doll's House*, Friedrich Hebbel and others had written plays that clearly anticipated the realistic genre. As early as 1874 the Duke of Saxe-Meiningen with his "amateurs" introduced sweeping reforms in staging, acting, and directing, all of which tended toward greater verisimilitude. In 1889 Otto Brahm established his Freie Bühne, a theatre devoted primarily to the production of realistic and naturalistic plays, just as André Antoine with his Théatre Libre had done in Paris.

Outstanding among naturalistic playwrights are Gerhart Hauptmann (1862–1946) and Arthur Schnitzler (1862–1931). One of Hauptmann's first plays, *The Weavers*, is an excellent example of naturalism. A dramatization of an historical event, the revolt of the Silesian weavers, its first scene pictures a long line of weavers on payday. One complains and is fired, a sick child faints, tales of unbearable hardship are related. As the play progresses we finally see these miserable and seemingly helpless beings rise against their employers, whom they consider responsible for their suffering. The volcanic force of the mass uprising wrecks factories, mills, and the home of the owner. Such a plot might easily amount to leftist propaganda and nothing more, but Hauptmann has tempered it with just the right blend of human sympathy and naturalistic objectivity. As in Lope de Vega's *The Sheep Well*, a group, rather than an individual, becomes the protagonist. In *The Weavers* drama of the masses came of age.

Among Hauptmann's plays that depart from naturalism *The Sunken Bell*, which in its symbolic and poetic quality strongly resembles much of Maeterlinck's work, is probably best known, although many prefer *Hannele*, which blends both the fantastic and the naturalistic. Into an ugly, realistic setting a kindhearted schoolmaster brings the dying Hannele, a child of fourteen. At this point realism disappears and we drift with the delirium of the feverish waif. She is Cinderella now, even to the tiny slippers; she finds beauty in death, with its crystal coffin; her drunken stepfather is punished; her schoolmaster becomes her Christ. She dies, lost in her own sad dream of goodness and the singing of angels. Such a plot could easily become sentimental were it not for the sordid naturalism of the real situation, the poetic quality of Hannele's escape into the dream world, and the ample motivation for all that she imagines. These qualities keep the pathos on solid footing and mark *Hannele* a play of rare beauty and appeal.

In some respects Arthur Schnitzler reminds us of Galsworthy, for he was likewise a professional man, a gentleman, always calm, always sympathetic, always objective. But whereas Galsworthy was a product of England, Schnitzler was a product of old Vienna, and love rather than social problems became his chief concern. A successful physician by profession, he still found time to write many plays, both comedies and tragedies. *Liebelei* (*Light o' Love*) reveals his infinite skill as a writer, and stimulates our admiration for a playwright who could make such a moving tragedy out of such slight material. Christine, a sensitive girl of the middle class, falls deeply in love with Fritz, an aristocratic young student, who, already embroiled in a dangerous love affair with a married woman, is scarcely aware of Christine's existence. Although Fritz means all the world to her, no one even troubles to tell her when he is challenged to a duel. He has already been buried before she learns what has happened. Out of such material Schnitzler weaves a play that is not only moving but also has much depth and reflective thinking. In other plays, notably *Anatol* (translated by Granville-Barker as *The Affairs of Anatol*) and *Reigen* (recently seen in America in an outstanding French film version, *La ronde*), Schnitzler works in a lighter vein. He intrigues us with satires on love. But while his outlook is critical it is also melancholy. He regrets life's lack of fulfillment, yet accepts it with philosophic calm. He is more intrigued by the joys we miss than the errors we commit.

Turning from the basically naturalistic theatre of Hauptmann and Schnitzler, we come to the Hungarian playwright, Ferenc Molnár (1878–1952). A popular success in his own eyes and in the eyes of the world, his plays have little of the depth or social protest so characteristic of his age. Some of the best of them, like *The Play's The Thing* and *The Guardsman*, are sophisticated comedies, brilliantly written, highly entertaining, and at times mildly satirical. In *The Guardsman* an actor grows suspicious of his actress wife. To test her he disguises himself as a romantic Russian guardsman and tries to seduce her. His consternation as he almost succeeds, his pompous indignation as he returns to confront her with her near infidelity, and his final confusion when she maintains that she knew him all the time and was only teasing, all this and much more makes *The Guardsman* rare entertainment even if not profound.

In *Liliom* Molnár gives us a play of a vastly different quality. It has the beauty, compassion, and understanding of a great poem. Liliom, a carnival barker, is an unforgettable mixture of the braggart and dreamer, of tenderness and brutality, of the strange good and evil that plague mankind. A failure when first produced, it later became a play of world importance.[8]

While Ferenc Molnár was departing from realism toward popular the-

---

[8] The musical comedy, *Carousel*, by Richard Rodgers and Oscar Hammerstein II is based on *Liliom*. It opened with great success in New York in 1945.

atrical success, other writers were turning from realism to antirealistic expressionism. Although Wedekind, like Strindberg, had moved beyond naturalism even before the twentieth century, it was not until after the shattering defeat of World War I that expressionism came of age in Germany. Of its many important plays one of the greatest is Ernst Toller's *Man and the Masses*. Toller was himself a tragic figure, an idealist devoted to communism but unalterably opposed to revolution or violence, a position that brought attacks from both the right and the left. His own struggle resembles the struggle of his heroine in *Man and the Masses*, which first appeared in 1921. Sonia, a woman of the upper class, leads the masses in a strike for peace. Her determination to avoid mob violence and bloodshed is contested by the Nameless One (mob spirit) whose plea for animal action and violence prevails, destroying the very peace for which the masses had revolted. In the end Sonia is imprisoned and sentenced to death.

Expressionism also took root in Czechoslovakia, especially in the work of Karel Čapek (1890–1938), whose *R. U. R.* (*Rossum's Universal Robots*) has been a popular favorite in America. More difficult to produce than *R. U. R.* but more exciting and imaginative, is *The Insect Comedy*, which Čapek wrote in collaboration with his brother Josef. A drunken tramp in a forest sees the insect world magnified into a biting satire on mankind. Throughout the first act the butterflies flirt and love. Throughout the second the beetles hoard their filthy wealth (piles of manure). Throughout the third act we view life's crowning stupidity, war. First the red ants, then the yellow ants, score victories, urged on by an ever-increasing tempo and cries of "Kill all the women and embryos"! Finally, as the gloating and victorious yellow commander stands supreme over all, bloated with victory, the huge boot of the tramp comes crashing down, and we hear the bitter verdict, "Stupid little insect"!

One other writer of central Europe claims attention, Bertold Brecht (b. 1898), the champion of epic theatre. Modern opinion varies as to his importance. To Eric Bentley he is one of the very few worth-while modern playwrights, while to Allardyce Nicoll his work is not "likely to cause more than an idle ripple on the surface."[9] A complete discussion of his much-discussed epic drama involves much philosophy and more semantics. The new student of theatre will not go far afield, however, if he views the epic play as fulfilling the same function as that of a speech intended to incite action. Actors sometimes further the author's purpose through direct ap-

[9] Allardyce Nicoll, *World Drama*, Harcourt, Brace and Company, Inc., p. 800.

peals to the audience, although for the most part they illustrate the author's point of view by acting out stories and events in presentational manner. *The Good Woman of Setzuan* and *The Caucasian Circle of Chalk* are among Brecht's most interesting pieces. Both deal with the near impossibility of being good in the evil framework of the modern world. Both have appealed with some success to intellectuals, but if Brecht's purpose is to influence the popular masses he has not yet achieved his goal.

ITALY: GOLDONI TO PIRANDELLO

Following the Renaissance, Italy's efforts in playwriting were largely drained away by opera on one hand and the *commedia dell' arte* on the other. The first notable exception came during the last half of the eighteenth century through the work of Carlo Goldoni and Carlo Gozzi, who resemble their famous English contemporaries, Oliver Goldsmith and Richard Brinsley Sheridan. Goldoni (1707–1793), like Goldsmith, had leanings toward cleverness, humor, and the sentimental. Gozzi (1720–1806), like Sheridan, tended to champion the comedy of laughter; but whereas Sheridan wrote comedies of manners, Gozzi delighted in extravagant fairy tales, which he spiced with a dash of social satire. The *commedia dell' arte* tradition is strong in his plays. In fact his most famous work, *The Love of Three Oranges*, does not have a complete script, much of the dialogue having been improvised by the actors. The fantastic delight of this mad tale is known to modern audiences primarily through the gay opera of Prokofiev. Its delight survives even though its satire is lost, a satire aimed at Goldoni, whom Gozzi caricatured as the magician who had banished laughter.

One acquainted with almost any of the plays by Goldoni will find Gozzi's implication that Goldoni had banished laughter to be extreme. Although a somewhat sentimental tendency to moralize is apparent in Goldoni's plays this quality is not nearly so pronounced as in most modern comedy. Adjectives like charming, sprightly, and vivacious more nearly describe his work. While Goldoni is not a Molière, his approximately two hundred fifty plays have created many hours of merriment, especially in Italy. His *Mistress of the Inn* is the story of a charming girl whose flirtatious ways reap benefits from three men far above her station. The manner in which she jilts them all and finally marries her servant is the essence of the fun. It is a play that a modern audience can still thoroughly enjoy.

From the death of Gozzi in 1806 we can skip to Gabriele D'Annunzio (1863–1938) before finding another reasonably outstanding Italian playwright. Like other countries Italy felt the influence of Ibsen and realism, yet the movement in that direction was comparatively weak. Perhaps realism is foreign to the Italian temperament; perhaps no great realistic writer happened to come along; or perhaps the colorful and powerful D'Annunzio shattered any tendency toward realism with his fiery, flamboyant romanticism, for D'Annunzio had tremendous appeal in Italy, even though the rest of the world has been inclined to find his plays a bit hollow.

But if D'Annunzio with his dashing romanticism is not so highly regarded outside of Italy as his native admirers might wish, the same cannot be said of Luigi Pirandello (1867–1936), who is generally regarded as the greatest Italian playwright since Plautus. Pirandello was a product of the disillusionment, loss of faith, and loss of hope that were so general following World War I. His loss of faith was not confined to conventional religion but included a loss of faith in realism, in science, and in humanity itself—at least as humanity exists today. In a search for some basis to existence and human behavior he cut through conventional barriers of form and thought, but his search found only a chaos of complexity that provoked bitter, grotesque laughter. In fact, some have regarded the fierce sanity with which he views life as closely akin to insanity.

His life had obvious bearing on what he wrote. Following the birth of their third child his wife became a hopeless neurotic. Among other things she persisted in the delusion that he was unfaithful, even though he stayed at home continuously and turned over to her all his meager earnings as a schoolteacher. He refused to commit her to a mental institution, although she made life a torture to both him and their children. In view of such experience it becomes easy to understand the origin of Pirandello's basic preoccupation with the question, What is the real; what is the unreal? In play after play he attacks this theme with brilliant variations and originality. In *Right You Are If You Think You Are,* we are introduced to a situation where a wife living with her husband in a top-floor apartment is never permitted to meet her mother, although the two converse daily—the one from the street and the other from the garret window. Suspicious neighbors in search of the truth demand an explanation, and the husband provides a very plausible one. His wife, he tells them, is not the daughter of the woman in the street at all. That was his first wife who died; this is his second wife. However, the mother has refused to accept the reality of her daughter's death, and since this delusion brings the older lady happiness the husband perpetuates it by preventing her from meeting his second wife face to face. Such an explanation is entirely satisfactory until the neighbors are given an equally convincing account by the mother, who informs them that the wife is really her daughter, but that the husband suffers from the delusion that she died and that he remarried. To humor him the mother submits to the strange practice of conversing with her daughter from the street. Finally the wife is asked to clear up the mystery, but she refuses to do so since "truth" would destroy the happiness of either her "mother" or her husband. The one other character who throughout the play acts as a mouthpiece for Pirandello and could clear up the mystery to satisfy the idle curiosity of both neighbors and audience breaks into loud laughter as the play comes to an end.

This is a far cry from the neatly contrived happy and "satisfying" endings of sentimental and well-made plays that comprise the vast bulk of theatrical entertainment. It is the bitter outcry of an idealist who has found modern life unbelievably confused and inadequate. Instead of tears, however, Pirandello chooses to laugh, especially at the neighbors and fools who are always so sure that they know, or will soon know, the answers.

While *Right You Are* most clearly reveals Pirandello's view of life, it is not necessarily his best or his most important work. *As You Desire Me, Naked, Six Characters In Search of An Author,* and *Tonight We Improvise,* are probably more famous. In the last two plays he fascinates us by exploring the differences between actual reality and stage reality. To most minds such a subject is nothing more than a theme for an academic lecture, but through Pirandello's wit and sensitivity, the intellectual is made dramatic, a grotesque mixture of intense tragedy and biting comedy. His plays may not be pleasant, nor are they ever likely to be popular, yet they seem bound to live, for no one has more vividly reflected the confusion and suffering of the twentieth century.

SPAIN: BENAVENTE TO LORCA

After sinking into unimportance following the golden age of Calderón and Lope de Vega, Spain in the twentieth century experienced a reawakening of the dramatic spirit. Among his countrymen Jacinto Benavente (b. 1866), Nobel prize winner in 1922, is the most famous modern playwright. Plays and other forms of writing have poured from his pen— shades of Lope de Vega! The plays are limited to no single type; comedy, drama, romance, and realism all may be found among his works. The best known in America are probably *Los intreses creados* (*The Bonds of Interest*) and *La malquerida* (*The Passion Flower*). The former is a delightful play with a *commedia dell' arte* flavor in both plot and style, while the latter is serious and intense. Although its violence and Freudian psychology no longer ring entirely true, its story, the psychotic hatred (really love) of a girl for her stepfather, still holds us with its color and fascination.

Contemporary with Benavente is Gregorio Martínez Sierra (b. 1881), a less colorful, less prolific, but more sensitive and in many ways finer writer. His delicate, almost feminine quality is well illustrated by his religious play, *The Cradle Song*. It has been extremely popular and it may be that this quiet, appealing story represents Martínez Sierra at his best.

But the most interesting writer of modern Spain, at least, in the eyes of those having some literary or theatrical background, is the poet Federigo García Lorca (1899–1936). In contrast to the amazing output of most Spanish playwrights, he wrote only twelve plays before he was executed during the Spanish civil war, but it may be that even this handful will outweigh the hundreds by Benavente. Some are lyrically delightful, like *The Shoemakers Prodigious Wife*, while others are powerful and bitter, like *The House of Bernarda Alba*. The latter is concerned with a proud and cruel mother, who enforces upon her daughters a seven-year period of mourning in memory of the death of her husband. Tragedy results as the daughters are unable to endure the unnatural restraints; but the violence and passion of the play gain beauty from the imaginative language as well as from the vividness of the characters. With his gifts for the comic, the tragic, and the poetic it is hard to estimate what Lorca might have accomplished had not Franco's bullets cut short one of the most promising careers of the twentieth century.

RUSSIA: PUSHKIN TO ANDREYEV

Neither oriental nor occidental, though well acquainted with the earth and with suffering, Russia has been a ponderous, sometimes awkward, sometimes brutal giant lagging behind other countries in development. Yet in an artistic sense she has commanded respect rather than derision because of her deep sensitivity, imagination, and hunger for the ideal. Song, poetry, and drama come naturally to the Russian people, although their troubled history has seldom allowed these impulses to grow to fulfillment. According to Gogol, "English drama reverberates with a beautiful and wise knowledge of life; French drama glitters and shines and flits away; German drama has a meaning unattainable to any one else; Russian drama, however, is torn from the heart itself."[10]

[10] Quoted by H. W. L. Dana in his chapter on "Russia" found in Barrett H. Clark and George Freedley, *A History of Modern Drama*, D. Appleton-Century Company, Inc., p. 370.

The Modern

Russian drama, which now belongs to the proletariat, began with the Czars. Peter the Great invited foreign actors with foreign plays to visit his court; Catherine the Great encouraged the drama, especially native drama, and even wrote several plays herself. Many others also made contributions, but for our present purposes the first writer to demand serious attention is Alexander Pushkin, who in 1825 wrote his great historical tragedy, *Boris Godunov*. Although not well known to Americans except in the operatic version by Mussorgsky, this play is a landmark in the history of Russian drama, both because it was written by Russia's greatest poet, and because it was patterned after Shakespeare. Thus Pushkin occupies much the same position in Russian drama that Lessing does in German drama. Both took Shakespeare as a model, and while Pushkin's tragedy *Boris Godunov* does not equal those of the English master, it is a richly imaginative work.

Eleven years later came Russia's first comedy of world importance, Nikolai Gogol's *The Inspector General*, a brilliant exposé of provincial graft and political corruption in old Russia. The Mayor robs the shopkeepers, the Police Sergeant is always drunk, the Hospital Superintendent feeds his patients on a diet of cabbage, the Judge raises geese in the courtyard, and the Postmaster opens all the letters. Panic strikes these guilt-ridden grafters when it is rumored that they are about to be investigated. To their horror they soon discover that a mysterious stranger from Moscow is already at the local hotel. The audience is next introduced to the stranger, Khlestakov, an unimportant little government clerk with no power whatever, except for his own natural endowment of shrewd wit and the uninhibited flexibility of his code of honor. As the Mayor and other local officials swoop in upon him, Khlestakov quickly sizes up the situation, senses that they have mistaken him for the Inspector General, and proceeds to play his cards to the limit. He is showered with attention. The Mayor's wife and daughter offer their affection. One after another the crooked officials ply him with bribes. At last, loaded with booty, he leaves the town just as the Postmaster arrives at the Mayor's house with a letter that he has intercepted from Khlestakov to a friend. In a hushed room filled with the culprits, the letter revealing exactly what Khlestakov thinks of each of them is read aloud. Then before they can recover from the shock of the letter, they are frozen into a final tableaux of horror by the sudden arrival of the real Inspector General.

Here is comedy once more returned to its Aristophanic function as a lash against corruption and folly. Gogol cuts almost as deeply as do Aristophanes, Molière, and Shaw. The play might have run into difficulties with censorship had not the Czar seen it and approved, much as Louis XIV had seen and approved Molière's *Les precieuses ridicules* almost two centuries earlier.

Unlike Gogol and Pushkin, who wrote but a few plays each, Alexander Ostrovski (1823–1886) wrote more than forty. Not well known outside Russia, he is highly regarded in his native land. He had spent the early years of his life working in a section of Moscow composed largely of the newly rich merchant class, and most of his plays expose the inherent weaknesses of these people. In *Enough Stupidity in Every Wise Man* we meet the clever exploiter Glumov, who, like Khlestakov in *The Inspector General,* unscrupulously exploits the dishonesty of those about him. Through an intercepted letter he likewise is exposed, but instead of flying like Khlestakov he stays and braves out the storm. He knows too much about his victims; they are too guilty to dare to touch him, and his brazen exploits go unpunished.

The next writer to claim our attention is one of the world's greatest novelists and short-story writers, Count Leo Tolstoi (1828–1910). He turned to the stage late in life, but even so made an important contribution, particularly in his terrible and tragic study of evil, *The Powers of Darkness.* Here is a story of lust and murder among Russian peasants, on a brutal, animal level, but the darkness is overshadowed by a final act of faith and conscience as Nikita, revolted by his own crimes, voluntarily gives himself up to justice and experiences the beginning of moral regeneration.

Tolstoi's last play, *The Light Shineth in Darkness,* unfinished at the time of his death, is autobiographical. Nicholas Ivanovich, believing in Christ if not in the church, and filled with compassion for humanity, tries to devote his final years to service. But in this evil world his efforts to do good result in suffering and misunderstanding. When he gives up his wealth to the peasants, his wife accuses him of having robbed his own children. When he leads a young man to pacifism, the youth is flogged. And so it goes until, like the Savior Himself, he pays with his life for his attempt to live real Christianity.

The Russian skill for picturing life as it is, but should not be, is seen in more subdued and sensitive tones in the work of Russia's greatest playwright, Anton Chekhov (1860–1904). Most critics regard Chekhov as the supreme naturalist, and yet even in translation his plays have a prevailing atmosphere, a quality of mood and longing that is almost poetic. Their naturalism shows up in a lack of contrived situation, a lack of violence, and a lack of the sensational. Very little happens, "life rusts away," hopes and dreams fade—unrealized; yet with the right kind of acting these plays hold audiences spellbound. The secret of their spell is hard to describe, but certainly one important element is characterization. So genuine and vivid do his characters appear that even common crises in their lives become dramatic and important, just as common crises in our own lives or within our own families seem dramatic and important.

The Cherry Orchard is generally regarded as Chekhov's masterpiece. An ancestral estate is to be sold at auction, but there is no last-minute rescue by a hero, no purchase of the estate by a villain. The Cherry Orchard is a symbolic, nostalgic story of the futility of the old Russian nobility and their inability to cope with the modern world, but they are treated with sympathy and understanding. Madam Ranevsky with her kindness, extravagance, and gracious ways endears herself to us from the start. On the other hand she is helpless and useless when it comes to practical problems in the new world of business and progress. The best she can do on the eve of the auction is to give one more lovely party. And so Lopahin, the newly rich business man, buys the Cherry Orchard—Lopahin, whose father had been a peasant on the estate, who had never forgotten Madam Ranevsky's kindness to him as a ragged boy with a bleeding face. The play lives because of the vividness and compassion with which Chekhov has drawn his characters. It is not necessary to have murders, mistaken identity, intrigue, and other theatrical paraphernalia. These characters become our intimate acquaintances; consequently even trivial events become moving.

Almost equal to The Cherry Orchard in both quality and fame are Chekhov's Uncle Vanya, The Sea Gull, and The Three Sisters. All have much the same qualities: the quiet tragedy, the wistful yearning, the living characters. To capture and portray these qualities, however, requires acting of a highly sensitive and convincing order. The declamatory, theatrical style that was in vogue when Chekhov first began to write was highly inappropriate, and largely because of this his first plays were unsuccessful. The failure of The Sea Gull in its first production was a particularly bitter blow, and Chekhov threatened to write no more for the theatre. Then, two years later, a Russian playwright, Nemirovich-Danchenko, and an amateur actor, Constantin Stanislavski, organized The Moscow Art Theatre. Among the plays offered during their first season was The Sea Gull, which opened December 17, 1897. Almost overnight both Chekhov and the Moscow Art Theatre became famous. Seldom has there been a more fortunate combination of playwriting and production. The deep "psychological naturalism" of the Stanislavski system of acting provided a perfect means of expression for Chekhov's naturalism. When the author was too ill with tuberculosis to come to Moscow for the production of his *Uncle Vanya*, the Art Theatre took the play to him at Yalta. A special opening performance of *The Cherry Orchard* was arranged in order that Chekhov might see the play on what proved to be his last birthday. To this day the emblem of a sea gull is the official insignia of the world's most famous producing group, The Moscow Art Theatre.

When the Moscow Art Theatre visited Yalta in 1900, Chekhov introduced them to a powerful and fascinating young author who had made his way up from the depths of poverty, suffering, and even imprisonment. His name was Maxim Gorki (Maxim the Bitter) (1868–1936). It was soon decided that Gorki should write a play depicting the lives of the submerged and broken failures whom he knew so well. Two years later Gorki finished not one but two plays. The first to be produced by the Moscow Art Theatre was *The Petty Bourgeois*, a devastating picture of the smugness of middle-class Russian life. But its fame is overshadowed by his second play, a masterpiece of its kind and still the most frequently produced drama in Russia, *The Lower Depths*. In a cellar below Moscow we meet the outcasts of society. A woman lies dying in childbirth, yet she is scarcely noticed. There is also the Baron and his streetwalker, the actor, the young thief, the receiver of stolen goods, and the bitter old philosopher, Satine. Into the midst of these derelicts comes a pilgrim, Louka. Under the spell of his wisdom and humanity we soon begin to discover that, in spite of their hopeless exteriors, these people of the lower depths all have a dream of goodness, and a bitterness that life should be as it is. Under his spell they begin to change and to gain new hope, but Gorki is too tough-minded and naturalistic to permit a happy ending. A quarrel flares up, the proprietor of the hovel is accidentally killed by the young thief, and Louka disappears as mysteriously as he had arrived. Without him the characters slump back into despair save for powerful, brutally unsentimental Satine:

. . . The old man's no humbug! What's the truth? Man! Man—that's the truth! He understood man—you don't! You're all as dumb as stones! I understand the old man—yes! He lied—but lied out of sheer pity for you. . . . I know what lying means! The weakling and the one who is a parasite through his very weakness—they both need lies—lies are their support, their shield, their armor! But the man who is strong, who is his own master, who is free and does not have to suck his neighbors' blood—he needs no lies! To lie—it's the creed of slaves and masters of slaves! Truth is the religion of the free man![11]

[11] Act IV (Jenny Covan translation).

Many of the things Satine says ring like the words of Gorki himself, for both have a fierce belief in the potential worth and dignity of man, and a revolutionary hatred of the system that was keeping so many in misery and poverty. A born champion of the oppressed, a destroyer of evil, and a revolutionist, Gorki became one of the notable figures in Russia as the Communist party swept away the old and gave promise of something new. He did much to champion and preserve the arts and was prominent in the struggle to give Communism an intellectual and idealistic basis. How far he succeeded seems doubtful, for it appears to us that the old forces of corruption that Communism sought to correct have saturated the new regime as well. As far as Gorki's own motives and integrity are concerned, however, they appear to have been beyond reproach.

Among the many other playwrights of importance during these years was Leonid Andreyev (1871–1919). A brooding, almost unbearable pessimism that casts the spell of a great symphony or poem pervades his *The Life Of Man*. Unlike Gorki, who cries, "Everything is in man—and everything exists for him!" Andreyev pictures man as hopeless and meaningless. From his birth in pain and darkness, we follow Man's pathetic and futile struggle to rise to success. We see grotesque and chaotic discord even in his hour of triumph. Finally we witness his failure, and at last his return to the darkness of death. *King Hunger* is a terrible and powerful allegory of the unsuccessful Revolution of 1905, but it has a more positive ring than *The Life Of Man*. In America Andreyev is best known for a much later play, *He Who Gets Slapped* (1916). Even in this work the author's gloom and obsession with suffering are compellingly portrayed, especially in the character of He, who prefers to endure the slaps and buffets of other clowns, rather than the more intense beating of the world "out there."

What has happened since the Revolution seems hopelessly confused, and judgments are hazardous. It is difficult to believe, however, that great plays could ever be written without freedom of thought and expression. If anything is characteristic of great playwrights it is the intensity, individuality, and honesty of their search for truth. Conditions permitting such a search apparently no longer exist in the Soviet Union.

AMERICA: GODFREY TO MILLER

In tracing the origins of drama in America, Spaniards can point with pride to the fact that as early as 1603 daily theatrical performances were being given in Mexico City. The French likewise might boast of performances of plays in their early Canadian settlements, for both the French and the Spanish transplanted theatrical culture to their new colonies as early as possible, just as they transplanted other elements of their national life.

But with the English it was different. Puritans and Quakers were deeply opposed to the theatre, and as late as 1792 even *She Stoops To Conquer* had to be advertised in *The Boston Gazette* as "A moral lecture in five parts in which the disadvantages of a neglected education will be strikingly described."[12] Even today the American theatre is regarded by many with a faint air of suspicion and hostility foreign to the other arts.

During the early years the chief exceptions to this prevailing hostility were found in the South. Both Virginia and Carolina, largely Episcopalian in faith, displayed comparatively tolerant and kindly attitudes toward all forms of culture, and it is in these states that much of the American theatre's early history is to be found. The earliest record of a theatrical performance goes back to 1665 when *Ye Bare and Ye Cubb* was performed in Virginia, and although those responsible for the production were hailed into court they were promptly acquitted. There are many other scattered theatrical records of historical interest, many of them in connection with early college productions, but for our purposes the outstanding theatrical event of the pre-Revolutionary period was the arrival in 1752 of Lewis Hallam with a company of fifteen professional actors from England. They opened on September 15th in Williamsburg, Virginia, with *The Merchant of Venice*, and in spite of restrictions and hardships survived, built theatres, and brought plays to the Colonies. It would be hard to overestimate their influence on our early theatrical history.

Hallam died while on a trip to Jamaica, but his widow and her second husband, David Douglas, carried on. The plays the company produced were standard English pieces including *King Lear, Hamlet, Othello, The London Merchant, The Conscious Lovers,* and *The Beggar's Opera.* The first American play to be performed by this company was *The Prince of Parthia* (1767) by Thomas Godfrey. Its fame rests almost entirely on its claim to being the "first" American play ever to be performed by a professional company. How good or how bad it is depends on one's point of view. Considered as our first play it is not bad at all, being closely akin to the English heroic tragedies of the Restoration. Considered on its own merit, however, it is a rather uninspired heroic tragedy on a foreign theme, without the slightest suggestion of anything like a new idea or fresh point of view from a new world.

---

[12] For a reproduction of this advertisement see Oral Sumner Coad and Edward Mims, Jr., *The American Stage,* The Pageant of American Series. Yale University Press, 1928, p. 39.

The Modern

Comedy fared better. Prior to and during the Revolutionary War, Mrs. Mercy Warren and others wrote a number of original satires on the British, and in 1787 Royall Tyler wrote *The Contrast,* the first American comedy to win professional production. Tyler's inspiration came from having seen a few plays, including a production of *The School For Scandal,* at the John Street Theatre in New York. He set to work and, with all the confidence of young America, proceeded in the space of three weeks to dash off a comedy of his own. The surprising thing is not that the result was imperfect but rather that even today an imaginative production of the old piece can still delight an audience. The title indicates both the theme and the plot. The sophisticated dandy, Dimple, provides a vivid character contrast to honest, plain-dealing Colonel Manly; Dimple's servant, Jessamy, is employed as a contrast to the American Yankee, Jonathan, while Charlotte is used as a contrast to the sentimental Maria. Some of the scenes have a surprising dash of wit and cleverness, while Jonathan holds the distinction of being the apparent original of a long line of stage Yankees who have been responsible for much native American humor.

Tyler's play with its American setting and American theme is also a contrast to Godfrey's *The Prince of Parthia,* with its foreign setting and foreign theme. In fact, although such a division is purely arbitrary and overly simplified it seems convenient to classify nineteenth-century American playwriting under these two headings: (1) plays on American themes and (2) plays on foreign themes.

Among the plays employing a foreign theme, three of the most outstanding examples are *Charles the Second,* a comedy by John Howard Payne and Washington Irving, *Francesca da Rimini,* a tragedy by George Henry Boker, and *Hazel Kirke,* a melodrama by Steele MacKaye.

Charles the Second (1824), dealing with a gay escapade of "The Merry Monarch" and his companion in adventure, The Duke of Rochester, is delightful. Although set in Restoration England it is entirely American in spirit. It has the robust good humor of Washington Irving, and the kindhearted sentiment of John Howard Payne (the author of "Home Sweet Home"). While we may regret that two such libertines as Charles and Rochester are not treated with the smacking wit and sharp satire they deserve, we should at least be thankful that the fun is maintained on a comparatively healthy and robust level. Though it lacks the sharp satirical wit of a Molière, a Congreve, or a Shaw, the comedy does avoid the more objectionable pitfalls of common sentimentality.

Of all the American tragedies written in "foreign" style, in fact of all American tragedies prior to those of Eugene O'Neill, *Francesca da Rimini*

(1855) is probably the best. The plot is based on a story first told by Dante and popular with playwrights ever since.[13] The action is set in Italy during the Renaissance. To promote peace between two warring families, it is agreed that beautiful Francesca from Ravenna shall marry Lanciotto of Rimini, a great warrior who is physically deformed. Knowing that she has never seen him and does not know of his ugliness, Lanciotto sends his handsome young brother Paolo to the lady with instructions to tell her everything before asking her to agree to the match. As Paolo arrives at Ravenna he is at first mistaken for the bridegroom. Francesca, for the sake of peace and out of respect for Lanciotto, consents to the marriage, but we already sense that she is in love with Paolo. We watch as their love flares into the open following the marriage; we watch their vindictive fool, Pepe, carry the news to Lanciotto, who is away on the field of battle, and finally we see Lanciotto return home, surprise the lovers, and kill them. The fact that all three principal characters are presented with sympathy and understanding, that Paolo and Lanciotto are deeply attached to one another, and that even Francesca holds Lanciotto in high esteem, is responsible for much of the play's power. Although it is not one of the world's great tragedies, *Francesca da Rimini* deserves more attention, in America at least, than it has hitherto received.

In contrast to *Francesca da Rimini,* which was neglected by American audiences, *Hazel Kirke* (1880) was for many years the most popular play on the American stage. It is a melodrama but one of the best, full of tears, laughter, suspense, and excitement. The scene is England. Young Lord Carringford has been saved from death by the rugged old miller, Dunstan Kirke. He is nursed back to health by the miller's beautiful daughter, Hazel, who is already pledged in marriage to a likable, middle-aged gentleman, Squire Rodney. Discovering that Hazel has fallen in love with the young Lord, Dunstan flies into a rage, disinherits her, and drives her from home. Not daring to let his aristocratic mother know of his love for a commoner, Carringford marries Hazel in secret, but unknown to him his servant arranges an illegal ceremony. In a climactic scene reminiscent of a similar scene in *Camille,* Lady Carringford, old and ill, visits Hazel, begs for the freedom of her son, and finally reveals that the marriage was a sham. With a tragic shame that only a nineteenth-century heroine could muster, Hazel rushes away from Carringford to hide from all who know her.

Back at the old mill Dunstan has gone blind, but his bitterness toward Hazel is still intense. Chancing to appear at the window, Hazel, whose

[13] Maeterlinck's *Pelléas et Mélisande* is one of the many plays based on this plot.

wanderings have led her back to her old home, hears his angry words, sobs out her tragic farewll speech, and throws herself into the river. Dunstan hears the cries for help, tries to save her, but is helpless. He is blind.

Since the play is a melodrama, Lord Carringford of course arrives in the nick of time, saves Hazel, and causes all to end happily. *Hazel Kirke* is not great literature; but in its day and for its audience it was great theatre. It set a box office record of 486 consecutive performances. One final fact: it seems to be one of the first melodramas on record with no villain, which may be an advantage or disadvantage, depending upon one's point of view.

᠍᠍ 73/33

Turning to plays featuring an American theme and an American setting we should first note that during the early nineteenth century there was a rash of Pocahontas stories, finally ending with John Brougham's *Po-Ca-Hon-Tas,* a burlesque opera of thoroughly "corny" vintage. A much more worthy American effort than these, or than any of the other Indian plays, is the tragedy *André* (1798) by William Dunlap, which treats a historical event, the execution of Captain André, with restraint and insight. The play becomes the more remarkable when one considers that this story with a British officer as its protagonist was written only fifteen years after the Revolution and at a time when feeling against the British and against spies must still have been intense.

Dunlap's importance, however, in the history of American drama goes far beyond the excellence achieved by *André.* He wrote over fifty plays, and although the bulk of them were translations and adaptations of foreign melodramas, a few like *André* were genuinely original. In addition to his work as a playwright Dunlap was one of America's most outstanding theatrical managers and producers. He also wrote an invaluable *History of the American Theatre,* published in 1832. These and other achievements have earned him a position second to none among the founding fathers of the American stage.

A landmark in American comedy is Anna Cora Mowatt's *Fashion* (1845). In many ways it resembles *The Contrast.* The complications of plot arise from Mrs. Tiffany's determination to cultivate foreign culture, a determination that almost succeeds in forcing her daughter to marry a French barber who is masquerading as a Count. There is once again the manly American hero, and while there is no stage Yankee in the literal sense, there is a hardheaded, straightforward old uncle, Adam Truman. On the whole this is a much better comedy than *The Contrast,* as of course it should be, since it was written more than half a century later and under far more favorable circumstances.

Mrs. Mowatt was not the only woman prior to the Civil War who earned a secure place in theatrical history. There was also Harriet Beecher Stowe, whose *Uncle Tom's Cabin,* through its stage version by George L. Aiken,[14] has a fabulous stage history. From its first appearance in 1852 until well into the twentieth century it established an amazing record of popular success. It was played as rousing abolitionist propaganda, as a tear jerker, a comedy, a musical, an animal show, a scenic spectacle, and a burlesque. From America's largest cities to her frontier hamlets, from her finest theatres to her tents and dime museums *Uncle Tom's Cabin* demonstrated its amazing power to attract an audience. The novelties and effects that were employed to keep the show alive were fabulous. At times the bloodhounds received more publicity than the actors. The river of ice over which Eliza flees with her baby, Little Eva's ascent into heaven, and other "scenic wonders" were exploited to the last ounce of spectacle. Tiny companies with as few as three players performed the "entire" script, while other companies expanded until they included such items as jubilee singers and brass bands. During the eighties a few even advertised themselves as "double" companies with two Evas, two Toms, two Topsies, etc. Although from a literary standpoint *Uncle Tom's Cabin* leaves much to be desired, its success on the stage was colossal.

Much of *Uncle Tom's* success was undoubtedly due to the fact that in America, as elsewhere, the nineteenth century was the great age of the sentimental and the melodramatic. One of the most prominent playwrights in this area was Dion Boucicault (1820–1890). His career began in his native Ireland, but in 1853 he came to America, where he finished out the remainder of his long and active years as an actor, playwright, and manager. Some of the plays he wrote are set in Ireland, many are adaptations from the French or German, but a few are clearly American. In the latter category the play usually read by college classes is *The Octoroon.* In this play there is an attempt to deal with the race problem; there is a solution to a murder by means of a newfangled invention, the camera; there is a juicy villain; there is a relentless Indian with the nose of a bloodhound; and there is an abundance of scenic spectacle climaxed by a steamship explosion!

[14] Aiken was only one of many to dramatize the famous story, but his version was by far the most successful. For a brief but excellent account of *Uncle Tom's* stage history see: A. M. Drummond and Richard Moody, "Hit of the Century: Uncle Tom's Cabin," *Educ. Theatre Journal,* IV, No. 4, Dec. 1952, pp. 315–322.

The Modern

A quarter of a century later the mantle of Boucicault descended upon David Belasco (1853–1931). Born in San Francisco, Belasco was destined to scale the heights in almost every phase of the popular theatre, and we shall meet him again as a director, scenic designer, and lighting artist. As a playwright he was for the most part an adapter and collaborator, but the results were invariably successful with playgoers. He was sentimental and melodramatic, but like Boucicault he was also effective.

One of his most sensational situations may be found in the second act of *The Girl of the Golden West*. The scene is The Girl's cabin in the mountains. Her sweetheart lies wounded and hidden in the loft as a posse enters to search for him. Unable to find him, the men leave except for Jack Rance, the sheriff and a gambler, who pauses in the doorway for a last word just as blood splashes on the table! His eyes go to the blood-stained ceiling. She knows he knows! In desperation she makes a gambling offer. They will play poker. If she wins, Rance goes away. If Rance wins he gets his man and The Girl besides. Audiences scarcely able to breathe saw the game that followed. Now the sheriff thumps down his last and deciding hand, "Three kings!" but wait! The Girl shows hers. "Three aces and a pair!" Audiences were so wildly partisan that they forgave her, even though they had just seen her pluck the winning hand from the top of her stocking!

So much for samples of the melodramatic and the sentimental. These are still with us, although much of the activity in this line has shifted from Broadway to Hollywood.

Shortly before the turn of the century certain stirrings toward a more literary drama may be discerned. According to Professor Quinn,[15] this movement toward modern drama began with Augustin Daly (1838–1899). Certainly Daly, like William Dunlap before him, deserves recognition for his outstanding work as a manager and for his encouragement of American playwrights, but the fact remains that most of his own works were either adaptations or melodramas. His most famous piece, *Under the Gaslight*, is a thriller in which he created a sensation of suspense by tying a man to a railroad track in the path of an onrushing locomotive.

But while Daly undoubtedly stimulated the movement toward American plays, the real beginning of modern American drama is much more apparent in the works of Bronson Howard (1870–1908). Though not a genius, Howard was a respectable, well-educated writer who devoted himself to the task of playwriting with more than customary skill and honesty.

[15] Arthur Hobson Quinn, *A History of the American Drama from the Civil War to the Present Day*, Vol. 1, F. S. Crofts & Co., 1936, p. 1.

His most interesting play is *Shenandoah,* probably the best play of the nineteenth century on the subject of the Civil War. Although written largely in the "well-made" style of its day, it nevertheless reveals some insight into the tangled loyalties of war.

Still closer to serious "modern drama" as we know it through the thesis plays of Ibsen, is the work of James A. Herne (1839–1901). Herne, like Belasco, MacKaye, Boucicault, and Daly was a very successful actor-manager. Consequently, it is not surprising to find that he wrote plays like *Hearts of Oak* and *Shore Acres* that were great theatrical successes. On the other hand, it is surprising to find that in writing his most important play, *Margaret Flemming* (1890), he cared little for popular success, but rather focused his attention on trying to say something about the double standard. Bits of naturalism, such as nursing a baby on stage, were both realistic and shocking. Herne's objective, as he himself so well phrased it, was to use "art for truth's sake."[16]

Among American playwrights during the early years of the twentieth century there are many of interest. Prolific and famous in his day was "the great Mr. Fitch," for Clyde Fitch (1865–1909), a college graduate, was often referred to as the "dean of American playwrights." In 1901, for example, he had four smash hits playing on Broadway. Even his best plays, however, such as *The Truth* and *The Girl With the Green Eyes,* although they treat social problems, tend to sacrifice truth on the altar of the theatrical and contrived. At best they are only equal to the secondary works of Pinero, but in spite of their shortcomings the plays of Clyde Fitch advanced the standards of American playwriting.

William Vaughn Moody (1869–1910), with only two plays, rates high among the playwrights of his day. *The Great Divide* is revealing and effective as it brings New England refinement with its narrow codes of conduct into conflict with the rough honesty and freedom of the West.

Fitch and Moody, along with George Ade, Augustus Thomas, Percy MacKaye, Owen Davis, and many others, did much toward keeping the theatre alive and prosperous during the first two decades of the century. At the same time they paved the way for the great period that was about to follow, a period of which Professor Allardyce Nicoll has said: "The totality of the American contribution to the Theatre between 1920 and 1940 must be deemed to go considerably beyond the British and French contributions of the same decades."[17]

[16] James A. Herne, "Art for Truth's Sake in the Drama," *Arena,* February, 1897.
[17] Allardyce Nicoll, *op. cit.,* p. 769.

The Modern

Among the many influences behind America's rise to a position of world importance in playwriting were the general factors in national life that had already made America a world power in such other areas as industry, invention, wealth, and military might. Even in the other fine arts America's contribution rose to significance much earlier than it did in playwriting, which lagged behind possibly because of the theatre's strangling commercialism, possibly because of its overzealous desire to please everyone in every audience, or possibly because of America's general lack of mental and emotional maturity. This last deficiency was more apparent in theatre, which is a group art, than in the more individual arts like poetry or painting, where a select few could set the standards. It has always been difficult for the theatre to rise much above the general level of its audience.

But American playwriting of the twenties owed debts to things other than the nation's general prosperity and growing importance. It owed a debt to the work of a group of realistic writers including William Dean Howells, Hamlin Garland, Henry James, and James A. Herne, who even before the close of the nineteenth century had started a movement toward noncommercial literary drama. It owed a particular debt to George Pierce Baker, professor of playwriting at Harvard and later at Yale, whose instruction provided guidance and inspiration for many an outstanding young playwright, including Eugene O'Neill. Finally it owed a debt to several independent producing groups that began as nonprofessional or semiprofessional organizations. Among these were the Washington Square Players, a group that finally evolved into the powerful Theatre Guild, and the Provincetown Players, a group that dedicated itself to the production of new American plays and was largely responsible for giving O'Neill his start.

To understand the contribution of these independent art theatres we should place them against the background of their times. The first two decades of the twentieth century had seen a titanic struggle between the Theatrical Syndicate and the Shubert Brothers for control of the American commercial theatre. These decades had also seen the stagehands' union and finally Actor's Equity battle to positions of power. Yet while these forces struggled against one another, the prize over which they fought was disintegrating. The popular audience was being lured away by an inexpensive and entertaining new form of theatre, the movies, until by the beginning of World War I the chance of securing a monopoly over a big-money theatrical industry was gone. However, there still remained a high-quality though limited audience, which was being bolstered by an increasing interest in theatre on the part of American schools and universities. On the whole the old managers and the new unions underestimated the growing competition of the movies on the one hand and the modest but potential possibilities of a new art-conscious audience on the other.

It remained for the nonprofessionals and semiprofessionals, inspired by young leaders like Robert Edmond Jones, Kenneth Macgowan, and Lee Simonson, to infuse the theatre with the new life and vitality that was to make New York one of the theatrical capitals of the world.

Coming to the new playwriting itself, the most prominent name is Eugene Gladstone O'Neill (1888–1953). The son of a famous actor, James O'Neill, he had abundant opportunities to secure both theatrical experience and education. On the other hand, life as a great actor's son had its problems and its loneliness. O'Neill was deeply influenced by the sea stories of Joseph Conrad and the expressionism of August Strindberg. He shipped at sea, deliberately searching for ideas and stories; these experiences provided the basis for his first group of plays, mostly one-act stories of the sea. Many of these early plays, *The Long Voyage Home, Ile, In the Zone,* and *The Moon of the Caribbees,* show vivid promise of what was to come. In 1920 came the production of his first full-length success, *Beyond the Horizon.* This is a story of two New England brothers and a girl. Robert Mayo, the dreamer, yearning for travel and adventure, is trapped into staying on the farm, while his brother, Andrew, who wanted to stay home, is driven to sea. The play may be overwritten and too long, it may be depressing rather than truly tragic, but at the same time it provided the American theatre with a new standard of emotional and intellectual maturity. It explored some of life's frustrations with new irony and insight, and it rated well above any previous American effort. It won its author his first Pulitzer prize and almost overnight established him as America's newest and most promising playwright.

During the next decade and a half many plays came from his pen. Looking at them as a whole, we are struck by O'Neill's restless search for new devices and new forms of expression. *The Emperor Jones* and *The Hairy Ape* stand out as America's first successful attempts in expressionism; *The Great God Brown* makes intermittent use of masks in order to contrast our real selves with the external selves we present to others; *Strange Interlude* returns to a free use of soliloquies and asides. Its playing time was also so long that in performance it was necessary to begin at 5:30 P.M., pause one and one-half hours midway in the show for dinner, then return for the second half, which lasted until after eleven. Even *Mourning Becomes Electra,* which many consider his masterpiece, shows the same restless tendency to experiment. It is extremely long, a trilogy based on Greek tragedy but set in New England during the Civil War, with Freudian psychology very evident in its tragic motivation. But of all the surprising plays that O'Neill has written, his most surprising was probably *Ah, Wilderness!*, for this is his one perfectly normal comedy: unpretentious, nostalgic, entertaining. It would be ironic indeed if this "slight" work should outlive his grim and oft-times ponderous tragedies. One other comparatively "normal" play comes close to revealing O'Neill at his best. This is *Marco Millions,* which places young Marco Polo, the epitome of Western success—handsome, confident, efficient, sure of all the answers—against the revealing wisdom and culture of the Orient. By so doing it exposes his essentially self-centered, materialistic hollowness. The scenic background is rich and colorful, the satire sound and stinging, and in the end the play rises to tragic heights that have seldom been equalled in the modern theatre.

Final judgment regarding O'Neill is a matter for the future. Opinion now varies from those who would place him beside the great playwrights of all time, to Eric Bentley who sees O'Neill as no more than "promising." At the time of his death he had completed three unpublished plays. He stipulated that one of them, *Long Day's Journey into the Night,* should not be released until 25 years after his death. Perhaps these plays will reveal new values, but whether they do or not, O'Neill seems assured of his place as America's first playwright of world importance.

O'Neill has not been alone in his search for new dramatic forms and techniques. Maxwell Anderson (b. 1888), commonly regarded as America's second most prominent playwright, has also been a restless experimenter, particulary in his use of verse, his struggle to revive tragedy, his effort to revive the historical play, and his belief that drama has a higher, more worthy function than merely to entertain. Anderson's crusade for a return to poetry is particularly interesting. It will be recalled that prose drama, with its language of everyday life, began with Lillo, reached respectability with Schiller and Lessing, and finally attained complete triumph with Ibsen. Now, as already pointed out, we see Anderson and others, especially Eliot and Fry, engaged in the struggle to return to verse. This is less of an innovation in Anderson's historical plays like *Elizabeth the Queen, Mary of Scotland,* and *Anne of the Thousand Days* than it is in a tragedy like *Win-*

terset, where the characters are American types including gangsters, or in *High Tor,* where the characters are mostly comic. There can be little doubt but that Anderson is right in his contention that great drama must rise above the poverty and awkward inadequacy of everyday speech. There is some question, however, whether a verse form is the essential element needed. Synge, O'Casey, Strindberg and others writing in prose have frequently achieved levels of expression, imagery, and rhythm that contain more real poetry than is to be found in most verse.

Not all of Anderson's plays are written in verse. The first to win success, *What Price Glory?* (with Lawrence Stallings), was an innovation of quite the opposite sort. It shocked many a polite audience with its hardbitten prose and profanity as it debunked the heroics and "glory" of World War I. *Both Your Houses* is another effective prose attack, this time upon political corruption in Washington. Sometimes it seems that Anderson, like O'Neill, may have succeeded best when he was least pretentious. The two plays just mentioned, plus his delightful *High Tor,* may well survive much longer than his more conscious attempts to raise the standards of American drama. Even if he has not always succeeded as well as he himself and others may have wished, he has made a great contribution to American drama.

Any survey of American playwriting must recognize the importance of Thornton Wilder (b. 1897), although this well-known author's dramatic fame rests largely on a single one-act play and three full-length plays. His *Our Town* probably comes close to being the best-known play in America. It has been a tremendous success on all levels, from Broadway to the most remote amateur groups. Its absence of conventional scenery, and its use of the stage manager to establish direct rapport with the audience places Wilder, like O'Neill and Anderson, among the innovators; but the play has qualities beyond novelty. It is an honest and revealing portrait of small-town American life. It has been criticised as sentimental, but American life is sentimental; Emily, George, and the others give us a far more genuine insight into twentieth-century American living than do the studies of neurotics, gangsters, and the sexually frustrated.

Wilder's one-act play, *The Happy Journey,* employs the same technique —stage manager and absence of scenery—that characterized *Our Town.* The mixture of sentiment, humor, and pathos is also much the same. In his other important full-length play, *The Skin of Our Teeth,*[18] which like *Our Town* won him a Pulitzer prize, his innovations are even more startling and

[18] Wilder is also the author of a highly entertaining farce-comedy, *The Merchant of Yonkers.*

enjoyable. Sabina, the maid, frequently interrupts the play to speak her mind to the audience. Our realistic notions of time and place also suffer as Wilder skillfully scrambles events of the ice age, the Biblical flood, and modern warfare to drive home his optimistic thesis that mankind is always squeezing by one crisis after another by "the skin of our teeth."

In contrast to Thornton Wilder's fundamentally optimistic view of American life stand the views of Elmer Rice, Clifford Odets, Tennessee Williams, and Arthur Miller. Elmer Rice (b. 1892), knowing poverty and social injustice, writes about them with passion and conviction. In *Street Scene* his attack takes the form of stark naturalism, but in most of his other plays, particularly *The Adding Machine*, he moves beyond naturalism into expressionism. The central character in *The Adding Machine* is Mr. Zero, one of the millions who stumble through a drab existence as cogs in an inhuman industrial machine. When Zero finds himself replaced by an adding machine he becomes unbalanced, kills his employer, is executed for the crime, is too narrow-minded to recognize happiness when it is offered to him in the Elysian Fields, becomes an adding machine operator in heaven, and finally is forced to return to earth to begin the torture of living all over again.

Clifford Odets (b. 1906) first won fame with *Waiting for Lefty*, a one-act play that grew out of a bitter taxicab strike in New York. The audience finds itself not in the atmosphere of a conventional theatre but in the tension of a labor hall. Characters rise from the audience to voice both grievances and appeals. The tension mounts until news comes that their leader, Lefty, has been murdered by hired assassins. When played during the depression audiences joined actors in the cry, "Strike, strike, strike!" which concludes the play.

In his full-length plays that followed, including *Golden Boy* and *Awake and Sing*, Odets quickly gained a reputation as the most promising of the young left-wing writers. He then moved to Hollywood and has only recently returned to Broadway with the very successful *Country Girl*.

Another writer who loomed brilliant and promising but has not yet fulfilled that promise is William Saroyan (b. 1908). Perhaps he has had only one thing to say—that the little people of the earth are fundamentally good and beautiful. He said this with poetry and great skill in his first short play, *My Heart's in the Highlands*. He said it again with great dramatic and ironic effectiveness in *The Time of Your Life*, but since then his variations of the same theme have been disappointing.

Of active present-day writers Tennessee Williams (b. 1914) commands our attention. His plays deal with the tensions, the frustrations, and the neurotic problems that grow out of modern life. *The Glass Menagerie,* his first work to win success, is like a haunting memory of the great depression. It has been criticized as sentimental and sad, yet it stands out as one of the most worthy achievements of recent years. *A Streetcar Named Desire* is his best play to date. In it we see the remnants of culture and sensitivity destroyed through conflict with the crude and animal forces of modern life. His next play, *Summer and Smoke,* is good, but falls short of *Streetcar.* His *The Rose Tattoo* shows a sense of humor as well as his usual psychological intensity.

Newest of America's major playwrights is Arthur Miller (b. 1915). *All My Sons* established him as the most talented dramatist to come out of World War II, but it was *Death of a Salesman* that gave him a secure place in the American theatre. *Death of a Salesman* is probably the most tragic and convincing story yet written on the shallowness of the old American ideal of "success." It is the tragedy not of a king or hero, but of a middle-aged traveling salesman, Willie Loman, who has smothered most of his finer qualities in a blind faith that somehow, someday, he or his boys will be a "big success." By the time the play opens his attempts to bluff through life on all the formulas—the hearty smile, good fellowship, winning on the athletic field, never admitting defeat—have worn threadbare, for the relentless facts of his failure have already begun to close in upon him. In one flashback after another we relive the sorrows and mistakes into which his shabby ideals have plunged him, and in the end this common man, who might have been a successful father and an excellent carpenter, is driven to suicide.

We cannot leave the discussion of American plays and playwrights without a word about musical comedy. While it is true that most musicals are "theatrical" rather than literary, momentary rather than lasting, and merely entertaining rather than penetrating, the fact remains that they are primarily an American contribution to the theatre, and that in some instances they have moved far beyond the usual entertaining nonsense and sentimental love themes into the realm of genuine satire. The high point of musical comedy to date was written by George S. Kaufman, Morrie Ryskind, and George Gershwin. In their *Of Thee I Sing* we follow J. P. Wintergreen as he rides triumphantly into the White House on a program of

The Modern

"Love!"—not dignified love of one's fellowmen, but Love! young, romantic —like the movies. Even at the play's climax, when the new President is about to be impeached by the old men of the Supreme Court, disaster is averted by the discovery that our hero is about to become a father, and the chorus bursts into the swelling refrain "Posterity is just around the corner!" Never before or since in America has the spirit of Aristophanes come closer to resurrection.

Kaufman and Ryskind also wrote an excellent musical about Franklin D. Roosevelt, *I'd Rather Be Right*. Kaufman, almost always writing in collaboration with others, has likewise given us some of our best legitimate comedies, among them *The Beggar On Horseback* (with Marc Connelly), *You Can't Take It With You*, and *The Man Who Came To Dinner* (with Moss Hart).

While no one else in the musical field has equaled Kaufman for satire and wit, it must be admitted that his theatrical success in the musical field has already been overshadowed by Rodgers and Hammerstein with their record-breaking hits: *Oklahoma!*, based on the play *Green Grow the Lilacs* by Lynn Riggs, and *South Pacific* based on the Pulitzer prize-winning *Tales of the South Pacific* by James A. Michener. The popularity of these and other musicals is indicated by the fact that although it now costs far more to produce a musical than it does to produce a standard legitimate play, men who have money to invest are becoming more and more inclined to gamble on the musical. Whether we like it or not, there is something about this genre that reflects America as nothing else does. But the story of musical comedy belongs in a book of its own.

CHAPTER V

Theory and Criticism

AVING GLANCED AT 2500 YEARS OF PLAYWRITING, WHAT HAVE WE learned? What are the basic elements of drama? Are there any lasting standards? Is the theatre a moral or immoral influence? What is wrong with being "merely entertaining"?

The search for answers to questions such as these frequently makes graduate study something far more exciting than most people suppose. The following pages do not pretend to cover even the basic fundamentals. If they stimulate a desire to know more, or even a desire to disagree, they will have served their purpose.

WHAT CHARACTERISTICS HAVE PLAYWRIGHTS IN COMMON?

For one thing they have a tendency to be born at the right time. Allardyce Nicoll reminds us that a giant of playwriting is usually surrounded by a group of lesser giants. Sophocles, Shakespeare, Goethe, Ibsen—none stood alone. Perhaps this is because a great playwright needs the stimulus of keen competition, or perhaps the great playwright and his fellows all grew from the same source, as for example, from the spirit of national exuberance that flooded Elizabethan England following the defeat of the Spanish Armada.

The great names have usually emerged not at the beginning, but near the beginning of a period. In other words, the spade work had been done, the giant had models to influence him, but not such perfect models that there was little hope of ever rising above them.

He has usually had early experience as well as practical experience in a living theatre. He has known his audience and has known his theatre. He has also tended to be a man of mature judgment with insight into life and character. This, as Nicoll observes, has resulted in his being a "late starter and long endurer." A surprising number of the best playwrights did not begin writing until their late twenties or thirties.

One other characteristic of great playwrights might well be remembered by the student who would shake the foundations of both theatre and philosophy with his first play; great dramatists have usually begun by first writing many skillful, well-made, and entertaining plays. *The Comedy of Errors* preceded *King Lear*.

WHO IS TO JUDGE?

In *The Playwright as Thinker*, Eric Bentley does a brilliant job of convincing us that popularity and box office appeal are inaccurate guides as to the worth of a play. Unfortunately he is not as successful in establishing an alternative basis of judgment. Bad as the judgment of audiences may be, scholars and critics down through the ages seem to present an even more dismal record. Critics do not agree on even basic fundamentals, although Aristotle, writing in the century following Sophocles, gives us a masterly analysis in his great critical essay, *The Poetics*. Liberally interpreted, this famous work does much to establish a foundation for criticism. Among other things it defines drama as an imitation of men in action; it divides drama into six elements: plot, character, diction, thought, song, and spectacle; and finally it establishes the drama's purpose, or rather the purpose of tragedy, as a purgation of the soul through the tragic emotions of pity and terror.

But any illusion that a study of Aristotle can make one either an infallible judge of plays or an outstanding playwright is shaken when we remember that the great Greek plays were written before, not after, his essay, and that Shakespeare, Molière, Lope de Vega, and so many of the best dramatists were either ignorant of his work or politely ignored it. It is even true that during certain periods, Aristotle's ideas, when slightly misinterpreted and slavishly applied, served to hinder the development of drama rather than help it. The mystery behind the creation of great art tends to remain a mystery.

ON WHAT BASIS SHOULD ONE JUDGE?

While we could discuss most of the subsequent ideas within the framework provided by Aristotle, it seems better to organize them under five simple questions frequently asked by those who attend plays.

1. Was It Entertaining?

Like the speaker, the playwright must first catch and hold his audience; other values, if any, are dependent upon this. We can go even further and say that entertainment alone has value, even though such value may be only momentary. Its aftereffects are neither harmful nor useful; it "Struts and frets its hour upon the stage and then is heard no more." We in the audience return home neither better nor worse for the experience.

What then is wrong with being "merely entertaining"? Nothing is wrong, but some other things are better. Moreover, in the twentieth century "mere entertainment" is cheap because it is so abundant. Commercialism and competition have forced radio, television, and motion picture productions to concentrate so much on momentary, interest-catching "entertainment" that we are surfeited by it. Pink ice cream and pop may be wonderful in small quantities, but not as an exclusive diet.

2. Is It Experience?

To some people "experience" implies an escape from life into the romantic world of vicarious experience, the world of daydreams and dream-fulfillment, the world as it should be. In small doses this form of escape may not be dangerous, but if overdone this world of melodrama, soap opera, romantic novel, and second-rate movies may seriously affect one's capacity to deal with real life. Few of us win the game in the last 30 seconds, slaughter the outlaws and escape unscathed, or end up in the moonlight with Miss America in our arms. The mature, well-adjusted personality must develop a tougher, more realistic sense of values. The right kind of theatre can help one develop such a sense of values. If a man gains wisdom through living, he can also gain it through art, for art is in large measure organized experience that men share together. A man who knows Shakespeare, Sophocles, Ibsen, Shaw, Strindberg, Chekhov, and O'Neill sees life honestly in myriad patterns and sees it both as it should and should not be. Such a man's ability to make wise decisions, to take disaster and disappointment in his stride, to realize that he is not alone, nor the first to have been humbled and troubled by existence, these qualities should make him a better, more stable, and more understanding human being.

3. Is the Language Effective?

There is no substitute for command over the magic of words. If anyone doubts this truth let him consider the following passage from Lee Simonson's *The Stage Is Set*.[1] Here are two of Hamlet's greatest soliloquies, "To be, or not to be" and "O, that this too too solid flesh would melt," rewritten as Simonson suggests they might be rendered by a modern playwright. Hamlet becomes plain Henry; he sits in a dirty back yard, where children have fashioned a melting snowman.

HENRY: Damn my stepfather; lecherous old bastard. If I could only kill him. But I'm a snivelling introvert. All I can do is complain. I can't do anything. . . . Mother—mother's nothing but a whore. NO! I shouldn't have said that. Forgive me, mother. . . . But it drives me almost mad to think of it. God! if I could only kill myself—get away from it all. There's nothing to live for. . . . I'm afraid! Afraid to do anything. Afraid of death. . . . Spooks. What they told me when I was a kid. Just afraid of the dark—but it sticks. It gets me. (*Looking at the snowman.*) I'm just so much mush—mush like you. . . . If I could only thaw with you tomorrow—thaw, just dissolve, trickle into the earth—run off into the sewer, etc.

Perhaps the barren quality of modern language is a reaction against the overexalted eloquence of the nineteenth century. Perhaps it is part of the machine age. Yet the reaction against such poverty of prose has already set in; we have already noted how Maxwell Anderson, T. S. Eliot, Christopher Fry, and others are returning to the poetic form. It should also be remembered that prose in the hands of writers like Strindberg, Chekhov, O'Casey, and Synge can achieve great vividness, rhythm, and imaginative richness of expression. In any event, whether in prose or verse, "word magic" must be present. It is one great difference between life and art. We are often clumsy, awkward, or inarticulate in life's great crises, but on the stage, never.

4. Is It "Moral"?

This question is difficult to deal with since there is neither common agreement nor logical definition of what we mean by "moral"; yet probably more plays are condemned on the grounds of being "immoral" than on any other. Any play running counter to established customs, laws, or especially the religious standards of a group is likely to be so condemned; yet curiously enough the great thinkers and religious leaders themselves have usually run counter to established norms. Of course they, like the playwrights, have often paid bitterly for their failure to conform. The problem is confusing. Ibsen's *Ghosts*, now a thoroughly respectable play, was once

[1] Lee Simonson, *The Stage Is Set*, Harcourt, Brace and Company, Inc., 1932, p. 435.

condemned as the essence of filth and indecency. Aristophanes' *Lysistrata* deals frankly with sex, but does so for the basic purpose of destroying the greatest evil in life, war. Many a seemingly pious melodrama may lead the spectator to conclude that the villain had the right idea had he not been unlucky enough to get caught at the end of the last act. *What Price Glory?* uses brutal profanity, but for the purpose of debunking war. The endlessly popular success stories with their inevitable happy endings that today meet with common approval may wreck more lives than all the Restoration comedies put together, for they lead one to expect the impossible of life.

This is not intended to imply that there are no lasting ethical values, but to suggest that such values cannot be determined so glibly and easily as many suppose. The problem is further complicated by the fact that sometimes one can attack the evils of life more effectively by examining them than by ignoring them. *Crime and Punishment, The Powers of Darkness,* and *Macbeth* are profoundly moral even though they depict terrible crimes.

One other observation seems valid. The great playwrights have usually been humanitarians and staunch believers in the brotherhood of man. They have tended to see beyond racial, religious, and national barriers. They have been liberals and frequently iconoclasts. Because of this they have shared the fate of other liberals and have felt the lash of scorn and abuse, especially in their own day.

5. Has It a Message?

We are told that to be great a play must do more than entertain; it must have something to say. Yet in America, at least, we are warned against propaganda. Just what is the difference between having something to say and being a propagandist? Probably to most people the play that presents ideas with which we disagree is propaganda. Mordecai Gorelik[2] points out that radical Soviet critics see nothing inartistic about agitational Communistic plays that we would regard as pure "red" propaganda, but they do look upon plays like *Winterset* as bourgeois propaganda. Though the problem remains complex and confusing, we can at least condemn certain types of propaganda, as for example, the type that slavishly follows the "party line," whether the line be communist, capitalist, or monarchist. We can also condemn the type of propaganda that is crudely and unskillfully presented, whether the message is the virtue of honesty or the horror of capitalism. But when the idea (or the propaganda if you prefer) is one's own and is presented with imagination, insight, and dramatic skill it may

[2] Mordecai Gorelik, *New Theatres for Old,* Samuel French, 1947, pp. 361 ff.

well become great art. In fact Gorelik presents the challenging thesis that the old "art for art's sake" writer is only great when he presents new and challenging ideas, whereas the "propaganda" writer is only great in so far as his ideas are presented with great art.

In concluding this section on plays and playwrights the reader should be warned that the preceding pages pretend to be no more than an introduction to the world of dramatic literature. Thousands of important plays and playwrights have not even been mentioned, nor is it to be expected that those who know drama best will agree with everything that has been said. Readers who are interested will find a wealth of material for further study —above all, the plays themselves. Books about plays may help in the process of acquiring an appreciation of the drama, but the play, as Lear would say, is "the thing itself."

Whatever literary or critical standards of judgment we apply, the fact remains that the contribution of dramatic literature to the sum total of human culture is tremendous. As Helen Hayes recently wrote:

When I consider how many of the world's greatest minds—Sophocles, Aristophanes, Shakespeare, Goethe, Molière, Ibsen, Shaw—have clothed their ideas in the dramatic form; when I consider how the theatre has cut through the barriers of national, religious, and racial prejudice; when I consider the enjoyment, the enrichment, and the enlightenment it has brought into the lives of countless millions down through the ages—I become very proud of my profession.[3]

[3] Helen Hayes, from a statement contributed for a brochure campaigning for the construction of a theatre at the University of Minnesota, 1952.

PART TWO

Acting and Directing

CHAPTER VI

Acting

OF THE ARTS AND CRAFTS THAT COMPOSE THEATRE, ACTING IS PROBA-
bly the most glamorous, fascinating, and controversial. From
Thespis to Bing Crosby, the fickle public has exalted beyond all
proportion those few who somehow caught its fancy, while ignoring, if not
abusing others of equal ability. Nor is the fickleness of fame the only confusing factor about acting: its theories are complex and contradictory, advocates of special techniques violently oppose one another, while the
crowning irony of all is that those with no formal training whatever sometimes excel others who have spent most of a lifetime in study and practice.

Some of the perplexity is due to the momentary quality of the art. Until
the movies came to provide a record of what was said and done, the actor's
art was preserved only in the memories of those who experienced it. Then,
too, the final appeal of acting is subjective. Acting is great only if it produces a great effect upon a given audience, but the audience is not a fixed
phenomenon. Its tastes and habits are as unpredictable as fashion in
women's dress. What one generation applauds with enthusiasm bordering
on ecstasy may be regarded by the next as sheer affectation or "ham." Our
grandparents applauded the actor who played to his audience, maintaining
a warm, friendly relationship. With the advent of realism such acting was
branded as "elocutionary" and the naturalistic approach became the vogue.
Today we in turn have grown impatient with the naturalistic actor, who
in his excessive fear of playing front or projecting his voice presents his
audience with the unexpressive profile and the mumbled speech of daily
life. Instead we cry that art should be greater, more vivid, more expressive
than life. In fact some nonillusionistic styles of acting such as those employed in epic theatre carry frank theatricality and actor-audience contact
to extents that would have startled even our grandfathers.

But in spite of the complexity and intangibility of the art, is it not possible to discern a few lasting standards and values? In spite of their many differences have not most of the greatest actors had much in common? Let us begin by a quick sampling of history, by looking briefly at a few of the stage "immortals."

THE HISTORY OF ACTING

Thespis was not the only actor in Greece whose name has survived; there are many, including Aeschylus and Sophocles, who, like Thespis, performed in their own plays. Wearing built-up shoes (cothurni), a mask with a high headpiece (onkus), and performing in huge outdoor theatres, these actors must have found great volume, rich intonation, and a certain degree of stylized movement necessary.

On the other hand, the common concept of classic acting as highly conventionalized and artificial may be misleading. Remember that Thespis was the "first actor," that Aeschylus was the first to use two actors on stage at the same time, and that Sophocles was the first to use three. Acting was a new art that had had little opportunity to crystalize into any stereotyped code of behavior. While this does not mean that Greek acting was "natural" it does suggest that it was comparatively fresh and original. Cole and Chinoy[1] cite examples that bear out the impression that classic acting was by no means devoid of impulse, inspiration, and emotion. Aesop, a Greek-born actor, performing in Rome, became so emotional while playing Atreus that he accidentally killed one of the servants; while the great Polus in playing Electra made the tragic heroine's grief convincing to himself and to his audience by carrying the ashes of his own son in the urn supposed to contain the ashes of Orestes.

Whereas Greek actors usually enjoyed relatively high social standing, those of Rome were almost without exception foreigners and slaves. One actor finally gained such prominence, however, that he was awarded his freedom. This was Roscius, who, interestingly enough, was primarily a comedian rather than a tragedian as most of the greatest actors have been. His success won him fame and the friendship of the great Cicero. To this day to call an actor a second Roscius is to pay him one of the most extravagant of compliments.

From the death of Roscius in 62 B.C. there is a span of 1600 years to the *Commedia dell' arte* players, who are the next to claim our attention. Perhaps we should have paused momentarily in tribute to some of the

---

[1] Tobey Cole and Helen Chinoy, *Actors on Acting*, Crown Publishers, 1949, pp. 14, 15.

medieval actors who must have hit peaks of naturalism. At least the actual crucifixion of a criminal in a Spanish Jesuit production in 1549 was some sort of an ultimate in this respect.[2] But for the most part roles in the mystery, miracle, and morality plays were performed by amateurs whose names have not survived. With the *Commedia* it was different. Here was acting in one of its most intriguing phases, for in these troupes the players were supreme. They used no scripts, no memorized lines, no elaborate scenic effects. Following nothing more than a rough scenario, these audacious performers faced their audiences prepared for anything. Songs, dances, quick wits, and alert imaginations combined to spin together some of the finest spontaneous theatre the world has ever known. According to one account:

> They were as chock-full of malice as of wit. . . . They were not willing, like silly school-boys, to recite only what they had learnt from a master. . . . They had only to receive a scenario, which someone had scribbled on his knee, to meet their stage manager in the morning to arrange the outlines of the plot . . . the rest they could invent themselves. . . . They had a store of proverbs, sallies, charades, riddles, recitations, cock-and-bull stories, and songs jumbled together in their heads. . . . They seized opportunity by the forelock and turned the least accident into profit. They drew inspiration from the time, the place, the color of the sky, or topic of the day, and established a current between their audience and themselves out of which the mad farce arose, the joint product of them all . . . Harlequin, armed with blacksmith's tools, draws four of Pantaloon's soundest teeth. He waits on Don Juan at table and wipes the plates on the seat of his breeches . . . There is only one plate of macaroni between them and they eat it in floods of tears. . . . Their extravagant fancy broke loose before an audience and burst into fire and soared to the sky, a marvel of balance. Explosions of wild laughter followed, and wild confusion, and a medley of caricatures, dreams, buffooneries, scurrility, poetry, and love.[3]

Although the above is obviously an imaginative rather than an objective record of what a *Commedia* performance was like, it does suggest the exciting possibilities. Actors capable of such brilliant improvisation must have been hard to find, even though most of them specialized in the playing of only one character. Among the players who mastered this art of improvisation was the beautiful, talented, well-educated Isabella Andreini (1562–1604), who won fame and admiration wherever she appeared. Foreshadowing the glamour that so often has attached itself to great actresses were the tributes extended at the time of her early death. The greatest of

[2] Lee Simonson, *The Stage Is Set*, Harcourt, Brace and Company, Inc., 1932, p. 49.
[3] Philippe Monnier, "The Venetian Theatre and the Italian Comedy of the Eighteenth Century," *The Mask*, January, 1911, pp. 104–105.

these came from her husband, the famous actor and manager, Francisco Andreini, who in his sorrow left the stage, never to appear again.

Our knowledge of acting during the Elizabethan period is limited. Of the many companies, the two main ones were The Lord Chamberlain's Men, with Richard Burbage as the leading actor, and The Lord Admiral's Men, which featured Edward Alleyn. Shakespeare was associated with the former company, Marlowe with the latter. There is some evidence that the Burbage-Shakespeare company championed a more lifelike style than its rivals. Certainly Hamlet's advice to the players indicates that Shakespeare was striving for a more convincing effect than that achieved by those who, "sawed the air with their hands, tore a passion to tatters, out-heroded Herod, and split the ears of the groundlings."[4]

It was Burbage (c. 1567–1619), who first created such great roles as Hamlet, Lear, and Othello, and there is no reason to believe that he failed to do them justice. A passing nod is also due to the boys who played Cleopatra, Lady Macbeth, Juliet, and the other great women who troop through Shakespeare's plays. They too must have performed well.

During the Restoration women first appeared on the English stage. Mrs. Bracegirdle, Mrs. Barry, and the fabulous Nell Gwynn were among those who emerged as favorites. These, along with such actors as Thomas Betterton, began to assume such importance that by the middle of the eighteenth century the actor tended to overshadow the play. This unfortunate state of affairs however, reflects upon playwrights and audiences rather than upon the actors, who during the eighteenth and nineteenth centuries in France, Italy, Germany, England, and America gave the world some of the greatest individual performances it has ever seen.

In England the most famous of these eighteenth-century actors was David Garrick (1717–1779). He entered the theatre, not as a stage-struck student of acting, but as an amiable, intelligent, witty business man. His approach was fresh, original, and "natural." "If this young fellow is right," cried Quinn, leading actor of the old school, "then we have all been wrong." It is interesting to note that Garrick had none of the arty, temperamental, or neurotic qualities that the general public seems so determined to associate with acting. He was a close friend of Samuel Johnson, Oliver Goldsmith, and other leading figures of his day. He was an excellent executive, one of the best managers the Drury Lane Theatre ever had. Unlike some stars who have been inclined to "hog the show," Garrick surrounded himself with an outstanding company and was responsible for giving a number

---

[4] For exact quotation see William Shakespeare, *Hamlet*, Act III, scene 2.

of actors, including Sarah Siddons, a boost toward success. As to his acting, he seems to have been extremely versatile. His contemporaries regarded him as equally effective in both comedy and tragedy, although today there is a tendency to favor the reports of his comedy. His style, while regarded as very natural in his day was, according to Cole and Chinoy, "not above the stops, starts, and drawn-out death scenes that drew applause."[5] He also played most of his roles in lavish contemporary costume, but in spite of what may seem minor shortcomings, he brought freshness, health, and common sense to the theatre of his time.

Anyone inclined to conclude from the example of Garrick that in order to act one must be emotionally stable and well adjusted is due for a shock when he considers the case of Edmund Kean (1787–1833), who followed Garrick by half a century. Kean was the typical artistic genius, and his genius had the usual roots in a life of suffering and misery. His debut at Drury Lane as Shylock reads like a romantic extravaganza. Almost overnight he had London at his feet, and within a few years had amassed a fortune. Tales of his tragic power are numerous. During a performance as Sir Giles Overreach, the famous role in Massinger's *A New Way to Pay Old Debts*, his final scene is reported to have achieved such a pitch of intensity that, "One of the actresses on stage, Mrs. Glover, overcome with fright at the horror depicted on his countenance, fainted; [Lord] Byron at the same time was seized in his box by a convulsive fit; whilst women went into hysterics and the whole house burst into a wild clamour of applause."[6] Coleridge remarked: "To see Kean was to read Shakespeare by flashes of lightning." Although quite obviously intended as a compliment to the brilliance with which Kean illuminated certain Shakespearean passages, this remark by Coleridge contains connotations that are apt in quite another sense, for Kean was erratic and undependable. He gave bad performances as well as inspired ones, made enemies in both England and America, and undoubtedly hastened his own death by alcohol and dissipation. But at his best there is no denying that he was a great genius— perhaps the greatest of the romantic, inspirational school.

England's greatest actor toward the close of the nineteenth century once again presents a character contrast to the eccentric genius of Edmund Kean, for Sir Henry Irving (1838–1905) was above all things respectable, dependable, and conscientious. Like Garrick, he excelled both as actor and

[5] Chinoy and Cole, *op. cit.*, p. 95.
[6] J. F. Malloy, *The Life and Adventures of Edmund Kean*, Ward and Downey, 1888, p. 248.

as manager. Born in poverty and obscurity, not unusually gifted in either voice or body, he achieved success through infinite care in perfecting details. His entire company could always be depended upon for an excellent and carefully rehearsed performance—quite an unusual achievement in his day. No one has ever done more to elevate the stage in the opinion of those outside the theatre. He insisted that the actor, as a member of a learned profession, was entitled to the same esteem and respect as the doctor, the lawyer, or the clergyman. His own conduct was exemplary. He presented what were considered masterpieces of literature with the strictest reference to historical accuracy. In recognition of his contributions, he was knighted in 1895, the first actor to be thus honored.

While we admire Irving for the above qualities, it must be admitted that like so many of the Victorians he was more respectable than profound. Shaw writes,

> To the author, Irving was not an actor: he was either a rival or a collaborator who did all the real work. Therefore, he was anathema to master authors, and a godsend to journeymen authors, with the result that he had to confine himself to the works of dead authors who could not interfere with him, and, very occasionally, live authors who were under his thumb because they were unable to command production of their works in other quarters.[7]

While Shaw may be a bit harsh, he hits at the core of Irving's weakness, which consisted of a romantic tendency to emphasize production, stage business, and by-play at the expense of character, sincerity, and the play itself.

Like England, France produced more than her share of great stars. To begin with, there was Molière himself, who rates along with Garrick and Roscius as one of the great comedians of all time, and who in his plays conducted a witty crusade against the affectation and bombast of players in rival companies. Then there was Michel Baron (1653–1729), one of Molière's young actors, who carried the "natural style" into tragedy as well as comedy and did so with tremendous success. Intoxicated by his fame, he is reported to have maintained that the world had known only two truly great actors, Roscius and Baron. In 1691, at the age of 38, he retired from the stage, convinced that there were no more worlds to conquer. Modesty in actors, although desirable, is apparently not indispensable.

Perhaps the most famous of the early eighteenth-century French actresses

[7] George Bernard Shaw, "From the Point of View of the Playwright," published in *Herbert Beerbohm Tree: Some Memories of Him and His Art,* collected by Max Beerbohm, E. P. Dutton and Co., Inc., 1917, pp. 240–241.

was the beautiful Adrienne Lecouvreur (1692–1730). Her acting followed the natural style of Baron and her tragic death (she was poisoned at the height of her fame) has inspired both poets and playwrights. According to Voltaire, she "almost invented the art of speaking to the heart, and of showing feeling and truth where formerly had been shown little but artificiality and declamation."

Another French actor, François Josef Talma (1763–1826), was likewise famous for his naturalness. But to confound once more our stereotyped notions of how actors behave, he, like Garrick, was admired for his qualities of common sense and good taste. His easy convincing style enraged his more formal contemporaries, and had it not been for the protection of Napoleon, he might have found himself barred from the French stage for having failed to observe the "rules."

From nineteenth-century France came Sarah Bernhardt (1845–1923) and Benoit Constant Coquelin (1841–1909). Bernhardt, "The Divine Sarah," was undoubtedly one of the world's great personality actresses. Temperamental and sensational on stage and off, she was always colorful and easy to publicize. With the help of a magnificent voice, she maintained her reputation as the world's greatest actress for nearly fifty years.

In contrast to the eccentric genius of Bernhardt, Coquelin was famed for his logic and mental control. He established what Stanislavski calls the representational school of acting, which advocates creative imagination, study, and emotion during rehearsals but insists upon complete objectivity during performance. In other words he believed that the performance should be a fundamentally intellectual imitation of what had been worked out during rehearsal. This unemotional approach was challenged by Sir Henry Irving and a great controversy ensued, which we will consider in some detail later.

Sarah Bernhardt's greatest rival was the Italian actress Eleonora Duse (1859–1924). The contrast between them was as marked as that between Garrick and Kean. Duse's private life was restless and tragic, but on stage she exhibited a sincerity and quiet greatness that will always be admired. Bernhardt always played Bernhardt, but Duse submerged her own personality in the role. Her objective was to "live the part"; her style, quiet simplicity and sincerity. Duse made one film, which has been preserved, and while she was ill at the time, over sixty, and hampered by a hopeless script, her acting has not aged. Present-day audiences who have seen the film have been struck by the truth and quiet dignity of her performance. In contrast, Bernhardt's films of the same period seem overacted and sometimes quite ridiculous. This leads to the conclusion that Shaw, as usual, was right, for he chose Duse as the greater of the two, maintaining that Bernhardt projected only her own charm, but that Duse projected the charm of whatever character she portrayed.

Using the sincere approach of Duse plus the inspirational power of the romanticists, another Italian actor, Tommaso Salvini (1829–1915) rose to a position where everyone who saw him seems to agree that in roles such as Othello he was unequalled. A deep, almost religious sincerity seemed to characterize his playing. Like Duse, his aim was to live the part. Tradition has it that long before the performance began he assumed the spiritual as well as the physical character of Othello and remained completely in character until the performance concluded. He began his portrayal of the Moor with such simplicity and quietness that audiences were at first unimpressed, but as the poisoned suggestions of Iago began to take effect, he gradually changed into one of the most powerfully tragic figures ever seen. It was from watching Salvini that Stanislavski received many of the impressions that were to lay the foundation of the Moscow Art Theatre and the "Stanislavski system" of acting.

In nineteenth-century America, at least three actors managed to gain international fame. The first, Edwin Forrest (1806–1872), was a man of enormous physical vigor, rough realism, tragic dignity, and a powerful voice. Strong willed, violent tempered, and egocentric, he made enemies in both England and America. His sensational squabble with the English tragedian William Charles Macready culminated in the disastrous Astor Place riot. The trouble that led to this outbreak had begun several years earlier when Forrest, playing in London, was hissed during a performance of *Macbeth*. Accepting the rumor that Macready was responsible for the insult, Forrest attended his rival's performance of *Hamlet* and deliberately hissed Macready. The audience was shocked, and the fiery tempered old English actor was so choked with rage that he was momentarily unable to continue the performance. Ill will continued to mount until during Macready's visit to America in 1849 the hot-tempered partisans of each clashed in a bloody riot inside and outside the Astor Place Opera House in New York.

It is perhaps fitting that such a rugged individual as Edwin Forrest should have been the first American actor to attract international attention. Certainly he had many of the "he-man" qualities commonly associated with the frontier.

In most respects Edwin Booth (1833–1893), America's second and per-

haps greatest actor, was a marked contrast to Forrest, for his style of playing is usually referred to as quiet, intelligent, and of great depth. The son
of the English-born tragedian, Junius Brutus Booth, Edwin grew up in a
theatrical environment. Although his father did not want him to act, the
fates ruled otherwise. By the time he was thirty-one Booth was generally
recognized as outstanding, particularly as Hamlet, in which he had established a record run of one hundred nights. At this climax of success came
the shock of his brother's assassination of Abraham Lincoln. Temporarily
he retired from the stage, but eventually he returned to give some of the
greatest performances the American theatre has ever seen. Hamlet was
still his most distinguished role. His melancholy temperament and essential loneliness gave to the famous character a depth and understanding
that may well have been unequalled. His acting was moody and uneven.
One might see a great performance or a mediocre one, but in spite of these
limitations, the fact remains that few, if any, have equalled Edwin Booth
at his best.

The third outstanding American actor of the nineteenth century was
Joseph Jefferson (1829–1905). If anyone doubts the actor's importance in
the creation of great theatre, he should pause to consider the case of *Rip
Van Winkle*. In the hands of anyone else, the play has always been mediocre, but with Jefferson as Rip it acquired the qualities of greatness. Both
as an actor and as a man, Jefferson excelled in human warmth, kindliness,
and understanding. His *Autobiography* contains some excellent hints on
acting, as well as much common sense about both the theatre and life in
general.

As for the twentieth century, it seems safer to avoid the hazards of arbitrary selection that would be entailed in the selection of four or five from
among the many outstanding actors and actresses of our day. Moreover,
it is doubtful that further discussion would greatly advance our basic
purpose in this chapter, which is to try to discover something about the
fundamentals of the art of acting itself. Several relatively complete analyses
of the background and training of successful actors have as yet failed to
throw much light on the subject.[8] Carefully conducted psychological
studies of actor personalities, aptitudes, and interests have fared little

[8] For a summary of these see Elsie Turner, *A Study of the Background and Training
of Fifty Prominent American Actors*, unpublished M.A. thesis, University of Minnesota,
1954. Another excellent source is Toby Cole and Helen Krich Chinoy, *op. cit.* The
authors draw no dogmatic conclusions; they allow the actors to speak for themselves.
The reader is free to study, to reflect, to test in terms of his own experience, and finally
to draw his own conclusions if he chooses.

better.[9] Actors and acting simply refuse to be neatly codified. As we have already seen, there seems to be no common pattern. Some, like Kean, were temperamental and neurotic; others, like Garrick, dependable and level-headed. Some, like Bernhardt, projected their own personalities; others, like Duse, the personalities of their characters. Some like Coquelin, tried to perform with mental objectivity; others, like Irving, tried to feel the emotions they portrayed. More detailed study would reveal that many great actors came from theatrical families, although many others did not; that some succeeded through unquenchable determination, although a few did not even want to act. We would find, however, that most did have some early experience with the stage, that most lived interesting lives, that most did not slavishly imitate the systems or techniques of others, and that most knew how to work and work hard. Yet even these rather obvious statements are subject to qualifications.

Leaving the actors themselves, we can turn to teachers and textbooks in an effort to learn of the art. Lee Strasberg,[10] tracing major developments in this area from the first known text to the present day, finds that the usual approach has been to emphasize bodily expression, to catalog the emotions, to write "a kind of grammar of expression; and an analysis of voice and its production." If we view acting as a response to an imaginary stimulus, then most of the texts throw their emphasis on the response, paying little attention to the stimuli—the motives and drives giving rise to the response. As a result, most teaching prior to the twentieth century remained on the mechanical level. Standard responses, being tangible, could be taught. The problem of supplying the stimulus or motivation was left to the actor. If he failed in this he was simply dismissed as having no "talent."

Many attempts were made to break away from these codes of acting. As early as 1753 Aaron Hill[11] wrote convincingly against the affectation and stilted artificiality of the stage, only to conclude his essay with a system of expression fully as mechanical as the old one. François Delsarte, in the

[9] Frances E. Drake, *A Study of Personality Traits of Students Interested in Acting,* unpublished Ph.D. dissertation, University of Minnesota, 1949. Contains summary of research in area of actor personality.

[10] Lee Strasberg, "Acting and the Training of Actors," in John Gasner, *Producing the Play,* rev. ed., pp. 128–163.

[11] Aaron Hill, "An Essay on the Art of Acting," *The Works of the Late Aaron Hill, Esq.,* Vol. IV, [no pub. listed] London, 1753.

second half of the nineteenth century, did the same thing, but did it much more thoroughly, and is associated with the stilted posturing characteristic of "elocution." More successful in his attempt to break away from the mechanical approach was Talma, who in writing on the subject threw emphasis on sensibility and imagination, as Remond de Sainte-Albine had done even earlier in his work, *Le Comédien* (1747), which Strasberg finds was the first text to break completely with the oratorical school. It remained, however, for Constantin Stanislavski (1863–1938) to crystalize an approach that was essentially different, one that threw emphasis on the stimulus rather than the response, on the creative rather than the technical. Let us hasten to add that Stanislavski was not unaware of the importance of the technical. His second book, *Building A Character,* deals primarily with technique. But his first book, *An Actor Prepares,* is the one that is unique, for it deals with the creative—the stimulus—that is basic to acting as it is to any work of art.

Essentially Stanislavski tried to establish a system or technique for setting one's creative and imaginative faculties too work. It is based on the assumption that if the actor is truly sensitive to the stimulus of the imaginary situation, his reactions will largely take care of themselves. Stanislavski recognized that in order for the response to be effective, body and voice should be relaxed and healthy, free and responsive to shades of thought and feeling, but the core of the response was left to the individual actor. It was not thrust upon him mechanically by rules, instructors, or the example of other actors. It was what the actor sensed that he would do if he were a given character in a given situation. As a result, such things as imagination, concentration, memory of emotion, dramatic action, objectives, and relaxation became typical units of study for students of the "Stanislavski system."

CAN ACTING BE TAUGHT?

Having briefly considered the history of acting, we shall devote the remainder of this chapter to the discussion of a few ideas and theories. These are not intended to provide a complete picture, but it is hoped that they may serve to clarify some of the confusion that tends to surround this most intangible of arts.

We might begin by asking the question, "Can acting be taught?" for frequently from old-timers and occasionally from moderns one hears the statement, "Actors are born, not made." As already mentioned, a newcomer may sometimes outshine others who have spent most of a lifetime struggling with the art. In such instances someone always comes forth with a solution: "The newcomer was born with talent, the others without." This is very convincing until someone asks, "But what is talent?" One who wishes to keep acting veiled in mystery can reply, "A strange gift with which some are endowed." If he wants to understand, however, he must search for some explanation that is more rational. The question, then, is: are actors born inherently different from other human beings? If they are, no one has as yet isolated the difference. Tests, reasonably numerous in recent years, have failed to disclose any particular traits or aptitudes of unusual significance.[12]

In general, the term "talent" is probably used as synonymous with general effectiveness. As such, the term is not objectionable. But if used to imply some mysterious or special gift, it may become little more than a protective escape for the incompetent teacher, who, unable to get results, dismisses the student as "untalented." Talent is probably nothing more mysterious than the total pattern of abilities and aptitudes—of voice, body, personality, past experiences, and a knack for abandoning oneself to the world of make-believe. In other words, the actor, like the speaker, is first of all a total human being, a complex bundle of habits, memories, and attitudes, not just a few specialized techniques learned in a dramatic school. This view is not intended to make "talent" appear trivial or easy; but it should make it appear rational though complex, rather than mysterious though simple.

At the opposite extreme from the contention that actors are born, that it is all a matter of talent, lies the equally extreme view that the beginner in acting should consider himself as humble and helpless as the beginner in other arts such as instrumental music, for example. This view, while useful in motivating a lazy student, is essentially false, for as already admitted, a beginner can and often does act and act rather well. Imagine a beginner in violin or piano offering a public concert after practicing a few hours per day for three or four weeks! The difference is not hard to understand. The beginning musician can be assumed to have scarcely touched a violin or piano, whereas the beginning actor has been using his instruments (body and voice) for better or for worse, since the day he was born. Acting, then, is not so much an entirely new skill as it is a matter of

[12] Frances E. Drake, *op. cit.*

adapting what one already has to a new situation. This has disadvantages as well as advantages. It throws a premium upon the intangible thing called attitude. It requires a delicate adjustment in that the actor must concentrate most of his attention upon the play—the imaginary situation—at a time when the real social stimulus of success or failure before an audience is enormous. It may be more difficult for the actor to perfect control of his instruments than for the musician to perfect control of his, but in the beginning the actor is far ahead.

To return to the question of whether acting can be taught, it seems obvious that acting is neither wholly a matter of inborn talent nor wholly a matter of learning all from the beginning. It can be taught, provided that we think of teaching in the largest sense of that term, as the guiding and controlling of environment. Narrowed to the space of a few hours in a classroom, it is hard to say. Wonders are sometimes achieved during a single class or a single rehearsal, but again it is no reflection on the teacher or the student if habits and attitudes acquired over a lifetime of living are not easily changed. The teaching of acting is a challenging, frustrating, but fascinating task.

TO FEEL OR NOT TO FEEL

As far as actual theories of acting are concerned, there are, as already implied, two basic schools of thought: (1) the technical or mechanical school tends toward an approach from the outside, emphasizing the use of body, voice, gesture, inflection, conventions, and techniques; while (2) the psychological or creative school tends to approach the problem from the inside, emphasizing understanding, motivation, imagination, purpose, and emotion. Conflict between these two approaches has often been heated. Before we examine them directly, it seems worth-while to consider a closely related controversy that has raged for decades, "Should the actor feel his part?"

This question was originally posed in 1770 by the French philosopher and critic, Denis Diderot, who insisted that the actor should remain completely insensible to the emotion he portrays. The controversy reached a climax in 1888 when the English critic William Archer published a book on the subject entitled *Masks Or Faces?*, but in spite of Archer's thorough attempt to solve the problem, he ended in a rather inconclusive compromise. Although the controversy still continues, several issues can be clarified.

1. *Nobody Defends Forced Acting*

Most of the conflict is probably semantic in origin—words simply do not mean the same thing to different individuals. For example, everyone who has worked any length of time in the theatre is familiar with the young actor who tries too hard, struggles to force an emotion, strains for dramatic effect, and gets excited about acting for the sake of acting. Helen Hayes, Katharine Cornell, Cornelia Otis Skinner, and many others cite such instances of overacting as examples of too much "feeling" the part. Stanislavski, on the other hand, cites similar instances as examples of a failure to feel. It is doubtful whether most actors are good judges of how much they feel or do not feel during a performance. There is some tendency for imaginative, sensitive, and rather emotional actors to argue against feeling, while the naturally "intellectual" and critical actors argue for it. We often assume that everyone needs what we need. Many actors who try not to feel during a performance still try to be sensitive, imaginative, and in tune with the play. Perhaps they are doing the very thing Stanislavski advocates without knowing it. In any event, most young actors who think they are being overcome by the troubles and emotions of the character they are portraying are simply being overcome by their own troubles and emotions. Musicians, speakers, readers, and even athletes are quite as susceptible to this type of emotion as are actors. In any event, neither Helen Hayes nor Stanislavski defends such straining or forcing, such lack of poise and control. It is a sure sign of the novice upon either the stage or the athletic field.

2. *Nobody Advocates Literally Living the Part*

Wild stories are frequently related regarding actors so carried away by their parts that they forgot they were only acting, and burst into uncontrollable rage or hysterical sobbing. While most overacting of this kind is probably forced acting, it must be admitted that on rare occasions the stimulus of the imaginary situation itself can cause an actor to lose voluntary control. The danger of such an occurrence is remote; it will probably happen only: (a) If the actor has recently lived through a situation similar to the one which he must portray. (A mother who has recently lost a child may find it difficult to play a scene on the stage involving the death of a loved one.) (b) If the actor has a sufficiently psychotic personality. (Our mental institutions have numerous patients convinced that they really are Napoleon, Joan of Arc, etc.) (c) If the actor has had one drink too many. (d) If the actor has outstanding potential ability. On a few occasions during the lifetime of a director, he is likely to discover a young actor or actress so sensitive and imaginative that voluntary control in an emotional crisis (of the character, not the actor) is difficult. Ordinarily, if there is intelligence, the problem of teaching such a student to maintain control is not serious. Richard Boleslavsky's chapter on characterization[13] contains some excellent advice on the subject, or a few more rehearsals will usually bring the emotion under control. Everyone agrees, however, that a real emotional breakdown before an audience is highly embarrassing.

On the other hand, the fact that such notable actresses as Helen Hayes and Katharine Cornell find it difficult not to feel too intensely the emotions of characters they portray may well indicate the very source of their greatness. Directors know it is no problem to most actors.[14] In other words control is only a problem to those with enough imagination to have something worth controlling. The average individual possessing but a wee mouse of an aesthetic soul need not shackle it with log chains.

3. Almost No One Advocates a Purely Mechanical Approach to Acting

While many teachers prefer to begin with mechanical techniques, they almost always introduce some sort of motivation or emotional stimulation before the training period is over. At first glance one who has never acted may wonder why this is necessary. Logic tells us that in the final analysis it does not matter whether the actor feels or not, so long as he presents a pattern of voice and action that will make the audience feel. If anyone doubts this, let him consider the shadows on a movie screen. It can scarcely be argued that they feel, yet they move millions to tears, laughter, excitement, and all the vicarious sensations of romantic love. But this is no solution to the problem of feeling or nonfeeling. The question still remains, Is the actor more likely to assume the correct outward pattern —one that will convince and move his audience—when feeling or not feeling?

[13] Richard Boleslavsky, *Acting: The First Six Lessons*, Theatre Arts, 1933, Chapter IV.
[14] There are certain curious aspects about the problem of losing voluntary control that are seldom recognized. Such a loss of control is generally considered to be an actor's problem, yet thousands of people in real life are momentarily overcome by their emotions, hundreds of speakers and readers momentarily lose control; but oddly enough, I am not certain I have ever seen it happen to an actor or actress during the actual performance of a well-rehearsed play. Do not misunderstand—I have seen many young actors practically beside themselves with stage fright or so excited they shed tears. I have seen them *act* till they tied themselves in knots, but none of them were "feeling" in the way Stanislavski uses the term. All were overcome by their personal emotions, not by the emotions of the character.

To repeat, almost no one believes that a purely mechanical approach alone is sufficient. In the final analysis, it will be seen that if the actor himself does not create imaginatively a pattern of expression for his part, he becomes nothing but a puppet, a slave to his director, teacher, or textbook, following the pattern of expression created by someone who does or did feel into the role imaginatively. Mickey Mouse is quite unperturbed by the fact that Disney does all his thinking and feeling for him. Most live actors prefer to create for themselves.

4. Do Not Confuse Feeling with Trying to Feel

Most opponents of Stanislavski completely misinterpret his method of arousing emotion. He ridicules the idea that love, hate, sorrow, etc., can be aroused directly by simply willing to do so. The actor does not try to create the emotion. He tries to imagine the stimulus. He tries to concentrate on the given circumstances, the imaginary situation, and to believe in their artistic reality. He does not say, "I am Hamlet," but "if I were Hamlet." He simply engages in make-believe on an adult, and often very serious level. A gifted and sensitive actor who approaches his art in this manner is likely to find himself emotionally and imaginatively moved, in tune with the thoughts and feelings of the character. It should be easier for him to act well when he emotionally believes in what the character says and does, just as it is easier for the public speaker to speak well when he believes in what he says and does. After all, Stanislavski's Moscow Art Theatre was noted, and is still noted, for the quiet sincerity, the deeply moving simplicity, and the convincing truth of its acting. This hardly resembles the type of acting condemned by most antiemotionalists.

To summarize thus far, no one defends the novice who strains and forces; no one advocates that the actor should ever lose voluntary control of himself, on stage or off. Very few would defend an entirely mechanical approach. Such direct advice as "feel your part" is bad since it leads to forcing, while "do not feel" can only lead to dry, mechanical imitation. Almost everyone, then, accepts a compromise position. John Dolman[15] wisely suggests that the actor should work for sensitivity, understanding, and imagination rather than for "feeling." According to George Henry Lewes, the actor should be "in a state of emotional excitement sufficiently strong to furnish him with the elements of expression, but not strong enough to disturb his consciousness of the fact that he is only imagining— sufficiently strong to give the requisite tone to his voice and aspect to his

[15] John Dolman, *The Art of Play Production,* Harper & Brothers, 1936, pp. 219 ff.

features, but not strong enough to prevent his modulating the one and arranging the other according to a preconceived standard."[16] Joseph Jefferson sums up the matter as follows: "For myself, I know that I act best when the heart is warm and the head is cool."[17]

Within this compromise group, however, there is one discernible differ‐ ence of opinion that merits consideration. Constant Coquelin, Helen Hayes, and many other leading actors advocate feeling during rehearsals but nonfeeling during performances, while Stanislavski insists, along with Salvini and others, that the actor should act with such conviction that he experiences feeling "not only once or twice while studying his part, but to a greater or lesser degree every time he plays it."[18] With experienced pro‐ fessional actors Coquelin's system may be effective; with young actors it is risky, for they are likely to convey unconsciously what they really think and feel to the audience. On the beginning level many an amateur conveys, not the drives and desires of the character he is playing, but his personal eagerness to succeed, his struggle to remember the next line, his elation when the comic line gets a laugh, his strained anxiety when it does not, and his embarrassment as the romantic love scene draws near. The pro‐ fessional may be able to think such irrelevant thoughts and cover them up with technique, but for the amateur the best way to make an audience understand, feel, and believe is for the actor himself to understand, feel, and believe. It is safer to work with nature than against it.

It should be repeated that practically everyone accepts the compromise position in the controversy. Somewhere in the process both inside and outside are necessary—both creative feeling and technique.[19] The re‐ mainder of this chapter deals, therefore, with the function, importance, and methods of these two approaches. The assumption is that both are de‐ sirable, although not necessarily of equal importance.

THE CREATIVE APPROACH

Most of the basic principles of this approach have already been sug‐ gested in the foregoing discussion of Stanislavski and the problem of

[16] George Henry Lewes, *On Actors and the Art of Acting*, Henry Holt and Company, Inc., 1878, p. 105.

[17] Joseph Jefferson, *The Autobiography of Joseph Jefferson*, The Century Co., 1889, p. 439.

[18] Constantin Stanislavski, *An Actor Prepares*, Theatre Arts, 1936, p. 13.

[19] *Technique* is used here in a limited sense in contrast to *creative*. Actually the crea‐ tive system is in itself a technique for releasing the actor's own creative energies—a method of arousing his sympathy, his emotional and intellectual understanding of the play and the character he is to portray.

feeling. As already noted, the basic assumption of the creative approach is that the actor, if sufficiently sensitive to the drives and motives of the character he portrays, will "instinctively" sense what the basic responses should be. To achieve this goal, Stanislavski devised his method which rests essentially upon the following elements:[20]

Freedom from Unnecessary Muscular Strain

Unnecessary tension can be disastrous. It not only interferes with the use of voice and body but also blocks the imagination. Freedom from undue strain is a fundamental prerequisite to creative work.

Concentration of Attention

Unnecessary tension and many other ills of acting tend to arise from the actor's failure to concentrate his attention on something within or appropriate to the imaginary situation. The actor needs to be in somewhat the same "inspired" state of mind as the author, the painter, or the composer are when their energies are absorbed by creative work; but whereas other artists usually arrive at this creative state in the quiet of their own rooms and under favorable circumstances, the actor must create at a given time, in a given place, and under very adverse circumstances—glaring lights, offstage distractions, and the strain of being observed by an audience. The actor's power to absorb himself in his fundamental task, thus driving the numerous distractions to the periphery of his consciousness, is of tremendous importance.

Object of Concentration: Motives and Dramatic Action

The term dramatic action is closely related to motivation and purpose— to a sensitive and compelling awareness of the wants, desires, and drives of a character. The objective on stage as in life always ends in some action, something done, something accomplished. We want to warm ourselves at the fire, to find an article that has been lost, to convince a friend of our innocence, to win the lady of our choice. In an effort to achieve such desires we may employ words, inflections, gestures, facial expressions, or whatever type of activity seems likely to gain the desired end. Under the Stanislavski

---

[20] Divisions of any kind in the Stanislavski system are highly arbitrary. Actually all the steps tend to be interwoven and interrelated. Thus the best way to relieve muscular strain is to concentrate on one's objective, while in order to concentrate on one's objective it is necessary to get rid of muscular strain. What Stanislavski was striving for was a creative attitude. The various creative techniques function only as a means to that end. If one does not work another may. If one does work it helps the others.

system the actor pays little direct attention to such things as inflections, gestures, and facial expressions. These it is assumed will take care of themselves if he has a vivid awareness of his objectives. In other words, the actor does not concentrate on *how* he should say his lines but on *what* he wants and especially *why* he wants it. This, while not the actor's whole task, is his major task.

Related to all this is another creative method that teachers have recently begun to emphasize. Essentially it consists of substituting images for words. Take the great speech by Enobarbus in *Antony and Cleopatra* in which he describes how the lovers first met. The great actor not only knows why he is telling the story but in his "mind's eye" tends to see images of the event, fabricated from his imagination to be sure, but nevertheless images that are quite as artistically real and vivid as would images have been had he really seen the meeting of Antony and Cleopatra. Evidence, while sketchy, indicates that the poor actor tends to see only the images of words from the printed script or something equally inappropriate.

Memory of Emotion

Recognizing that we can interpret life and literature only in terms of our own experience, Stanislavski developed techniques for recalling and employing the emotional memories of past experiences. This technique is especially useful when a scene, although the actor knows it is well written, fails to arouse his interest or his belief. Searching out and quietly recalling some similar experience from the actor's own past may produce the conviction or the attitude that is necessary.

The personal experience that the actor recalls is not necessarily identical with the one he must portray. According to Boleslavsky,[21] a memory of how one once annihilated a particularly obnoxious mosquito can provide the imaginative actor with a sufficient emotional basis for the convincing portrayal of bloody murder on the stage.

Artistic Honesty and Belief

To act well the actor must have a basic belief in what he does. If the play is poorly written, the good actor finds it difficult to be convincing. Or again if the actor tries to say to himself, "I am Hamlet," his statement is preposterous and his imagination dries up. As already pointed out the solution in the latter instance lies in what Stanislavski calls the magic "if"—"If

[21] Richard Boleslavsky, *op. cit.*, p. 44.

I were Hamlet—." Here is an honest, rational, assumption that frees the imagination and sets it to work.

The above account of the steps in the Stanislavski system is admittedly oversimplified and incomplete. Exponents of his method have not entirely agreed among themselves, which is as Stanislavski would have wished. He himself was always changing and experimenting. He warned friends in America not to imitate the Moscow Art Theatre but to create for themselves.[22] Creation was the one indispensable element and he remained true to this until his death. Let us hope that his many followers will preserve his liberal, tolerant, and common-sense views.

In actual practice, most classes using the creative approach to acting are conducted on an improvisation basis. The student is given a character, a situation, and a motive. His reactions, including the words he uses, are left to him. This forces him to think on his feet, to be spontaneous, and to be alert, especially when improvising with a group. This is something like a modern version of the *Commedia dell' arte.* In rehearsal directors using the Stanislavski method usually try to work *with* the actors rather than dictate to them. There is a strong tendency to experiment, to ask questions, and to search for answers in regard to what the character is doing and why. Scripts may be discarded temporarily and a situation from the play worked up as an improvisation. Actors and director often work quietly and in small groups. Some directors even refuse to plan the movement, leaving this as well as the reading of the lines to the actor.[23]

Whatever the merits or demerits of the creative approach when dealing with professional acting, it has several obvious advantages when dealing with education:

1. *It requires the student to create for himself.* He must use his own imagination. He cannot fall back on standardized patterns and clichés. One of the great attractions of a good amateur performance is its freshness and sincerity. This is hardly possible where the young player, rather than creating for himself, is required to follow the pattern of expression set down by a Delsarte, a textbook, or a director.

2. *It opens the way for endless variation of expression.* Directors and teachers who try to pour everyone into a standardized mold should pause

---

[22] Joshua Logan, "Introduction" to Constantin Stanislavski, *Building A Character,* Theatre Arts, 1949.

[23] There are many exceptions. Great directors of opposing schools are often more alike than they realize. See p. 149.

with horror when they realize what they would have done to a potential Will Rogers, an Edna Mae Oliver, or a Charlie Chaplin. The true teacher must have a method so flexible that everyone can develop in his own way. It was Joseph Jefferson who said, "The pupil should first be allowed to exhibit his quality, and so teach the teacher what to teach."[24]

3. *It is safe.* Even if it fails to get results, it does no harm. The actor almost never learns anything that he will have to unlearn. Unfortunately this is not true of the mechanical system, where even sound techniques are often offset by their tendency to become stilted, artificial mannerisms that have caused many of the best professional, community, and university directors to prefer candidates with no training whatever.

THE TECHNICAL APPROACH

No responsible person, including Stanislavski, would argue that the creative approach alone is enough. After all, acting is not life. There are obvious differences, and these differences are commonly referred to as the techniques of acting.

Projection

What is said and done on stage must be seen and heard by the audience. Even in the most intimate scenes "sweet nothings" must be murmured in a voice that projects to the balcony! The simple requirements of audibility and visibility form the basis of numerous stage conventions and techniques: "turn front," "kneel on the downstage knee," "deliver important lines forward," and dozens of others. Obeyed slavishly and without judgment, such rules can become stilted, conspicuous, and ridiculous. Taken simply as a means of achieving the general ends of being seen and heard, they contain the wisdom of long experience, and the earnest beginner will welcome the help they can give.

The Actor's Body

Related to the problem of audibility and visibility are the instruments of expression themselves, the voice and the body. The value of a free, responsive voice and a rhythmic, expressive body cannot be overemphasized. How to develop such a voice and such a body is another matter. Actually voice and body are closely interrelated, or more accurately, the production of voice is simply one of the highly specialized functions of the body. Consequently, teachers usually begin the training of either by first considering the body, for it is more general, less complex, and more tangible than

[24] Jefferson, *op. cit.*, p. 448.

voice. Improvement in one is likely to effect improvement in the other, for the root cause of difficulty in both, as far as the beginner is concerned, tends to lie in unnecessary muscular strain, which in turn is probably due to such psychological factors as anxiety, fear, stage fright, insecurity. One approach toward improvement, then, lies in the realm of doing something to relieve these unnecessary tensions. Better psychological adjustment may help; some hints will be discussed later under the heading of "Stage Fright." Direct physical exercises may also be beneficial. At least a physio-logical-mechanical approach in dealing with the major muscle systems of the body is not so dangerous as it may be in the case of voice. But whether the approach is mechanical, psychological, a combination of the two, or something else entirely, it should, if successful, relieve unnecessary ten-sion. Note, however, the word "unnecessary," for the body must not only be relaxed, it must be expressive. The athletic champion is also free from "unnecessary" tension, but do not forget that the real reason he is a champion is that he runs faster, jumps higher, hits harder than anyone else on the field. The same is true of the great actor. It is focus, control, and coördination of energy that count, not absence of energy. Some help toward gaining such a free, expressive body may be found by returning imaginatively to the uninhibited, expressive days of childhood. Freedom in use of the body may also be gained from athletics and dancing, but whatever the technique, the objective to strive for is a body that, without strain or affectation, expresses feelings and ideas, not just with the face muscles, not just with the voice, not just with the hands, but with the co-ordinated power of the entire body. Good acting, while never strained, has vitality.

The Actor's Voice

The training of the human voice has suffered from far too much quack-ery, superstition, and exploitation. On the other hand, marvelous results have frequently been achieved. The same teacher may, with the same methods, succeed with one student but ruin the voice of another. All in all, the problem is too complicated to be considered here, save for a few general principles.

1. The whole process of speech is an overlaid function. Each part of the vocal mechanism used in expressing ideas also serves some more primitive function in connection with such acts as eating or breathing. Speech is achieved only by burdening this mechanism with an enormously compli-cated and ever-varying pattern of tensions and relaxations. The complexity involved in speaking a simple sentence is overwhelming. A clumsy, semi-

ignorant teacher may do infinite harm in throwing this complicated system out of adjustment.

2. Largely because of the stress of modern living, there is a tendency for voices to be strained, breathy, high-pitched, and poorly placed. Physiologically this is due to unnecessary tension in muscles that should be relaxed; psychologically it is due to the fears, anxieties, and lack of security responsible for these tensions. Most good voice teachers are masters at gaining relaxation and confidence. The bad ones may do little more than make the student acutely conscious of voice. This consciousness frequently leads to still more tension, which in turn leads to a still worse voice.

3. Amazing improvements are frequently made in voices simply by working for confidence and better psychological adjustment. Many a voice that rings with assurance and energy in the friendly environment of the playground becomes embarrassingly weak and ineffective in the strained, unfamiliar environment of the stage or platform. Even the inexperienced teacher can attempt to transfer the confidence and assurance of the one to the other. Anything that relieves fear and strain will almost invariably help the voice—at least it can do no harm.

4. A general desire to speak with greater audibility and clarity than in ordinary life can also be motivated without particular danger. Most people use a better than ordinary voice when speaking on the telephone, probably because they "instinctively" feel the need for more clarity and care. Students often make remarkable vocal development during the production of a single play, simply because they sense the necessity for better than normal voice production.

Except for a few common-sense techniques such as these, it is probably best to leave the training of voice to experts. Speech defects, especially serious ones like stuttering, should be referred to qualified speech clinicians. Well-meaning tampering is dangerous.

Stage Fright

As already indicated, one of the actor's most difficult jobs is to keep his faculties concentrated primarily on the illusive and intangible process of giving convincing theatrical life to his character. This job is hampered by numerous distractions, the worst of all being the actor's consciousness of himself, which usually attacks in the form of stage fright. In the final analysis, this is a personal problem, one that each speaker and actor must conquer for himself. Perhaps the following hints will help—if not, forget them.

1. It is reassuring to know that stage fright is natural, and in mild forms

even desirable. After all, an appearance before a large audience *is* a social crisis, and nothing can convince the intelligent person otherwise. Nor is the nervousness always an indication that one is self-centered. It may result from fear of letting down the cast, the director, or the school, rather than fear for one's own reputation. To some degree then, nervousness is a sign of intelligence and sensitivity, and both of these qualities are desirable if not indispensable.

2. It is comforting to know that the chemical and bodily changes that occur during stage fright are the same as those that are necessary for the heightened activity of outstanding acting. Athletes, actors, and speakers commonly find that their fear leaves them as soon as they really get into the game, the play, or the speech. Adrenalin poured into the blood under the stress of fear becomes an asset as soon as the individual begins meeting the challenge of his job.

3. Plenty of well-motivated action often helps since it absorbs excess nervous energy and also serves as a distraction technique. One can be reasonably certain that an actor whose first entrance calls for him to "turn on the lights, notice the room, cross to the fireplace, begin making the fire, hear the telephone, and cross to answer it, still dangling a stick of wood in one hand," will not have difficulty with his opening lines.

4. Charles Lomas, writing on the subject of public speaking and stage fright,[25] concludes that the best possible solution is for the speaker to interest himself in his subject. The same conclusion certainly applies to acting. Focus your interest on something within the play. Try to make the character's ideas and arguments serve the same function as your own ideas and arguments would in a speaking situation. Put your mind to work.

The psychological significance of this is much greater than most people suppose. It rests on the reasonably well-established theory that when the higher brain centers are active, the emotions, which tend to be localized in the lower brain centers, fall under control. It follows that nothing can be more helpful than a belief in something about the play: its message, its importance, your character's wishes and desires—anything that gives your mind something reasonably tangible to grasp, to work on, to believe in— something outside of and more important than yourself. An idea that arouses some emotional conviction is best, partly because it makes concentration easy, and partly because such emotional interest will supplant the emotion of fear, which is the essence of stage fright.

[25] Charles Lomas, "The Psychology of Stage Fright," *Quarterly Journal of Speech,* February, 1937, pp. 35–44.

5. One of the best and most practical methods of opposing stage fright is for the young actor to develop gradually. One who begins by working backstage, then progresses to mob scenes, then to bit parts, then to minor roles, next to supporting roles, and at long last to leads, is unlikely ever to experience the crippling terrors of acute stage fright.

Condensation and Elimination

Perhaps the most important techniques in theatre grow from the fact that art has form and purpose. Life tends to ramble on endlessly with a complexity largely beyond human comprehension. Its meaningful moments are usually hopelessly cluttered with the ordinary, the uninteresting, and the distracting. Everything in a play, on the other hand, should have significance and interest. Most of the play's problems of condensation and elimination have already been solved by the playwright before the actor enters the picture, and yet much remains to be done. Distracting, meaningless movements, though perfectly natural in life, can ruin a show. Ideas half-formed and fragmentary, as they may be in life, are seldom effective on stage. Mumbled and repeated words, not noticeable in most conversations, can be disastrous to the actor. In mob scenes, unity of effect must sometimes be achieved through the director's insistence that everyone share in the hero's victory, even though, from the standpoint of logic, some characters would be hostile or indifferent. On stage there is a tendency to "freeze" when the other person speaks. Stage reactions (of surprise especially) tend to be broader than is characteristic of most sophisticated modern adults. In other words, much of the movement and business that a good stage director requires of an actor is primarily for the purpose of composition, picturization, or rhythm, and is not necessarily the most natural thing that the character would do.

Glancing back at the two approaches to acting, the creative approach seems to be fundamental. Generally speaking, the actor can never be too imaginative, too understanding, or too sensitive to the stimulus of the imaginary situation. Stanislavski deserves credit for having evolved a system for developing this indispensable part of the actor's equipment that many had previously considered as fixed and innate. On the other hand, it must never be forgotten that art is not purely a matter of responding to imaginary stimuli. It must be an *effective* response. Such basic things as visibility, audibility, and the demands of composition are indispensable to the actor who would serve his function in the total process of conveying the play to the audience.

CHAPTER VII

Directing

NLIKE THE TERMS "ACTOR" AND "PLAYWRIGHT," THAT OF "DIRECTOR" dates only from the latter part of the nineteenth century. The more obvious functions of the director have, of course, always had to be assumed by someone. In Attic Greece that someone was often the playwright; in England it has frequently been the most outstanding actor of the company. Along the way other combinations have functioned with varying degrees of success in supervising rehearsals and getting the play on the boards. But the idea of a director, or *régisseur* as he is called in Europe, is practically a twentieth-century development.

The need for such an artist arose from the abuses of the old system. A few extreme examples will illustrate: In 1886 Edwin Booth and Lawrence Barrett combined their energies to give the American theatre what was generally regarded as the greatest company it had ever seen. Kitty Malony, starry-eyed young actress with the group, has faithfully recorded the events of the season, including numerous instances that give us insight into the rehearsal practices of the day.[1] "Ten days," she tells us, "proved enough to get the company letter perfect in *Richelieu, Macbeth, Hamlet,* and *Othello.*" A few more rehearsals and the entire repertoire, which also included *Richard III, Katherine and Petruchio, Merchant of Venice, The Fool's Revenge, Brutus, Don Caesar de Bazan, A New Way to Pay Old Debts,* and *King Lear,* was ready to be performed! True, this was not the same as preparing each of these plays for a present-day opening. These were standard pieces. Actors already knew most of the lines, business was largely traditional; yet even so the lack of rehearsal seems to us appalling. During this rehearsal period Mr. Booth himself gave only cues; if a full speech was necessary, "Mr. Doud read it." Consequently Miss Malony is

[1] Katherine Goodale, *Behind the Scenes with Edwin Booth,* Houghton Mifflin Company, 1931, pp. 11–29.

Burbage

Siddons

Garrick

Talma

Kean

PLATE 9. Great Actors

Booth

Irving

Bernhardt

Duse

Salvini

Jefferson

PLATE 10. Some Great Actors of the 19th Century

Appia   Craig

Meierhold

Duke of Saxe Meiningen

Stanislavski in 1883

United Press Photo

Belasco   Reinhardt   Kazan

PLATE 11. Some Outstanding Figures in the Art of Directing

Taglia Cantoni. Fracasso. Cap. Bonbardon. Cap. Grillo.

Cap. Babeo. Cucuba. Cap. Spessa Monti. BaGattino.

PLATE 12. Commedia dell'arte: Costumes and Slapstick

Mrs. Jackson, 1775

Adelaid Neilson, about 1882

Vandamm

Julia Marlowe, 1888

Kathryn Cornell, 1933

PLATE 13. Costumes for Juliet. Note how costumes reflect the period in which they were worn even more than the period they were intended to portray.

Famussov in *Trouble from Reason*

Rippafratta in *The Mistress of the Inn*

Prince Ivan in *Tsar Fyodor*

General Krutitsky in *Enough Stupidity for
Every Wise Man*

PLATE 14. Make-Up and Characterization: Constantin Stanislavski

Queen Victoria

Queen Victoria

Queen Victoria

Mary of Scotland

PLATE 15. Make-Up and Characterization: Helen Hayes

Left: Richard Halverson, student actor, without make-up.

Right: Application of nose putty and base or foundation.

Left: Application of highlights. Those on the left side of his face have been blended.

Right: Application of shadows. Those on the left side of his face have been blended.

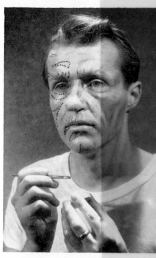

Left: The addition of eyebrows, wig, powder, costume accessories, and inner characterization results in a complete characterization.

Right: The addition of beard, mustache, and blackened teeth transforms Halverson into the King in *Huckleberry Finn*.

PLATE 16. Steps in a Character Make-Up

able to relate how on the opening night she stood enthralled in the wings to see Mr. Booth *for the first time* as Richelieu. She describes the excitement and uncertainty of being propelled through the trap *for the first time* on the opening night of *Macbeth,* and the near-disaster when on the same night she almost ruined the show by having not the faintest idea of how to make up for her part as one of the bloody apparitions.

Another incident, which occurred two years later, also indicates the prevailing attitude toward rehearsals. Lester Wallack, the great actor-manager, was dying. Accordingly, a benefit performance of *Hamlet* was arranged for May 21, 1888, which was to feature all the greatest living stars. Rose Eytinge, a famous emotional actress of the day, was selected to play the queen opposite Edwin Booth's Hamlet. Since there were to be only two rehearsals and since Miss Eytinge had never before played opposite Mr. Booth, the great tragedian suggested that she attend a special rehearsal of the closet scene. Rose Eytinge regarded the suggestion as an unpardonable insult to her acting ability. She withdrew from the cast even though her name had already been printed on the programs. The idea that she, Rose Eytinge, should attend a special rehearsal in order to play Gertrude opposite Edwin Booth's Hamlet was to her insufferable.[2]

Such examples could be multiplied. Even in my own early days of show business we felt that to rehearse beyond one week on a new play was to risk "going stale." Moreover we saved our best bits and real "inspiration" until the audience was there. But further examples are unnecessary. It suffices to point out that the following practices in play production were the rule rather than the exception during most of the nineteenth century.

1. The rehearsal period was short: only a few hours for a repertory piece, seldom more than a week for a new one.

2. Costume and make-up were largely left to the actor, and consequently were motivated by a desire to attract attention. At best they exhibited a confusing multiplicity of interpretations.

3. Scenery was usually conventional and but slightly adapted to the needs of the play.

4. Small parts and crowd scenes were practically ignored or were trusted to any supernumeraries who happened to be available. To some extent this is still the practice in both ballet and opera. Some of the funniest stories in theatre may be traced to the antics of these unrehearsed supers, but while

[2] Her story apparently found its way into newspapers across the country. The author found an account of the incident in the *St. Paul and Minneapolis Pioneer Press,* June 3, 1888.

such stories may provide delightful parlor entertainment afterward, it is safe to say that these supermishaps were invariably a source of distraction, if not disaster, to the audience's enjoyment at the time they occurred.

Obviously the difficulty with such theatre was the absence of some artist with power over not one actor, not a group of actors, not the scenery, sound, lights, costumes, properties or make-up, but responsible for *all* these things, responsible for seeing that all worked together to create an organic whole, the play itself. It was with the emergence of such an individual that the director or *régisseur* was born.

THE APPEARANCE OF THE DIRECTOR

Just who deserves the title of the first director has never been determined. As in most things there is no sudden clean-cut beginning. There is, however, much to justify beginning with the Duke of Saxe-Meiningen, a royal amateur whose well-directed company first appeared in Berlin on May 1, 1874. A strict disciplinarian, his rehearsal period was long and thorough. There were no stars; every part was considered important, and the crowd scenes, hitherto left to the mercy of supers, became the object of some of his most effective work. Scenery, lighting, costumes, make-up, and properties were carefully planned and blended into the total effect. Above all, worn-out traditional stage business was discarded, and new action was painstakingly adapted to express character and situation. During the last quarter of the century the Duke's company toured extensively throughout Europe. Its influence was enormous, for it demonstrated the excellence that could be achieved when concentration was centered through a director upon the whole rather than the parts.

Reinforcing this practical demonstration of the director's importance were the writings of two men, Adolphe Appia and Gordon Craig. Appia (1862–1928), an artist and a scholar, owed many of his ideas to Richard Wagner. Wagner had been one of the first to cry out for a fusion of all the stage arts, and in many respects his ideas along with his great music dramas stand as landmarks in any history of directing. It was Appia rather than Wagner, however, who gave the clearest expression to the thesis that scenery, lights, acting, music, and the rest must be fused into an organic whole. Scenery, he insisted, should be three-dimensional in order to harmonize with three-dimensional actors. Lighting, under his imaginative touch, became a powerful dramatic element reinforcing the dramatic effect of both the actor and the scenery and blending them into a unified whole.

But Appia was essentially a scholar, modest and rather quiet, and his excellent works, such as *Die Musik und die Inscenierung,* were not widely read.[3] It remained for Edward Gordon Craig (b. 1872), son of Ellen Terry, to add the flare of showmanship and exaggeration that was to catch the attention of theatres large and small throughout the world. Today there are those who still worship Craig as a genius and others who regard him as little more than an utterly impractical and overbearing windbag. Truth obviously lies between the extremes. To be sure, he exaggerated. To him the director was a superartist to whom even the playwright was subservient. He even went so far as to suggest that the living actor should be replaced by an *über-marionette,* a sort of three-dimensional Donald Duck, capable of doing anything and everything that the imagination and genius of his director could conjure up. At the same time, it was probably Craig's flare for boldness and exaggeration that attracted attention. Everyone soon knew of him and through him of a new theatre artist, the director.

During the years immediately before and shortly after the turn of the century several great directors emerged. In Paris, André Antoine at his *Théâtre Libre* brought to the theatre a new naturalism, simplicity, and conviction. In his opinion the stage director was to the drama what description was to the novel. He planned the stage movement with painstaking care in naturalistic settings that often employed the principle of the fourth wall. Max Reinhardt, in Germany and later in America, contributed productions that were imaginative, theatrically effective, and spectacular. He almost achieved Craig's dream, the director as superartist, for one of his greatest productions, *The Miracle,* used a wordless script, while most of his other efforts resulted in productions that were more characteristic of Reinhardt than of the author. In America, David Belasco brought realism to a height never before thought possible. To achieve this he introduced a long and well-organized period of rehearsal, which included a thorough coördination of every element of the production, especially the technical effects. But it is perhaps in Russia that the various styles of directing may best be studied, not necessarily because Russian directing is better, but because in Russia the various theories of directing are more radical, revolutionary, and sharply defined.

Greatest of all Russians directors was Constantin Stanislavski (1863–

---

[3] Most of Appia's writing has not been published in English translation. Much information is available in the Adolphe Appia memorial issue of *Theatre Arts Monthly,* August, 1932, and in Lee Simonson, *The Stage Is Set,* pp. 351–381. Appia's essay, *Art vivant ou nature morte,* is available in English in *Theatre Annual,* 1943. His article, *Comment reformer notre mise en scene,* is available in Toby Cole and Helen Krich Chinoy, *Directing the Play,* Bobbs-Merrill Company, 1953, pp. 111–119.

1938). Like Meiningen, who influenced him, Stanislavski came into the theatre as an amateur, thoroughly dissatisfied with the cheap and shallow ways of the commercial stage. Most of his principles of production resembled those of Meiningen or went beyond them. Whereas Meiningen usually rehearsed for about five weeks, Stanislavski stretched the period to as much as nine months[4]—two years in the case of *Hamlet*. With Stanislavski's company, the Moscow Art Theatre, the importance of bit parts became almost a religion. A fundamental axiom of the Art Theatre was, "There are no small parts; there are only small actors," and accordingly the greatest stars, even Stanislavski himself, frequently appeared in bit parts. Devotion to the play rather than to the actor's personal success was crystallized by such standards as: "One must love art; and not one's self in art."[5] Numerous technical improvements were also made, chiefly in the area of greater authenticity and realism, but it was in the realm of acting that Stanislavski's greatest contribution lay. In this he differed from Meiningen, who had been something of a despot. While it has been said that Stanislavski could imitate the Duke's despotism when necessary, his basic method, as already discussed in the preceding chapter, centered in stimulating the actor to create for himself. This probably accounts for much of the group loyalty and continuity that has characterized the Moscow Art Theatre. Actors with imagination and ideas had a chance to share in the creative process and many of the greatest remained loyal to the company, giving it a character of permanence quite unusual in the world of the theatre.

In sharp contrast to the group effort and fundamentally naturalistic style of Stanislavski[6] stands the work of Vsevolod Meyerhold (b. 1873). Although Meyerhold was one of Stanislavski's most brilliant pupils, he finally became irritated by the quietness and naturalistic restraint of the Moscow Art Theatre, and broke away to set up a system of his own. Briefly, he regarded the theatre not as a pale imitation of life but as something greater, more expressive, and more theatrical than life. He probed for the essence of human behavior rather than the mere reproduction of conventional behavior as seen in daily life. There was no pretense; everything was frankly theatrical. Actors often spoke directly to the audience; no attempt was made to mask spotlights or to disguise the elaborate scaffolding used to

[4] It should be remembered that other plays were in performance during such periods.

[5] For these and other guiding principles see Constantin Stanislavski, *My Life in Art*, Little, Brown and Co., pp. 298–299.

[6] Stanislavski was not a slavish naturalist; some of his plays were exciting excursions into such frankly theatrical styles as stylization and expressionism.

support ramps, springboards, and other paraphernalia on which his actors (more acrobats than actors) were expected to perform.

Meyerhold's method of directing was as revolutionary as the style of his productions. He was the dictator, the superartist from whom all ideas sprang. At rehearsals his common statement was, "Observe me and do likewise."[7] He created all the parts; the actors merely imitated. His theatre was brilliant because he himself was brilliant. When he disappeared his theatre likewise disappeared.

But even in Russia not all the best directors are identified with a definite style. One of the greatest, Eugene Vakhtangov (1883–1922), tended to take a compromise position, to base his work on the deep inner sincerity of acting characteristic of the Moscow Art Players, but to heighten and sharpen this with some of the theatricality of Meyerhold. Vakhtangov's results were brilliant, and although he died in 1922 at the age of 39, his theatre still continues as one of the finest in Russia.

Some such compromise as that made by Vakhtangov seems characteristic of the best modern directors everywhere. As Cole and Chinoy have observed, most American directors are essentially pragmatic,[8] and the same seems to be true in some degree of all successful directors. Stanislavski, although devoted to the principle of encouraging actors to create for themselves, often demonstrated ideas. Belasco and Reinhardt, both commonly remembered as having been rather despotic, insisted in their writings that actors must be treated with great consideration. Several of America's best present-day directors, including Elia Kazan, Harold Clurman, and Joshua Logan, although basing their work on the Stanislavski system, have not hesitated to modify the system to fit their own needs or the demands of a given production. In directing, rules and systems are of value only to those with sufficient judgment to know how and when to apply them.

Even such a brief view of a few directors from Saxe-Meiningen to the present day is enough to suggest that the director is of tremendous importance in shaping the destiny of the modern theatre. This is particularly true in the noncommercial productions of present-day American high schools, colleges, and communities. In fact it is reasonably safe to say that the quality of a school production will depend very little upon the school's size, location, or general type, but almost entirely upon the skill and imagination

[7] See Norris Houghton, *Moscow Rehearsals,* Harcourt, Brace and Company, Inc., 1936, Chap. 4.

[8] Tobey Cole and Helen Krich Chinoy, *Directing the Play,* Bobbs-Merrill Company, 1953, p. 65.

of the director. Even on the community theatre level, one invariably associates the name Gilmor Brown with Pasadena, Frederick McConnell with Cleveland; and the list might be expanded. It is conceivable that a sincere group of professional actors could get together and without a regular director produce an excellent play, but in the nonprofessional theatre the director is practically indispensable. He may stimulate the actors to create the play for themselves, after the method of Stanislavski, or he may create it for them, after the manner of Meyerhold, but his skill (or lack of it) will soon determine the success or failure of the entire group.

DIRECTING: THEORY AND PRACTICE

Because of the complexity of his task, a good director is hard to find. The job calls for a rare combination of talents, for the outstanding director should combine the qualities of a sensitive and imaginative artist, a skillful and patient teacher, and an efficient, well-organized executive. These qualities, of course, need not be mutually exclusive. Skill in organization should help the teacher as well as the executive, and imagination should assist the executive as well as the artist. Unfortunately, in real life this is seldom the case. The artistic genius often lacks the patience and understanding of the teacher, as well as the disciplined organizational ability of the executive. In some other arts, for example in painting and writing, this presents no serious problem. The painter can, if he chooses, wear strange clothes, work twenty-four hours one day and none the next, be irritable and neurotic to the point where few people can bear to associate with him, and yet if the art he produces is great, he will be great. Theatre, on the other hand, is a group art that demands teamwork. Even a mild amount of temperament or eccentricity—an amount that in a painter, an author, or even a farmer or minister, would go unnoticed—is in a director a disaster. Artistic and imaginative ability alone is not enough; ability as a teacher and executive is likewise fundamental. We must consider all three.

The Director as an Artist

Perhaps the first question the would-be director should ask himself is, "How much can I see on the printed page?" One person can examine the little black and white marks that make up a page from *King Lear* without receiving either mental or emotional stimulation, while another reading the same material may be moved to the very depths of his soul. Or one may read a page from *The Taming of the Shrew* and think, "How utterly dull," while another may howl with delight. Obviously the good director must be related to the latter type. He must be capable of extracting the play's dramatic essence from the printed page. One can no more hope to direct effectively without a vivid concept of the play than a speaker can hope to speak effectively without something to say.

This ability to extract full value from the printed page is not a mysterious inborn gift that one has or has not, for it changes with experience. For example, I am now deeply moved by the last scene of *Marco Millions*, in which the Great Khan weeps over the body of Kukachin, although when I first read this scene as a college sophomore, it left me unimpressed and slightly annoyed. To tune in on the rich world of experience that others have recorded on the pages of dramatic literature, one must have lived. This has little to do with having been exposed. Some can go through two world wars, famine, and five wives, yet experience less than other apparently sheltered souls who have known no greater warfare than a childhood battle with wooden guns, no greater hunger than a childhood craving for ice cream, and no greater love than a secret passion for some faraway movie star. It is reaction to experience that counts. Sensitivity and a lively imagination can work wonders with very little.

Nor must the value of plain hard work and will power be ignored. Many of the best directors probably receive little more from a hurried first reading of a script than would the average reader. Once they decide to produce the play, however, they read and reread, visualizing characters, environment, action. Some stimulate their imaginations by removing the play from any limitations of the stage, visualizing characters as real people in a real world. Others employ an opposite technique, visualizing opening night— crowds, orchestra, lights, curtain, and finally the play in every detail—as it might appear on the stage in the perfection production. But regardless of method, the director's enthusiasm, dreams, and imagination must somehow be aroused.

Before calling his first rehearsal, the director usually crystallizes his imaginative concepts of the play into some form of promptbook. This ordinarily begins with his analysis of the play, where he scrutinizes such things as theme, purpose, motivation, and characterization. He may picturize and even diagram the conflict or the emotional pattern of the play—the rise and fall of excitement, the crises, the climax—for one of the most deadly things about a bad production is its tendency to stick to one level. This level may be fast and strained, or it may be slow and anemic, but either is equally ineffective and monotonous. The skillfully directed play will command attention through its infinite variety. The rise and fall of its action is made to stimulate and restimulate the audience. Any technique of analysis that will help the director search out such variety, even before rehearsals begin, is of great value.

Into his promptbook the director may next insert preliminary plans for the technical side of the show: ground plans, sketches, property plots, light plots, sound plots, costume plots, and make-up plots. Somewhere in the process he also considers the problem of editing. Opinions differ as to how much (if any) editing is legitimate. Certainly the scatter-brained egotist who "improves" and rearranges a script as impulse dictates should be barred from the theatre. On the other hand, few would defend the timid soul, so conscientious that he dares not change a single phrase. Perhaps the sanest attitude is to try to understand and respect the author's basic purpose, the "thing meant,"[9] then do everything possible to convey this to the audience. This will almost certainly result in some cutting and rearrangement. As an example, consider the problem of profanity in a high school production. Certainly it is not the author's intention to shock half the audience and to distract the rest through their concern over what the shocked half will do, yet this is exactly what will happen in most high school auditoriums if the profanity is left in an otherwise good script, for it will overshadow the meaning behind the profanity. The "thing meant" will be lost if the words are retained.

The final, most difficult, and most important step in preparing the promptbook lies in planning the action. This is generally considered to be the director's responsibility. The author may help, the actors may help, the casual visitor at rehearsal may help, but the final decisions as to when and where the actors sit, cross, stand before the window, or lounge beside the fireplace rest with the director. While much of the stage business may be developed during rehearsal, the basic stage movement is usually planned well in advance and recorded, either by diagrams or by a sort of homemade shorthand, in the margins of the promptbook. In general, planning in advance has all the obvious advantages that accompany sound preparation for any task. This is particularly true where the cast is large, the actors inexperienced, or the time limited. Some directors especially devoted to the Stanislavski system will argue that the actor should be allowed to create his own pattern of movement according to his own impulses, but it is illogical to suppose that an actor who is not seriously inhibited by being told exactly

---

[9] See Alan H. Gardiner, *The Theory of Speech and Language,* Oxford University Press, 1932, pp. 29–33, for a discussion of "thing meant."

what to say would suffer from being given a basic pattern of where and when to move. Moreover there is no reason why action planned by the director cannot be modified and adapted to the style of each particular player as rehearsals progress. In fact the only valid argument against planning in advance is that it requires much will power, imagination, and hard work. As Shaw says, "writing dialogue (of Hamlet, for instance) is a pleasurable act of creation, whereas deciding whether the ghost shall enter from the right or left is pure drudgery, the author may leave the drudgery to the director. He mostly does."[10]

As already implied, the amount of advance planning may be modified when working with only two or three actors, with experienced actors, or when time is unlimited. Stanislavski during the early years of the Moscow Art Theatre planned his productions in amazing detail. As the company matured and the pressure of time subsided, he relaxed his system, and together with his actors worked out most of the stage business and movement during rehearsals. Even toward the end of his career, however, he still prepared himself for a production with a thoroughness completely foreign to most American nonprofessional directors.[11] In fact one common characteristic of all great directors appears to be their capacity for creative energy, imagination, and hard work. As already pointed out, methods and techniques of directing are of only secondary importance. It is the quality of the man himself that counts.

Principles that govern the planning of action are too involved for discussion here. Good business and movement, when skillfully planned, employ such elements of composition as emphasis, variety, balance, proportion, grace, and harmony. Action can also be vivid in picturization—in its storytelling qualities. In fact, a silent film of the well-directed play will usually reveal the essence of the story even without words or sound.

Well-planned action and lots of it is especially important when working with beginners on the high school or college level. Since vitality, spontaneity, and physical activity are characteristic of youth, the wise director will capitalize on these qualities instead of struggling against them. The tense, nervous amateur who swings back and forth, fidgets, and forgets his lines is usually found in a play that is too static. Nothing is more effective in relieving unnecessary tension than well-planned, well-motivated ac-

[10] G. B. Shaw, "Shaw's Rules for Directors," *Theatre Arts*, August, 1949.
[11] See Constantin Stanislavski, "Director's Plan for Othello," in Tobey Cole and Helen K. Chinoy, *Directing the Play*, Bobbs-Merrill Company, 1953, pp. 221–241.

tion. It is a pity that so many amateur directors are gravely deficient in this respect.

The Director as a Teacher

Thus far we have seen that the director, like other artists, must begin by gaining a concept of whatever he desires to express, in this case a penetrating concept of the emotional and intellectual potentialities of the play. We have also seen him crystallize certain phases of this concept into a carefully planned pattern of stage action. In addition, he will have given much imaginative thought to the setting, costumes, lighting, and other technical factors that will eventually assist the actor in expressing the play to the audience. In other words, if the imaginative factor in the director has been great enough, a vivid concept of the play and its possibilities exists in his mind, and to some extent in his promptbook, before the first rehearsal is called.

If this much is accomplished, the struggle toward producing an excellent play is well begun but by no means finished. Many who can conceive a play with an insight bordering on genius cannot direct. They simply lack the patience and skill necessary to teach others, mainly the actors, to convey this insight to an audience. This is especially true in the nonprofessional theatre where the director succeeds or fails according to his ability to get acting out of beginners. Some directors seem able to get a better than adequate performance out of almost anyone. The poorer the acting material, the more challenging the potential improvement; consequently the more intriguing the game of searching out the technique, psychological or mechanical, that will touch off results. Perhaps the best high school director I have ever known was a powerful redheaded woman with tremendous vitality, a hearty sense of humor, a booming voice, and a love for students big or little, timid or brazen, bright or dumb. Her infinite capacity for understanding was equal to any of them. Her plays, while sometimes lacking in polish, never failed to delight the audience, and her actors never seemed uncomfortable, unhappy, or "untalented." This is not to imply that all directors must of this type! Some of the best are quiet and refined in their approach. Each must discover and develop his own most effective style. But even so, there will probably be a few basic qualities common to all.

1. *Enthusiasm.* Though one might have a brilliant concept of the play and yet fail as a teacher, the reverse is not likely to be true. One can scarcely hope to do a brilliant job of teaching if his concept is a failure.

Nothing is more characteristic of good teaching than an enthusiasm for and understanding of the thing one wishes to teach. Thus a genuine enthusiasm for the play and its possibilities is indispensable if one wishes to enlist the enthusiasm and energy of young, inexperienced players.

2. *Patience.* Most directors suffer a mixture of anxiety and shock the first time they hear a beginning cast read the lines of a play, especially one on which they have been working for some time and have somewhat idealized. To give vent immediately to these feelings of frustration may do irreparable damage. It is hard to tell what an actor can do until he picks up a reasonable degree of confidence. Too much negative criticism early in rehearsal will probably tie the beginner in both psychological and physiological knots.

3. *Understanding.* It is not unusual for the artist to understand the play but find himself unable to understand the student. The teacher must understand both, especially the student. For example, anyone can spot the beginner who swings back and forth, but it may take a skillful teacher to sense *why* he swings back and forth and do something that will correct the habit. Most good teachers are masters at projecting themselves into the shoes of their students. Then, sensing the problem both from the student's point of view and from their own, they are in a position to prescribe a cure. They realize quickly that the matter of individual differences must be reckoned with. One actor needs a firm hand, another encouragement; one has no ideas, another too many; one fails to learn his lines because of laziness, another because of a deep psychological fear that he may forget. No two sudents are exactly alike, but the teacher who understands can almost always help.

4. *Inspiring confidence.* Probably the greatest problem faced by the director of beginners is that of giving his actors a bearing of ease and confidence. We may admire timid, quiet people in many walks of life, but not on the stage. On stage the voice and bearing must exhibit that combination of ease and strength characterisetic of poise and confidence. There is no set formula for arriving at this happy state. An actor's confidence is often increased by giving him plenty of well-motivated action, by encouraging him to project with a clear, resonant voice, and especially by catching him up in the spirit of the scene—the purpose and drive of the imaginary situation. Most successful directors also have a knack of meeting their actors on a friendly, informal basis, as friends and fellow workers rather than underlings. Especially when working with sensitive beginners, artificial discipline, false assumptions of superiority, and sarcasm can be devastating to

confidence, and consequently must be avoided.[12] These are only random suggestions. But in any case, the knack of inspiring confidence is a trait that must be acquired if one would succeed in directing beginners.

5. *Motivation*.[13] There was a time in my life when, quite unconsciously, I felt that the director's function was to see how many things he could find wrong with the rehearsal, then point these out to the players. Fortunately an old-timer set me right with the advice, "Let 'em have their heads, boy. No one can get his mind on the play up there with you yappin' all the time." Anyone can watch an average rehearsal and fill many pages with little notations of things that are wrong. It often requires a genius, however, to decide which notations should be mentioned, which ignored, and which lumped together around some basic principle.

To illustrate, one of the most effective bits of directing that it has been my good fortune to execute came during a rehearsal of Drinkwater's *Abraham Lincoln*. The play was already in its last week of rehearsal, and the cabinet scene at the outbreak of the Civil War was still lifeless and unconvincing. I listened to the scene with more than usual anxiety and, as in the past, filled several pages with notes of specific errors. Fortunately they were never used. The scene was so bad that I finally gave up and began asking myself, "What is behind this? What is lacking?" At the end of the scene I stopped the show, discarded my notes, and launched into a brief pep talk. Theatrically speaking, we were lucky. Pearl Harbor was only three months behind us, and the memory of the tension and anxiety of those hours when the bombs first began to fall was fresh and vivid. Strangely enough, everyone had been so busy trying to act that he had never stopped to realize that the crisis facing Lincoln and his cabinet at the outbreak of the Civil War was only an intensification of what Pearl Harbor had been to all of us. This mass application of memory of emotion served to motivate the entire scene. Other things were added that probably helped, among them a distant military band and crowd noises, but the numerous specific errors were never mentioned. When we tried the scene again, the difference was one of the most amazing things I have ever experienced in the theatre; for not only the lines previously noted, but almost every line in the scene, took on new life and meaning.

Even such a brief discussion as this should make it clear that in the make-up of a director the element of teaching is of extreme importance. A

---

[12] An exception is the dangerous, though sometimes effective, practice of driving out fear in an actor by inflaming him with anger.

[13] Material in this section is largely a reprint from an article by the author, "Some Hints on Directing Beginners," *Dramatics Magazine*, February, 1948.

thrilling concept of a play is of no value unless the director can get others to convey his concept to an audience, and this achievement requires skill as a teacher. It also requires skill as an executive.

The Director as an Executive

All through the process of preparing the promptbook and rehearsing the actors, the director's ability as an organizer and executive will have been important. The very act of planning in advance such items as action, settings, costumes, properties, and lighting is indicative of the good executive as well as of the imaginative artist.

Executive ability is also essential in the matter of tryouts and casting. Some directors succeed not because of ability to teach acting but because they attract such outstanding talent in the first place. Many factors must be considered in casting: type, experience, acting ability, and especially teamwork. In attempting to select actors on these and other bases many systems of tryout have been evolved, ranging from well-rehearsed, memorized scenes to informal interviews. None are perfect. All have advantages and disadvantages. When available, the best guide is probably the actor's achievement in past performances—provided of course that the tendency to type the actor according to his first role is avoided, and that newcomers are given a chance to be seen.

Tryouts are successful if they not only screen out the best people but also keep injured feelings to a minimum. Elaborate and long-drawn-out tryouts, while excellent in the first respect, may be devastating in the latter. Skillful judgment is needed to know where to strike the happy medium.

Executive ability will also be important in scheduling rehearsals, getting actors to come on time, having the hand props arrive when needed, and handling the endless adjustments that must be made if morale and efficiency are to be maintained.

But in addition to such general duties, there are specific instances when executive ability assumes major importance in the director's activity. In most nonprofessional theatres, the director is not just the director of a single play, but rather the director of the theatre. This means skill in handling board meetings, committee meetings, faculty meetings. It probably means speaking before civic and school groups as well as working with newspapers, business men, electricians, janitors. Entire books devoted to this side of the director's work have failed to cover completely the myriad patterns and ramifications of management and publicity. Only one or two fundamental hints can be suggested here.

As the successful actor must project himself into the personality of the character, and as the successful director must project himself into the personality of the student actor, so the successful executive must be able to project himself into the place of those with whom he deals. If he can do this, he will understand why the local furniture merchant will resent careless use of borrowed properties, why the physics teacher will resent having students cut class for rehearsal, why the band director will be upset by a cluttered rehearsal stage. The art of getting along with others is largely the art of understanding other points of view, plus having enough imagination and ambition to avoid trouble before it occurs.

The successful executive in the theatre must also have high ideals, ideals devoted to the good of theatre, rather than to personal achievement. The theatre's objectives and values should be clearly defined. Even unpleasant action can be forgiven if it is done for the good of some worthy principle or cause. It can never be forgiven when it is done for personal gain.

Another area in which the director's skill as an executive is of paramount importance lies in the supervision and coördination of the technical side of the production. In the college and community theatre, the director will usually have a technical director, plus assistants in each of the technical divisions, who relieve him of the labor and much of the responsibility. But no matter how elaborate the organization, he must make certain that all elements are coördinated and harmonized. In dealing with a specific show, the good executive does not wait until dress rehearsal to begin organizing the elements of the production. His first technical meeting is probably held with his staff well in advance of the first rehearsal. The first meeting after the play is cast is often a general meeting including crews, cast, technical and business staffs. Briefly but clearly the work to be done is outlined. Everyone should be made to feel important and given to understand the value of his particular task in relation to the whole. Designs of scenery and costumes should if possible be shown. Above all the director should catch and stimulate interest. This short general meeting may well be followed by group meetings where each staff member has a chance to meet and organize his own particular crew.

As rehearsals progress other meetings should be called whenever necessary, according to the needs of the show. Through it all the director enjoys an enormous advantage if he is skilled in each of the arts and crafts that go into the production. This is especially true in the high school, where he himself will usually have to supervise directly whatever is done. Even in the university or community theatre he should be able to meet each member of the staff on equal terms; he must know what can be done and know it so well that there is no need to bluff. On the other hand, he should avoid any attitude of superiority. If he has tact, the staff and crews will welcome his visits and his suggestions.

If some such program of planning and organization has been followed, the opening dress rehearsal need never be the hectic affair it too frequently is. The hundreds of elements that go to make up the play should fall into place quite naturally and noiselessly. Bursts of temper and frantic last-minute crises are usually signs of bad executive ability on the part of the director.

On the opening night some directors prefer to be back stage, quietly (we hope) making last-minute checks to be certain nothing has been overlooked. Others prefer to shift their energy to the front of the house, checking on ushers, programs, ventilation, and everything that contributes directly or indirectly to the comfort and enjoyment of the audience. In either case, if his work was well organized, the director should find little to do—he may even be able to relax and enjoy the fruits of his efforts.

Although the preceding account of directing is brief, it is hoped that it suggests something of the scope and magnitude of the director's task. The perfect director is, of course, an unachieved ideal. Some directors succeed because they are artistic geniuses of such brilliance that in spite of temperament and disorganization they still manage to produce exciting results. Others with mediocre imagination as artists succeed through excellent management, through the loyalty, morale, and enthusiasm they stimulate in those about them. Still others succeed because of their gift in teaching, especially in teaching beginners to act.

No two directors are exactly alike. Techniques and systems that work for one may be useless in the hands of another. Stage directing, like other arts, displays a chronic antagonism to standardization, and although the beginner can learn much from others, there are still many secrets that he must discover for himself. Textbooks, theories, or formulas can never replace intelligence, imagination, and a desire to bring stage life and expression to what the playwright has written.

CHAPTER VIII

Costuming and Make-Up

M ANY READERS WILL BE SURPRISED TO FIND COSTUMING AND MAKE-UP grouped with acting and directing rather than with the technical crafts of the theatre. There is good reason for such surprise, particularly at the separation of costumes from scenic design, for the same artist is frequently responsible for both. In fact the entire visual effect of a given scene may depend on neither one nor the other but upon a combination of the two—the brilliant splash of the queen's crimson costume against an otherwise drab scenic background. Yet in spite of all this, there is a strong case for relating both costume and make-up to the actor. Historically and traditionally, at least, this has been the usual practice. Even in our own age of specialization, neither costumes nor make-up have an independent life of their own. They must both be worn by actors, and if skillfully designed and skillfully worn, both tend to merge into the creation of an exciting new being, the character.

The relationship between clothing and character is much deeper than most laymen suppose. Rare is the girl who has never had sagging spirits restored through the magic tonic of a new dress. Rare is the man who has not felt and acted more trim and athletic in a new sports outfit. New autumn plaids for the homecoming game, new organdy gowns for the spring dance, each cause—or reflect—personality changes. Clothes may not make the man or the actor, but they certainly influence and help express both of them.

Costumes and make-up, including masks, are among the oldest, most fundamental elements of drama. In fact they become almost the whole show when one returns to the primitive rituals and ceremonies that are its roots. Although the Greeks, as we shall see, may have largely ignored scenery, we are certain that they did not ignore costumes and masks, and there is evidence to indicate that these were among the most striking that the legitimate theatre has ever seen. On his feet the Greek tragic hero wore high, heavy boots, his body was draped with a long, dignified robe, while his face was covered by the high mask of his tragic character. The result was often a character who, some believe, stood almost seven feet high, a figure of dignity and magnitude—no ordinary mortal, but a tragic hero, a god or a king.

In contrast, the comic actor was padded and masked in a way that emphasized the grotesque and the ludicrous. Remember that Aristophanes frequently derived his titles from his choruses (*The Frogs, The Wasps, The Birds*), which must in turn have derived much of their interest and color from their fantastic masks and costumes.

This tendency to rely heavily upon masks and costumes for the visual effect of the production was also standard practice in ancient Rome and among the *Commedia dell' arte* players. Masks as well as fantastic costumes were likewise used during the medieval passion plays. Serpents with bodies of willow, dragons that threw flames, and a wildly imaginative assortment of devils contributed to the somewhat surprising tendency of these pious plays to center the spectator's chief interest in hell.

The transition from predominantly masked to predominantly made-up faces took place during the Renaissance. By the time of Shakespeare the mask had largely disappeared, although it was frequently used in the Court Masques of James I, and actually has never been entirely discarded. At about the same time as the mask was losing favor, actors began to abandon the use of specialized stage costumes, playing everything in contemporary dress. This practice was continued during most of the seventeenth and eighteenth centuries. An actor wearing contemporary clothing would portray King Lear, Antony, or Sir Foppling Flutter in somewhat the same frank manner that the concert artist today sings Faust, Herod, or Don Juan in full evening dress. There were exceptions, but as a rule the actor simply wore the best he had, regardless of the part. Some companies, in fact, managed to acquire castoff clothing from the nobility, thus enabling them to appear in an elegance and splendor they could not otherwise have afforded. Some attempt was made, however, to fit the costume to the character. Thus the beggar usually appeared in contemporary rags, the servant in contemporary livery, and the prince in contemporary robes, but at least in England, attempts to reproduce historical periods were practically unknown until 1773 when David Garrick's great rival, Charles Macklin, attempted to costume *Macbeth* in Scottish robes. (Lady Macbeth still insisted on using "modern" dress.) Odell reports that Garrick's pride was stung to the quick by the fact that Macklin and not he had introduced this innovation. Accordingly Garrick "new-dressed" his King Lear in old English garments for his farewell performance of the role at Drury Lane.[1]

By the beginning of the nineteenth century the idea of period costuming was generally accepted in England as it had already been accepted several decades earlier in France. Even so, most stage costuming during the nineteenth century was restricted to a few period styles that tended to be unimaginative, standard, and conventional. Costumes for three or four periods plus those of one or two national groups made up the stock of most commercial costume houses. The usual practice, however, was for each actor to provide his own wardrobe, and half a dozen favorite costumes were probably sufficient for most of the roles played during an actor's lifetime.

With the coming of men like the Duke of Saxe-Meiningen, Stanislavski, and Belasco, standardized theatrical costumes were abandoned in a realistic search for greater and greater authenticity. While slavish adherence to historical accuracy, as it was sometimes practiced by such realists, is no longer regarded as important, we must nevertheless admire the painstaking care that Saxe-Meiningen and others lavished on costumes, as well as the conscientious effort they made to tie costuming into the organic pattern of the play as a whole. No longer did each actor appear on opening night in the robe of his choice, regardless of scenery, other costumes, or lighting, for his costume, like his acting, was made to function as one element in a larger pattern.

COSTUME DESIGN

To one gifted with a knack for designing clothing, the theatre offers an exciting outlet, for stage costumes can be bold, colorful, and striking. They can display a theatrical flare, a dramatic imagination, and a streamlined simplification not possible in ordinary dress. In addition to a feeling for style in clothing, the costume designer must know period styles and be able to reflect character. Obviously everything he does must spring from the needs of the play. There can be no such thing as a good costume that does not fit the play and the character, or does not harmonize with the setting, with other costumes, and with the lighting. Consequently the costumer must work in constant coöperation with the director, the scene designer, and other members of the technical staff.

[1] George C. D. Odell, *Shakespeare from Betterton to Irving*, Charles Scribner's Sons, 1920, pp. 452–454.

Costuming and Make-Up

Sometimes color is important and sometimes texture, in establishing the period of a costume. But ordinarily the essential element is the silhouette, as the accompanying sketches (Fig. 1) indicate. Obviously, a keen sense of silhouette is one of the first skills the student of costuming should try to acquire. This is only a short cut, however, for in the long run there is no substitute for knowing as much as possible about major periods.

The problem of adjusting designs to character is more important than that of adjusting them to period. *The Taming of the Shrew* can be played in modern dress without serious damage, but to costume Petruchio in delicate colors or effeminate lace, no matter what the period, would probably destroy the basic idea of the play as a whole.

In achieving costumes that reflect character, rules and formulas cannot replace taste and good judgment. A knowledge of color symbolism, for example, may be valuable, yet costumers can make fools of themselves by following too literally such oversimplified conventions as purple for royalty, pale blue for innocence, and red for vitality. The costumer, like the scene designer, must never forget that any given color is largely a relative matter. The color of the other costumes, the scenic background, the lights, and even the properties all have their influences.

One curious feature of style in clothing is its tendency to be in a more or less constant state of change. In the modern world this is undoubtedly encouraged by clothing manufacturers and fashion designers, who obviously profit by stimulating the purchase of a new wardrobe as often as possible. But a more fundamental explanation of our shifting fashions lies in a strange psychological cycle. A new style is designed and modeled by the most shapely figures available. Movie and stage stars quickly adopt it, and soon, through association rather than merit, everyone scrambles to display the "new look." Inevitable disillusionment follows as the new sensation goes into mass production and is draped over the strange assortment of shapes that make up the average and less than average specimens of the species. A reaction sets in. Everyone now has the new style, most of them still look awful, and psychologically we are ready for the cycle to repeat itself. The last to discard the new style, by now the old style, are usually the underprivileged, the eccentric, and the poorest physical specimens of the race. Thus the impression of the style just past is generally negative and a number of years may have to pass before we can view it impartially.

Whether one accepts the above explanation or not, the costume designer will do well to use care in dealing with styles that have aged less than a quarter of a century, unless he wishes to create a comic effect. Women

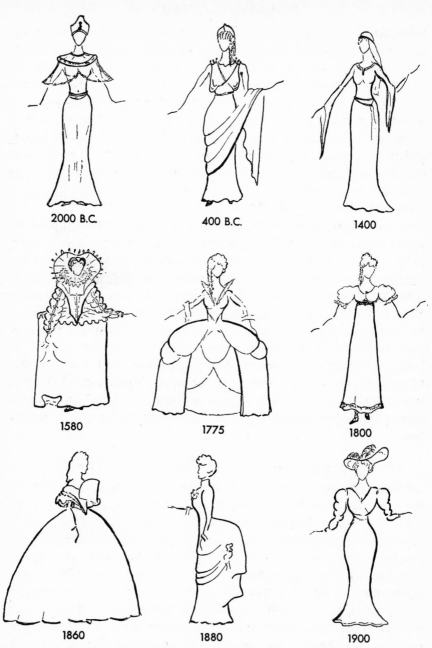

2000 B.C. 400 B.C. 1400

1580 1775 1800

1860 1880 1900

Fig. 1. Some Historic Costumes for Women. Note how a few lines, primarily those revealing silhouette, can capture the period of the costume. (Based on designs in Fairfax Proudfit Walkup, *Dressing the Part*, Appleton-Century-Crofts, 1950.)

during the twenties used to laugh at the horrible wasp waists that had been worn during the Gibson Girl era. Women during the forties laughed at the shapeless sacks worn during the twenties, but were beginning to find the Gibson Girl styles rather pleasing. Beyond a certain period of time costume styles again become interesting and perhaps beautiful, but those of the immediate past are likely to seem simply dated and old-fashioned. It is usually wise, therefore, to present most plays less than 25 years of age in modern dress unless they are period pieces to begin with, or unless some other reason makes it necessary to adhere to the style of the period for which they were written.

The costume designer should not only be wary of the style that has just become dated, he must also be conscious of the powerful appeal of the current vogue. Even in designing period costumes the modern style should wield its influence. Authentic period costumes are almost never effective. Good stage costumes for a Greek play produced in 1920 reflect the flapper silhouette as well as the classic lines of ancient Greece. The same Greek play if well costumed in 1949 would reveal the unmistakable influence of the "new look." The good costume designer knows the past, but instinctively modifies it by the present (Plate 13). He finds it easy to adapt his designs according to the taste of the times. He does not try to rationalize the problem, for it is not necessarily logical. He simply accepts the fact that final judgment in matters of style and beauty is largely a subjective matter that lies somewhere in the irrational subconsciousness of the audience.

CONSTRUCTION AND CARE OF COSTUMES

If the producing organization is small, does not employ a regular costumer, and for the most part produces modern plays, it is probably best to rent costumes when they are necessary. In such cases the problem is one of selecting the right costume company. Nationally known costume houses have large stocks from which to choose, and they know their jobs. On the other hand they may be rather expensive and also inaccessible to most groups either for fittings or individual consultation. Friendly relations with a local costumer, if there is one, can be advantageous. Personal contact, personal interest, and more moderate prices can often go a long way toward counterbalancing the inherent advantages of larger, nationally known concerns. In any case start early enough so that there is time to shop. A policy of asking for bids is wise, although quality, not price alone, must be considered.

But no matter where costumes come from, some efficiency in receiving them, caring for them, and returning them is essential. On the whole, costume houses have far greater cause for complaint than do most nonprofessional theatres. What can a costumer do if the order itself is garbled, inaccurate, and vague? He can hardly be blamed for not sending his best, when he knows how thoughtless, careless, and destructive the untrained and confused amateur can be on opening night. He can hardly be blamed for exorbitant prices when only part of the costumes come back, and those days late and in filthy condition. Most commercial costumers tend to be artists rather than business men. They love costumes and often love theatre. If you are renting, take care of what you get, show intelligent interest and enthusiasm, start early, and you will probably be delighted with both quality and prices that your costume house will provide.

For larger theatrical organizations like community and university theatres, renting costumes is almost never so satisfactory as making them. Materials used in constructing costumes usually cost about the same as rental for a week's run. If most of the work can be done by volunteer committees or by students, the saving over a period of years become impressive, for the wardrobe grows rapidly. In the school, moreover, the training and satisfaction that accompany original creation are of utmost importance.

A discussion of techniques of costume construction has no place here, though one or two basic ideas particularly applicable to the nonprofessional theatre are worth mentioning. Uniforms, for example, are beyond the skill of most amateur costumers, yet excellent results may be achieved by buying old uniforms (army, navy, band) and remodeling them to suit the play. They can be cut, fitted, dyed, and decorated with gold braid and medals. In fact, the gifted costumer is a genius at remodeling all sorts of wearing apparel. If the theatre has a real place in the community, and if it has adequate storage facilities, it is amazing how much of value can be acquired over a period of years if friends of the theatre know that gifts of old clothing are welcome. Some such gifts may be worth keeping just as they are. Others should be refashioned as needed. Good judgment will have to dictate what to keep and what to remake, but in either case gifts are valuable.

When working with stage costumes, the designer and the seamstress must be constantly aware that the play's action may dictate special techniques. The gentleman who must fight a duel may require a considerably different costume from one who does nothing but stand or sit in a formal drawing room. Elaborate costumes must sometimes be modified to permit quick changes. Such special requirements can be met if the director and costumer recognize and plan for the emergency in advance. Undetected until final dress rehearsal, quick changes can be disastrous.

In making new costumes, the selection of materials requires training, experience, good judgment, and a knack of shopping for bargains. Since the effect from a distance is always what counts, intricate patterns and delicate textures are lost. The good costumer is constantly alert regarding drape, weave, texture, and cost of materials. Skillful dyeing, top dyeing, spattering, and spraying can sometimes give to inexpensive materials a luxurious and expensive stage appearance. Designs can be painted or appliqued. There is no limit to the ingenuity of some costumers. Gorgeous pieces of costume jewelry can be fashioned from scraps of metallic cloth set with ordinary marbles. Some costumers turn out stunning effects at practically no cost, while others, working in elaborately equipped shops with expensive materials, achieve mediocre results. The fault, dear Brutus, lies truly within ourselves.

As to general organization, there is no set pattern, although most larger university and community theatres proceed about as follows. The costume designer first studies the play and then meets with the scene designer and director well in advance of the first rehearsal. By the time of the first general meeting[2] the designs should be ready, the basic work schedule outlined, crews organized, and measurements taken of the actors who must have costumes. A few days later materials should be on hand and construction under way. Further meetings with the director and the scene designer are almost always necessary. Actors must be fitted, unexpected problems solved, changes in scenery or lighting noted.

Approximately a week before opening night comes the dress parade. Actors don costumes and appear on the set under the lights before the costumer, the director, and their assistants. Fittings, adjustments, and changes should be agreed upon and carefully noted. As dress rehearsals begin, costumes are usually checked out to the actors, who then assume responsibility for their care until the run is completed. Unless a good tradition has been established, some pressure will have to be applied if the average actor is conscientiously to discharge his responsibility. Even in the best of theatres constant checking is necessary if costumes are to be hung up and cared for. Lost buttons, broken snaps, and other problems should be reported immediately.

Following the last performance costumes are checked in; those worth

[2] See chapter on "Directing," p. 158.

keeping are then sent to the cleaners and stored for future use. The costumer in an active theatre has a full-time but fascinating job.

MAKE-UP

To most actors there is magic excitement in the smell of stage make-up. This is not due to its perfume, but rather to its association with the exciting glow of the hour or two immediately preceding performance. In fact, one of the values of make-up may lie in giving the actor something useful and definite to do during the nerve-racking preperformance period. This is not true of all actors. Some prefer peace and solitude, but the majority, if left alone with nothing to do, begin to worry, tense up, and anticipate various horrors of failure. The chatter, activity, and bravado of dressing rooms tend to buoy up such spirits. This make-up period also requires the actor to arrive at the theatre well before curtain time, thus providing a slight margin of safety in case of emergencies. It also gives dinners a slight chance to settle.

But the psychological value of make-up is deeper than the activity and atmosphere it provides prior to the opening curtain. Many actors, particularly when playing character parts, find that make-up stimulates them toward a more confident and effective performance. In some cases they almost hide behind masks and dare to say and do things that would embarrass them if said and done in naked faces.[3]

But although the application of make-up has certain psychological values for the actor, its more obvious functions lie in the fact that from an audience standpoint it counteracts stage lighting, delineates character, and in a large auditorium helps to project the features of the character to the audience. Of the three, delineation of character is by far the most important. Age, nationality, and personality are among the vital factors that make-up can help to convey. Note the word "help." No make-up artist on earth can paint a convincingly harrowed and tragic expression over a bright, happy, unimaginative face. Just as make-up helps the actor, so the actor must help the make-up, and actors who are famous for characterization have flexible faces and sensitive "souls." It is ordinarily a skillful combination of make-up, costume, and expression that achieves the desired effect.

Not all make-ups require marked changes in appearance, however. Those commonly known as straight make-ups aim at little if any funda-

[3] For an interesting example see Constantin Stanislavski, *Building A Character,* Theatre Arts, 1949, pp. 3–28.

mental change. In other words, the actor has been essentially type-cast as far as appearance is concerned, and it is only necessary to accentuate what he already has. Usually this results in an attempt to bring out one's most attractive features according to the tastes of the time, but the tastes of the time vary. Twenty-five years ago the make-up of stage heroes tended heavily toward the romantic, even the pretty side. Eyebrows and eyelashes were generally lined, cheeks heavily rouged, and lips accentuated. Today such a make-up would be used by a male actor only if he were playing the role of some effeminate fop. The modern hero tries to imitate the ruddy, sunburned, complexion of the "he-man." Tomorrow—who can say?

But whatever the prevailing style, students of straight make-up have an excellent chance for frank evaluation of their own features. Hints on make-up as well as hints on hair styling and on how to wear clothes have frequently turned rather plain people into very attractive ones, on stage and off.

The process of applying a straight make-up begins with the application of a base. Grease paint in tubes is standard, although the more expensive type known as pancake has several advantages. The objective in either case is to achieve an even, healthy complexion, and this usually requires a color more pink or ruddy than normal to counteract the prevailing amber of artificial lights. Next come subtle highlighting and shadowing to correct possible bad features, followed by application of rouge and eye shadow. After this the make-up is carefully and thoroughly powdered with a shade of powder a bit lighter than the base. Lipstick is then applied, and finally eyelids and eyebrows are lined with varying shades of brown, or on occasions blue, green, or black. Some insist that a touch of red in the corner of the eye gives it life and sparkle. For women who are to appear glamorous, mascara and even artificial eyelashes may be useful. A pleasant trick of the trade is to wash gently in cold water following application of the base—an operation that cools, smooths, and sets the foundation. Needless to say, the style and grooming of the hair, the press and fit of the costume, and the ease and carriage of the actor do much to complete the effect.

After the show the make-up is first dissolved with cleansing cream. It is then removed with cleansing tissue or a make-up cloth; finally the face is washed with soap and water, and the job is complete. Good make-up should not be harmful to the normal skin or complexion.

Character make-ups are more interesting than straight make-ups since they produce marked changes in appearance (Plates 14, 15). In addition to the techniques already mentioned the character actor employs a number of others. In many cases he may actually alter the shape of his face by the use of nose putty or other plastic material (Plate 16). If nose putty is used it is first worked in the fingers until soft and pliable, then applied to the dry skin. Beginners often find that the putty insists on sticking to the fingers rather than to the nose, cheek bones, or chin as intended. The experienced actor avoids such a messy catastrophe by occasionally dipping his fingers into the grease paint that is eventually to be used as a base. He continues to work and mould the putty until the edges blend into the skin and the desired shape has been achieved. He then smoothes the base color across the rest of his face and the foundation for the make-up, complete with new putty features, is prepared.

The second, and perhaps the most difficult technique that the character actor employs concerns the application of highlights, lines, and shadows. How does he decide where to put these? That is where skill, art, and practice come in. If a formula or a few definite lines would suffice, then anyone could put on an excellent make-up, but this is not the case. It is more difficult to apply a good character make-up than it is to sketch the faces on paper, for the sketch artist can begin with a clean blank piece of paper, whereas the actor must rework features and characteristics already there. Shadows and highlights can go anywhere on paper according to the dictates of expression, but in make-up they must generally coincide with the natural tendencies of the actor's own face. In fact many actors proceed by assuming the attitude and facial expression of the character they intend to portray. Then, noting where the wrinkles and shadows tend to fall, they lowlight these with brown or old red. Noting where the highlights appear, they accent these with white or a tint of the base. These shadows and highlights are then skillfully blended until the shadows and lines appear to be wrinkles or sunken areas, not scratches of paint, while the highlights are blended until they appear to be ridges or bulges of flesh, not daubs of white.

In old-age make-ups it is almost always necessary to paint out the natural lines of the eyes and mouth, replacing them with lines that give the illusion of wrinkled flesh. One who knows the art of make-up also pays careful attention to highlights and shadows on arms and neck. An old-age mask painted on the front of the face of an otherwise robust youth gives an unintentionally ludicrous effect.

Having applied nose putty, foundation, highlights, and shadows, there is little more that a woman can do except to powder the make-up, fix her hair, adjust her costume, and get into character, although for certain old-age types artificial eyebrows may work wonders, and of course accessories like spectacles have their value.

Men have the advantage, for not only eyebrows but beards and mustaches of every imaginable design can be added. These are ordinarily made from crepe hair, which comes in a braided form. This is usually unraveled, dampened, and stretched to remove most of the curl. Strands of this are then shaped, combed, and clipped. They are glued to the face with spirit gum. If well done the job is convincing at close range as well as from the auditorium. Generally a color of the crepe hair is selected that matches the hair of the actor, although on some occasions the process is reversed and the actor colors his hair to match the crepe. The most common change in hair coloring is to grey it. For dignified old age, white mascara or liquid hair whitener is ordinarily used, although for certain outdoor, dried-out types, corn starch may be superior. Metallic powders sprayed with lacquers are sometimes employed, not only to grey the hair but also to transform actors into blondes, redheads, or brunettes. There are occasions when wigs for both men and women are indispensable.

Many special techniques have not been mentioned here, including some new developments such as the use of rubber make-up. Many theatres rely on the services of a professional make-up artist in order to achieve the necessary degree of skill in this element of the production, but it is really the actor's problem. He may receive aid, and he should welcome the advice of the make-up specialist, but after all he should know his own face and character better than anyone else does. His pride in developing a complete characterization should stimulate him to purchase his own make-up and develop professional skill in its application, for make-up is frequently an indispensable element in projecting a character to the audience.

PART THREE

Theatres, Artists, and Technicians

CHAPTER IX

Theatre Architecture

*W*HILE THE PLAY AND THE PLAYERS ARE THE CENTRAL ELEMENTS OF the theatrical experience, there are other items whose contributions cannot be ignored. One is the playhouses in which the plays are performed. Undoubtedly the grandeur and exaltation of Attic tragedy were reinforced by the beauty and simple dignity of the Theatre of Dionysus under the open sky. Undoubtedly the poetry and dynamic flow of action in Shakespearean tragedy were assisted by the excellent accoustics and functional efficiency of the Globe and other Elizabethan playhouses. Undoubtedly the realism of Ibsen and Chekhov was reinforced by the naturalistic intimacy of the picture-frame stages of the late nineteenth century. Consequently some knowledge of theatre architecture, some sense of its evolution, some concept as to which of its elements are universal and essential and which accidental or nonessential, become necessities to anyone who would more fully understand and appreciate the art of the theatre.

THE ANCIENT GREEK THEATRE

There is no information as to what kind of a stage or in what kind of a theatre Thespis may have performed while winning the first Greek tragic contest in 534 B.C. Horace mentions something about a cart, and from this fragment of evidence, some have conjectured that Thespis probably stood on a cart in the midst of his chorus and "acted" for an audience that gathered about him (Fig. 2). Others maintain that he stood on a table, and although neither idea can be backed by evidence, the fact remains that Thespis would have been wise to stand on something for this would have set him apart from and above his chorus where he could have been better seen and heard by his audience. The business of providing the actor with a better chance to be seen and heard is the fundamental function of all stages.

FIG. 2. Perhaps Thespis stood on a cart.

Most theatre architects, however, have been concerned about providing functions other than audibility and visibility. For example, the most important architectural element of the early Greek theatre was religious, an altar to Dionysus. This in turn was surrounded by a large circle, the *orchestra,* within which most of the actors performed. Greek audiences, like all audiences, were also concerned with comfort, which soon led to some sort of seating arrangement. A hint as to what this first seating arrangement may have been comes from an historical fragment. We know that about 499 B.C. the Athenians suffered a minor disaster when some wooden stands collapsed during a theatrical performance. This has led some scholars to conclude that early Greek performances might have been given on level ground, probably within the city, where some form of scaffolding for seating would have been necessary. But in any event, whether because of this disaster or because of theatre's growing importance as a community function, or because of other factors now lost to us, we know that within a few years the standard form of the Greek theatre, with its auditorium resting on the solid ground of a hillside, had evolved.

The Theatre of Dionysus at Athens, where the plays of Aeschylus, Sophocles, Euripides, and Aristophanes were first performed, is the most famous of the classic theatres, although many others were scattered across ancient Hellas. Its development seems to have been about as follows. Sloping down behind the Acropolis was a hillside that formed a natural amphitheatre for the audience. At the base of this hillside were laid out the two indispensable essentials of the Greek stage, an altar to Dionysus and an *orchestra* circle about 90 feet in diameter (Fig. 3). Although there is no reliable evidence, logic leads us to believe that wooden seats were next added on the hillside. Whether there was any scene building (*skene*) in the back-

FIG. 3.   Perhaps Aeschylus wrote his earliest plays for a theatre something like the one above.

ground during the early years seems doubtful. The main evidence indicating the lack of such a building is derived from the plays themselves, for the earliest extant plays of Aeschylus are all set in the out of doors, while his later plays, and also the plays of Sophocles and Euripides, are usually (but not always) set before a building or palace. It is therefore logical to suppose that a scene building was added in the neighborhood of 470 B.C., or shortly after Aeschylus wrote *The Persians,* the last of his plays that could easily have been played without a building as a background.

But whatever its evolution may have been, we have a good idea of what the typical Greek theatre was like, for the ruins of many that were built of stone during the Hellenic and Greco-Roman periods that followed the great Attic period still remain. The best preserved of these is the one at Epidauros, built, or at least begun, during the fourth century B.C. As the photograph (Plate 17) indicates, there is little guesswork as to the features of either the auditorium or the *orchestra*. These have been well preserved. The *skene*, scene building, has disappeared, however, as it has from all theatres of the Attic and Hellenic periods, and archeologists have quarrelled bitterly as to what the form of this important feature may have been. In general they agree that the *skene* had at least three doors (Fig. 4) and that in later Greek and Roman times the uses of these doors became traditional, the center door, for example, always leading into the palace of the

FIG. 4. Perhaps Euripides wrote for a theatre something like the one above.

protagonist or central character. There is also general agreement as to the names of some of the parts. The entryway on either side (between the *skene* and auditorium) was called the *parodos,* and it was through one of these that the chorus made its entrances and exits. At some period in the *skene's* evolution side wings (*paraskenia*) and a forestage (*proskenion*) were added. The top of the forestage (the *logeion*) probably served as a stage on which the actors performed, although this conjecture has been the subject of much bitter controversy.[1]

As to the numerous stage machines and effects employed by the Greeks there is little reliable evidence. The three major devices appear to have been the *eccyclema,* the *periaktos,* and the *mechane.* The *eccyclema* was a low platform, mounted on wheels or castors in such a manner that it could be rolled out through the central doorway to reveal scenes that had supposedly taken place within the *skene.* Thus Aegisthus kills Agamemnon inside the palace, yet a few moments later he appears before the chorus to justify the deed while seemingly standing over the body of the fallen king. Such a scene was probably made possible by placing the body of Agamemnon on the *eccyclema,* then rolling the whole bloody spectacle out on the forestage and into view of the audience (Fig. 5).

The second device was the *periaktos.* Its exact form and usage is shrouded in much guesswork and uncertainty, but it appears to have been a prism-shaped unit with different scenes or decorations painted on its three faces. By placing several of these *periaktoi* between the pillars along the front of the *skene* and then revolving them, something approaching a change of scenery may have been possible.

The third device commonly used was the *mechane.* This was apparently

[1] For a summary of arguments on the subject see Carless Jones, "Establishing a Basis for the Study of the Greek Theatre," *Quarterly Journal of Speech,* **22,** 85–92 (1936).

FIG. 5. Highly Conjectural Sketches of Three Greek Stage Devices: right, the *periaktos;* below left, the *mechane;* below right, the *eccyclema*.

some sort of crane or derrick used primarily to raise and lower the gods. The effect must have been rather crude and obvious. In fact, Aristophanes may have been poking fun at the *mechane* as well as at Socrates when in *The Clouds* he suspended the great philosopher in a basket.

So much for the typical Greek theatre, which in its time served the cause of Dionysus so nobly. As the years went by, changes occurred. We have already seen that after the death of Aristophanes the chorus declined in importance, and that the old religious significance of the theatre died away. With these changes a full orchestra circle was no longer of importance. Consequently, in the Hellenic period the *skene* began to encroach upon the edge of the orchestra, while after the Roman conquest theatres usually reduced the orchestra to a semicircle and dispensed with the altar altogether. Auditoriums also tended to grow smaller; at last even these could no longer be filled, and the great open-air structures were abandoned to the elements.

THE ANCIENT ROMAN THEATRE

In general there are marked similarities between the typical Roman theatre and the Greek theatre from which it descended. It should not be imagined, however, that all the plays in either Greece or Rome were performed in "typical" theatres. None of the great Roman playwrights wrote for such theatres. Seneca, it will be remembered, wrote closet dramas to be read or declaimed in polite circles, while both Plautus and Terrence wrote for a temporary wooden type of theatre about which next to nothing is known except that it had a long narrow stage representing a street with several houses. Some of the temporary wooden theatres were of a type used to celebrate military victories rather than for the production of plays. M. Aemilius Scaurus is reported to have built a wooden theatre in 58 B.C., seating 80,000 spectators. Three stories high, it contained 360 columns and 3000 statues. If these figures are correct, which seems doubtful, then Americans are not the first to have been extravagant.

As early as 154 B.C. a Roman theatre is reported to have been built of stone, but the Roman Senate, strict and "puritanical" during the early years of the empire, condemned the structure and had it torn down. One hundred years later (55–52 B.C.) the great Pompey constructed the first permanent theatre—permanent because Pompey cleverly placed a shrine to Venus at the back of the auditorium, thus implying that the curved rows of seats were not the seats of a theatre but steps leading to a sacred shrine. This theatre became the model for others that were eventually constructed throughout most of the Empire (Fig. 6).

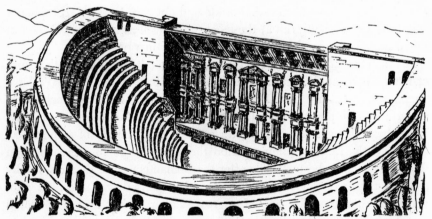

FIG. 6. Typical Roman theatre.

The form of the Roman theatre inevitably invites a series of comparisons and contrasts with the Greek.

1. Unlike the Greek auditorium, which rested upon a hill, the Roman auditorium was usually a freestanding structure built up on level ground.

2. The scene building and auditorium of the Roman theatre were joined to form a single architectural unit.

3. The auditorium was reduced to an exact semicircle, whereas in the Greek theatre it had extended beyond the semicircle.

4. The orchestra was reduced in size and also reduced to a semicircle.

5. The seating capacity, despite Rome's natural tendency to substitute quantity for quality, was usually (but not always) smaller than it had been in Greece. This was obviously because of the low social and artistic status of the theatre in Rome, in contrast to its vital importance in Greece.

6. The scene building of the Roman theatre was enlarged and lavishly decorated.

7. There was a long narrow stage with a roof above it.

Other practices of the Roman theatre, such as the stretching of colored awnings across the auditorium, the use of a curtain across the front of the stage, even such sumptuous items as carpets and air conditioning (cold, perfumed water that ran down the aisles) have been described by none too reliable sources.[2] But while there may be some doubt about the decorations and other minor items, our basic information about Roman theatres is excellent, for the ruins of many still stand (Plate 17). Romans, like Americans, could build wonderful playhouses; their weakness lay in what they said and did in these playhouses.

THE MEDIEVAL THEATRE

Of the many stage types that appeared during the medieval period, only three major forms will be considered here: (1) the temporary platform stage of the strolling players, (2) the simultaneous stages used in producing the mystery and miracle plays, (3) the wagon stages used in producing the English and German mystery cycles.

As to the stages of the strolling players, there were infinite variations, but the essential feature was a raised platform with a curtain as a background behind which actors could retire from the sight of the audience (Fig. 7). The spectators usually stood in front or on three sides of this platform, although there were exceptions. Thus when this type of theatre eventually made its way into the courtyards of the London inns, its stage was set up at one end of the yard in a manner that allowed most of the guests to watch the performance from the surrounding windows or balconies, a practice that eventually influenced the form of the Elizabethan public playhouse. It is interesting to note that the *Commedia dell' arte* players clung to their

[2] Primarily Vitruvius and Pollux.

FIG. 7.   Temporary platform stage.

simple platform stage even when their skill won them invitations to appear in courts throughout Europe.

The simultaneous stages were first developed within the churches. The basic idea consisted of shifting the audience rather than the scenery. A sequence of booths or stations was constructed (Fig. 8), each station depicting a given scene; audiences then moved from one to another as crowds in a zoo move from the elephants to the lions to the monkeys.

As the theatre moved outdoors, the simultaneous setting was retained, but the number of stations was modified, so that instead of surrounding the audience they were confined to an arc, with heaven occupying the station to the actor's right, and hell the station to his extreme left. Little or no provision seems to have been made for the comfort of the audience, although some spectators may have managed to find seats on the steps and balconies of the adjoining buildings.

This medieval idea of placing all scenes on stage at the same time appears again in the early Renaissance theatres of France, and is still seen (Plate 18). *Romeo and Juliet* was played very successfully on such a stage at the University of Minnesota, while the new theatre at Baylor University in Texas is fundamentally a modern adaptation of this simultaneous system. At the Baylor theatre the audience finds itself surrounded by four stages. In doing a given play the action might begin on the main stage, then shift to the auxiliary stage at the right, then to the stage at the left, and finally to the one at the rear, which also doubles as a lobby. The audience follows

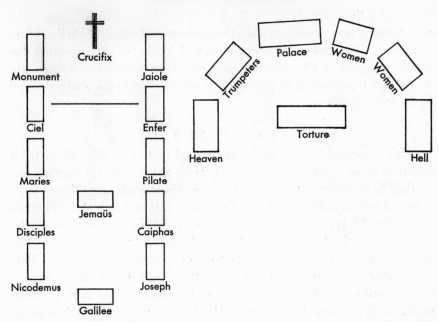

FIG. 8. Simultaneous Settings. At left is an arrangement for stations of a medieval play, *The Resurrection*. (Based on illustration in E. K. Chambers, *The Medieval Stage*.) At right is arrangement for the martyrdom of St. Apollonia.

all this by simply revolving in swivel chairs to face which ever stage is being used.

The famous wagon stages that were used in both England and Germany provide an interesting variation of the simultaneous stage. Each stage or station for a given production was completely prepared before the performance began, but instead of setting it up simultaneously in the same location with all the others, each was mounted on wheels and moved from one audience to another throughout the city. These wagon stages were of two-story construction; the lower story was used as a dressing room and the upper as a

FIG. 9. A pageant wagon.

the area for the action (Fig. 9). Each trade guild was usually assigned the responsibility for one wagon. Thus the garment-makers might do the Adam and Eve episode, the carpenters the story of Noah. On the appointed day people gathered in city squares, and one after another the wagons appeared. Each performed its play, and then moved on to the waiting crowd in the next square.

THE RENAISSANCE THEATRE

Italy's rebirth of interest in things classical quite naturally stimulated a rebirth of interest in the architecture of classic theatres, and as we shall see, resulted in the construction of the Olympic Theatre (*Teatro Olympico*), a beautiful and important playhouse that still stands. But Italy did more than restore the old. It contributed two very important books, the famous *Architettura* (1551) by Sebastiano Serlio and *Practica di fabricar Scene e Machine ne' Teatri* (1638) by Nicola Sabbatini. Above all, however, Italy contributed a new type of theatre, one that ignored both the forestage-façade tradition of the classic stage, and the simultaneous stations of the medieval. It developed the Farnese Theatre, commonly referred to as the first modern playhouse, since it had a proscenium, a front curtain, and employed painted scenery that gave a pictorial illusion of place.

Classic Tradition, the Forestage-Façade Theatre

Returning to the Olympic Theatre and the classic tradition, we find that this playhouse was the result of a deliberate effort on the part of a Renaissance group, the Olympian Academy, to construct a highly authentic replica of a classic theatre. The designer was the famous architect Palladio. He died after the work was begun, but the building was completed by his son in 1584.

While essentially a classic theatre, there are several highly interesting differences between the Olympic Theatre and those of Greece and Rome. In the first place Palladio's theatre moved indoors; in the second place the central doorway of the stage was greatly enlarged, and thus became sort of an embryonic proscenium arch, for behind this arch, as well as behind the side doorways, permanent perspective vistas were soon to be added (Fig. 10). Thus even the Olympian Academy was not able entirely to resist the new excitement of pictorial perspective, which was already thoroughly established in painting and had begun to find its way onto the stage.

But while the Olympic Theatre shows a pictorial influence, its basic form is clearly classical, for it is definitely an example of what we may call

FIG. 10.   The stage of the Olympic theatre.

the forestage-façade tradition; in other words, the basic form is that of a raised platform stage backed by an ornamental architectural façade (Plate 19). It is thus related structurally not only to the classic theatre, but also, as we shall see, to the Renaissance theatres of Holland, England, and Spain. Note, however, that although related, it is not the ancestor of the theatres in the countries just named, for it was not built until 45 years after the theatre at Ghent (1539)—see Fig. 11—and 8 years after James Burbage opened his first Elizabethan theatre (1576). Yet directly or indirectly all had a common heritage in the classic theatres of Greece and Rome. Although appearances vary, all show the same basic features: a platform stage backed by an ornamental façade containing three or more openings. In the case of the theatres of Holland, England, and Spain, however, the influence of the classic stage appears to have been indirect and probably unconscious. George Kernodle[3] advances the theory that certain elements of the classic stage had been transmitted into art, and through art (painting, sculpture, and the *tableau vivant*) to the stage. The *tableau vivant* (a static scene posed by living characters) was especially important and may well have exerted a major though indirect influence on the type of Renaissance theatre that developed first in Holland and later in England and Spain. The Olympic Theatre's claim to distinction, therefore, lies in the directness of its relationship to the classic stage, for it was built with the expressed purpose of reproducing the classic form.

Information regarding the exact nature of the English Elizabethan playhouse is extremely meager, for the theatres of Shakespeare's day were built

[3] George R. Kernodle, *From Art to Theatre*, University of Chicago Press, 1944, Chap. 1.

FIG. 11.   A Dutch theatre at Ghent, 1539.

of wood and have long since disappeared. Bits of evidence—a few old prints, a few descriptions, part of a building contract, and internal evidence from the plays themselves—provide most of the information on which our ideas are based.

The auditorium of the Elizabethan playhouse seems to have been entirely native and original. As already suggested, it apparently grew from the English innyard where the strolling interlude players had once performed while the guests watched from their windows and the commoners watched from the ground. In any event, the Elizabethan public playhouse likewise remained outdoors and still placed its groundlings in the court-yard, while patrons who could afford to do so watched from the galleries or boxes that surrounded the acting area (Fig. 12).

FIG. 12. Two Views of John C. Adams' Reconstruction of The Globe Theatre. Redrawn by the author from illustrations by Irwin Smith in Marchette Chute, *An Introduction to Shakespeare*, E. P. Dutton, 1951.

The typical Elizabethan stage appears to have taken the following form: The forestage or apron was very prominent. In most cases, but not always, it was wedge-shaped and extended well into the open pit or yard. Above this there may or may not have been a porchlike structure, the shadow, which was supported by two pillars. Behind and on either side were proscenium doors with proscenium balconies above them, while in the rear center were two larger openings, the inner-below and the inner-above. The inner-below and perhaps the inner-above were equipped with traverse curtains that could be opened or closed, thus dividing the propertied inner stage from the unpropertied forestage (Fig. 13).

This Elizabethan stage was one of the most functional and efficient ever devised. As an example of the way in which it operated, consider the first act of the *Merchant of Venice*.

Scene 1. A street in Venice. (Curtain would be closed. Actors would play on forestage.)

FIG. 13.   The Elizabethan Stage: A, unlocalized; B, localized.

Scene 2.   Belmont, a room in Portia's house. (Curtain would be opened, revealing inner stage set with scenery and properties to suggest Portia's house. Portia and Nerissa would be discovered inside, but as dialogue begins they would undoubtedly move onto forestage where they could be better seen and heard.)

Scene 3.   Venice, a public place. (Same as scene 1.)

Scene 4.   Belmont, a room in Portia's house. (Same as scene 2.)

Scene 5.   Venice, a street. (Same as Scene 1.)

Scene 6.   Venice, a room in Shylock's house. (Scenery and properties would have been changed behind the curtain as scene 5 was in progress, and the curtain now opens, revealing Shylock's house.)

And so the plays go, not always with such formal alternation between forestage and inner stage, but always in a manner that would enable the players to keep the action moving. Sometimes the balcony windows above the proscenium doors were used (*Romeo and Juliet*); sometimes the inner-above was used (the monument scene in *Antony and Cleopatra*). In any event, we cannot avoid being impressed by the functional efficiency of this stage, a stage that made possible the uninterrupted flow of action so necessary to the playing of Shakespeare.

Other features of the typical Elizabethan playhouse included machinery for flying effects, traps for ghosts, a flag that was raised when the show was in progress, and many sound effects including a cannon. In fact, one of the most famous of all playhouses, Shakespeare's playhouse, The Globe, burned to the ground when some of the smoldering wadding from a cannon ignited the thatched roof.

These public playhouses were many and popular, but they were not the only theatres to be found in England at that time. Plays were done in halls at the universities. They were also performed in private indoor theatres, which were apparently patterned after the outdoor theatres except for the addition of a roof and the consequent necessity for artificial lighting. By far the most famous of these was the Blackfriars Theatre, where the boy players of St. Paul's sometimes made themselves thorns in the flesh of Shakespeare and his companions, until 1608, when they lost their royal patronage and gave up the theatre to Burbage. Finally there were the court masques, in which the new Italian pictorial-perspective theatre was the dominant form. Some of the theatrical spectacles prepared by the great designer and architect Inigo Jones (1573–1651), for presentation at court during the reign of James I, reached extravagant heights of lavishness in both costuming and scenic splendor. We shall consider these further in our study of scenic design.

During the years when the Italians were building the Olympic and Farnese theatres, and at a time when the English were doing a booming business in their "wooden O's," the Spanish were crowding into their *corrales* to see the plays of Lope de Vega and Calderón. The Spanish auditorium had much in common with the Elizabethan playhouse. The Spanish native form had been a court yard or a *corral* the same as the English native form had been the innyard, and the results were similar—a series of galleries surrounding the level ground of the *corral* where the commoners stood. The stage itself was also of the same fundamental forestage-façade design. It tended to be simpler and to omit the proscenium doors, although it did use an inner stage and a curtain. Scenery, if any, and properties must have been meager, and yet it was on this stage that the plays of Spain's Golden Age were first performed.

The Proscenium Tradition

As mentioned earlier, the unique contribution of Renaissance Italy to theatre architecture was the Farnese Theatre at Parma, which was completed in 1618 or 1619. As George Kernodle points out,[4] the roots of this playhouse are to be found in the visual arts, particularly in the newly developed pictorial perspectives of Renaissance painting. Perspective painting, which had become highly developed in Italian art during the fifteenth

[4] See George R. Kernodle, *op. cit.*, Chap. 6.

century, made its way into the theatre in the early sixteenth century. These early perspective settings, for example those by Serlio (Fig. 14), were designed for a stage platform but were not placed behind a proscenium

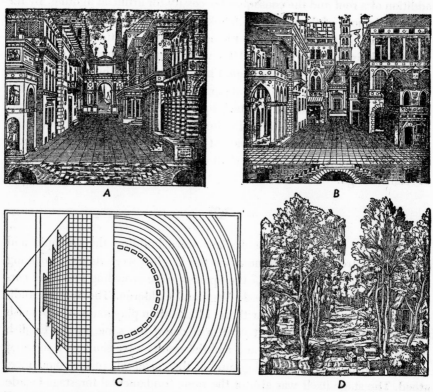

FIG. 14. Serlio's Famous Drawings: A, tragic scene; B, comic scene; C, ground plan for a theatre in which such settings might be shown; D, satyric scene.

arch. Kernodle also makes it clear that the proscenium of the Farnese Theatre did not appear as a sudden invention,[5] nor was it simply a further enlargement of the central doorway of the Olympic Theatre. Instead the proscenium developed gradually as the sixteenth century progressed. In other words, the Farnese Theatre is the "first modern theatre" only in the sense that it marks the culmination and combination of trends already developed. To repeat, it moved the stage behind a formal proscenium, equipped this stage with pictorial scenery that could be shifted, and further separated the audience area from the playing area by means of a front curtain, thus giving the world a new pictorial-proscenium type of theatre,

[5] *Ibid.*, Chap. 7.

a type that was soon to be generally accepted throughout most of the western world (Plate 20).

It was not long until both France and Italy began to display a preference for the pictorial-proscenium form. In France the native basis for the theatre had been the tennis court, which consisted of one or more galleries surrounding a playing area. To convert this into a theatre, a platform stage was erected at one end much as it had been in the English innyard and the Spanish *corral*. Unlike the English and Spanish, however, the French displayed an early preference for the proscenium arch. This may have been because the great period of French playwriting came after, not before, the Farnese Theatre.

As the centuries progressed there was a tendency for both opera houses and theatres to become larger, especially to increase stage floor area and flying space (the space above the stage area), thus making provision for elaborate and spectacular effects. The Hall of the Machines (*Salle des Machines*, 1662) constructed in Paris during the seventeenth century, although it eventually proved to be a white elephant, serves to illustrate the extent to which some of these tendencies went. On the great opening night the King and one hundred members of his court were placed on one of the huge platforms and hoisted into the air. Approximately 1000 stage hands were required to man completely the complicated effects. The stage was so enormous (its depth was 132 feet) that years later, when the *Palais Royal* burned to the ground in 1763, the company moved into the then abandoned Hall of the Machines for temporary quarters; but instead of using the entire building they found the stage alone of sufficient size to serve as both stage and auditorium.[6]

The Compromise, England and America After 1660

Consciously or unconsciously the theatres of Restoration England combined the two basic forms of the Renaissance stage. From the French and the Italians, or perhaps from Inigo Jones, came the idea of the proscenium opening with its scenic perspectives. Perhaps from the same sources came the idea of definitely moving indoors, of adding seats for the "groundlings" and new elegance to the decorations. On the other hand, Restoration theatres retained much that had been Elizabethan. They retained the forestage or apron where most of the action took place. They retained the proscenium doors, and in some cases, proscenium balconies. They even re-

[6] C. Lowell Lees, *The French Influence upon Garrick's Staging Methods*, unpublished M.A. thesis, Northwestern University, 1932, pp. 57, 58.

tained the old inner-below, which was simply enlarged and called a proscenium opening. Compare the sketches of a typical Elizabethan stage (Fig. 13) with the Dorset Garden Theatre (Plate 21), which was opened in 1671, and you will see that the break between the Elizabethan and Restoration theatre is not nearly so great as most people suppose. In fact, could we compare Dorset Garden with the old indoor Blackfriars Theatre of Shakespeare's day we might find no essential distinction whatever.

During the eighteenth and nineteenth centuries the theatres of England, like those on the continent, increased in size. They eventually introduced gas lighting, and finally electricity, but the essential English form, the apron with its proscenium doors, was stubbornly retained even into the twentieth century.

Theatre architecture in America has generally followed the English tradition. What is commonly regarded as the first American theatre was built in Williamsburg, Virginia, in 1716. However, the most famous of the early theatres was the John Street Theatre, New York (1767). It was built by David Douglas, who has been called "the builder of theatres," for he constructed them almost wherever his famous company (The American Company, originally organized by Louis Hallam) played. Both William Dunlap in his *History of the American Theatre,* and Royal Tyler, through the mouth of Jonathan, his famous Yankee character in *The Contrasts,* have left us descriptions of the old John Street playhouse. It was set far back from the street, was painted red, had a pit, a gallery, and a stage "of good dimensions." In 1798 The Park Theatre, a much finer playhouse than the old John Street Theatre, opened its doors in New York. It burned in 1820, but a new theatre, The Second Park Theatre, was soon completed where the old one had been. A famous painting of the interior, (Plate 21), indicates that there was little difference between the basic form and quality of this theatre and theatres of the same period in London. The apron, flanked by proscenium doors and windows, is prominent, as are the rows of boxes that encircle the auditorium.

The reader, however, should not make the mistake of thinking that all plays in America were performed in regular theatres. In all countries and in all ages, stages have been improvised with complete disregard for basic architectural trends. For example, the first plays seen in the territory of Minnesota were performed by soldiers stationed at old Fort Snelling. These soldier shows, which began as early as the winter of 1821–22, used barracks or mess halls—whatever was available. When the first professionals came up the river to St. Paul in the summer of 1851 they improvised a theatre in a hall located above a store. The companies that followed used similar makeshift facilities; one even played in the Court House. It was not until 1857 that a building was constructed especially for theatrical purposes. This was the People's Theatre, which cost a sum total of $750. Rough and crude as the frontier itself, it burned to the ground a few years later. Not

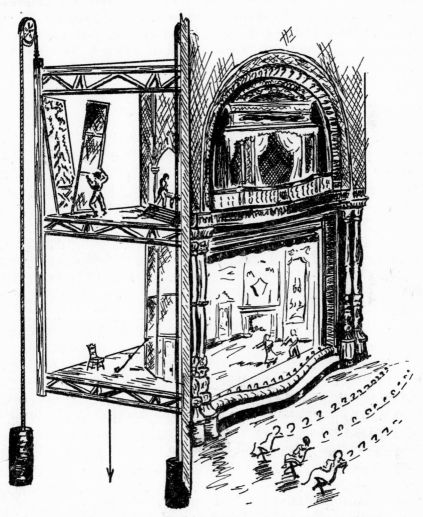

FIG. 15.   Elevator Stage. The Madison Square Theatre, 1879.

until 1867 did St. Paul get an adequate theatre, and even this was located on a second floor, with only one exit in case of fire or panic.

A complete history of theatre architecture in other nineteenth-century American cities would doubtless show thousands of innovations and variations. None, however, appears to have been new or fundamentally different except the Madison Square Theatre (1879), which was built by Steele MacKaye and contained an elevator stage capable of shifting entire scenes by simply raising or lowering them (Fig. 15). While the idea was not particularly successful in America, it did have an influence in Germany, and it marks the beginning of modern mechanical shifting devices. Of these the most effective to date have been: (1) the revolving stage, which traces its origin from Japan through Germany and from there to the rest of the world, and (2) the wagon stage, which traces its origin all the way to the *eccyclema* of ancient Greece.

The Broadway Playhouses

Today most American theatres, including college and high school auditoriums, tend to be patterned after the standard Broadway playhouses of the early twentieth century. Since these were constructed for the purpose of crowding as many paying customers as possible into about a 75- by 100-foot rectangle of fabulously expensive Manhattan real estate, it is easy to understand why they are so extremely limited as far as space for lobby, foyer, stage, and dressing rooms is concerned. We can likewise understand the absence of shop and storage facilities, for in New York it is much less expensive to construct scenery elsewhere and then truck it into the theatre. There is no need for storage space, since the house is rented to one show at a time, always in the hope that the new production will run indefinitely. When the show closes, everything is disposed of and the stage is completely cleared for the next tenant.

Even so, these Broadway playhouses are surprisingly well designed, considering their period and the purpose for which they were constructed. Most of the auditoriums are small, averaging about 1200 seats. Each has a main floor, a balcony, and often a gallery. This arrangement, plus the fact that most of them are quite wide, brings everyone reasonably close to the actors. Acoustically these small houses are excellent, and thus the primary functions, audibility and visibility, are well satisfied. The stages of these Broadway theatres, although cramped for space, are as good or better than those of most of other present-day proscenium theatres.

To those unfamiliar with the backstage area a quick view of its major features seems necessary. Architecturally a theatre consists of two major units, an auditorium and a stagehouse (Fig. 16). The wall of the stagehouse, which divides it from the auditorium, is known as the proscenium. This contains the proscenium opening or proscenium arch through which the play is seen. Immediately behind this opening is a steel or asbestos curtain, which rides up and down in metal grooves, and is used to divide the stage-

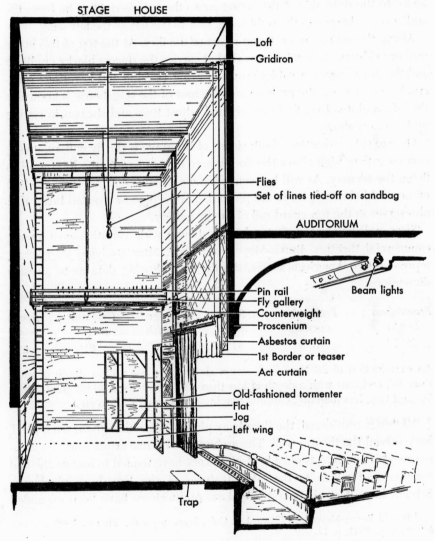

STAGE HOUSE

Loft
Gridiron

Flies
Set of lines tied-off on sandbag

AUDITORIUM

Beam lights

Pin rail
Fly gallery
Counterweight
Proscenium
Asbestos curtain
1st Border or teaser
Act curtain

Old-fashioned tormenter
Flat
Jog
Left wing

Trap

Fig. 16.   Cross section of a typical modern theatre (simplified).

house from the auditorium in case of fire. Any portion of the stage floor that projects into the auditorium beyond this curtain is known as the apron, a feature practically nonexistent in most Broadway houses. Stage space directly behind the proscenium opening includes the acting area, which, of course, varies according to the size and shape of the setting that encloses it. This area usually contains several traps (sections of the floor that can be removed), which provide for such scenic necessities as Ophelia's grave. Space to the right side of the acting area (the actor's right as he faces the audience) is known as the right wing, that to the left as the left wing.

Above the acting area is flying space or the flies. At the top of this is the grid or gridiron, an iron framework that carries the sheave blocks (pullies) and the lines (ropes or cables) used in flying (raising and lowering) scenery. Space between the gridiron and the roof of the stagehouse is known as the loft, and it is here that men rig and adjust lines and sheaves in setting up for a new show.

On one side (sometimes both sides) of the stage is the fly gallery, a long narrow gallery high above the floor where flymen handle the lines used in flying the scenery. As will be seen when we discuss shifting, lines are tied off around belaying pins in the pin rail, a large pipe or wooden beam that also serves as the top guard rail of the fly gallery.

Sizes and dimensions of stagehouses show a wide variation even among commercial theatres. Burris-Meyer and Cole, after studying thirty-eight representative American stages, supply the following data as to average dimensions:

Proscenium height	Proscenium opening	Stage depth	Stage width	Gridiron height	Apron width
28′ 1″	37′ 7″	31′ ½″	70′	61′	2′2″

An examination of 26 New York stages shows only one with a depth of more than 40′, and four with a depth of less than 25′. Two have a width greater than 90′ and two, less than 50′. Gridiron heights vary from 29′ 9″ to 80′.[7]

All things considered, the Broadway playhouses, although far from ideal, have served the theatre well. The architectural crime arises from the manner in which architects outside of New York have tended to imitate the bad features and eliminate the good features of the Broadway playhouse. Schools have been the worst offenders. Auditoriums have been expanded

[7] Harold Burris-Meyer and Edward C. Cole, *Scenery for the Theatre*, Little, Brown & Company, 1941, p. 11.

into barnlike caverns seating as many as 6000; stages have often been compressed to little more than a speaker's platform; lobbies and dressing rooms have been reduced and even eliminated, while shops and storage facilities have generally been omitted, just as they are in Broadway playhouses, but without the same good reasons.

Community and School Theatres

While the tendency to imitate the worst features of Broadway architecture has been the rule among school architects, there nevertheless have been many exceptions. As the twentieth century advanced, these exceptions have become more and more numerous until today the trend is reversed, and most of the new and exciting advances in American theatre architecture are to be found in college and community playhouses.

Architects have finally begun to realize that college and community theatres serve different functions than commercial Broadway theatres; that they are built on less expensive land and can better afford to expand horizontally; that they are concerned with the production of a season of plays and therefore need a building that is a self-contained producing plant. This means ample space for shops, storage, and rehearsal, plus offices for a permanent staff. In addition it usually means classrooms and teaching facilities. Finally, since the theatre is intended as a cultural center for the school, the community, or both, there is need for rather spacious lobbies, comfortable lounges, and perhaps provision for such things as art exhibits.

Among the better modern theatres still retaining the fundamental proscenium form are the Cleveland Playhouse and the theatres at the Universities of Iowa, Wisconsin, and Indiana (Plate 22). The interesting feature of the Cleveland Playhouse (Fig. 17) is that it incorporates two theatres into a single building in such a manner that both stages are adjacent to the same workshop and storage facilities, while the front of each house is served by the same lobby, lounges, and box office. Indiana University likewise has two auditoriums within a single building. As can be seen from the ground plan, the stages join, making it possible to shift scenery and properties from one to the other. The large auditorium seats 4000, the small one 400. One interesting innovation is the orchestra pit, which contains a lifting platform that allows it to be used below the main floor as a pit, level with the main floor as added seating capacity, or above the main floor as a stage apron. The University of Wisconsin theatre was built in connection with the student Union, thus blending into the social, recreational, and cultural

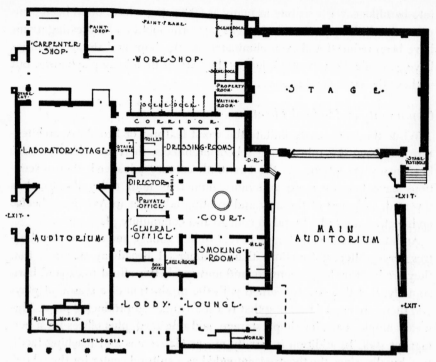

Fig. 17.   Ground plan of The Cleveland Playhouse.

affairs of the campus. Its seating capacity can be varied from 1300 to 700 by drawing large curtains across either the balcony or the rear section of the main floor. There is a glass-enclosed viewing room where a performance can be seen and discussed by classes without disturbing actors or audience. There is also a small laboratory theatre on the second floor with a seating capacity of 185.

For production of legitimate drama, perhaps the best standard proscenium-type theatre built to date on a college campus is to be found at the University of Iowa. The auditorium seats 500. It has a steep slope (stadium seating), and the rows are so far apart that no aisles are required (continental seating). Because of these features everyone in the audience has an excellent view of the acting area. There is a revolving stage that rests on a foundation independent of the rest of the building, thus eliminating noise and vibration. Two sets of steel tracks permit huge wagons, slip-stages, to be moved easily and accurately into place. Shops located at one end of the stage are separated from it by folding doors. Lounge, green room, and rehearsal space are located under the auditorium.

Theatre Architecture

Arena Theatres

But not all modern theatre construction has followed conventional patterns. In 1940 the University of Washington opened its Penthouse Theatre the first playhouse to be constructed exclusively for arena type productions (Plate 23). In this theatre there is no proscenium, and the audience completely surrounds the playing area. There are earlier examples of this idea, of course. In fact, enthusiasts for arena staging maintain that primitive man himself probably placed the performer at the center of such a circle. They also point to circuses, bull rings, and arenas of all types to support their claims as to the basic naturalness of such an arrangement.

In the early 1920's Adolphe Appia recommended that a theatre should be a large flexible space, while Robert E. Jones and Kenneth Macgowan wrote with imagination and enthusiasm about the possibility of producing Shakespeare in one of the small circus arenas of Paris.[8] In October of 1924, Gilmor Brown opened his Pasadena Playbox, a tiny intimate theatre, in his own living room, where plays might be staged in whatever area of the room seemed most desirable. It was also in 1924 that Jacques Capeau established a playhouse without conventional stage or proscenium in a warehouse on the outskirts of Paris. In Russia a few years later Nikolai Okhlopkov developed his Realistic Theatre. Okhlopkov gives the following account of how the idea was conceived.

One day during the Russian Civil War I stood on a railway station platform. From one direction a troop train drew in and stopped. In a moment another troop train arrived from the opposite direction and halted across the platform. Soldiers poured out to refill their tea-kettles, buy a bun, or stretch their legs. Near me one man alighted. From the other train came another soldier. They saw each other, ran forward and embraced, unable to speak for emotion. They were old comrades, dearest friends, whom the war had separated. There on a station platform, as one went one way and the other another, they met for a moment, clasped hands, and parted. In that instant I knew that that was what I wanted my theatre to be—a meeting where two dear friends experience an emotional union, in which for that moment all the rest of the world may be forgotten. Ever since I have worked for that. In my theatre, actor and spectator must clasp hands in fraternity.[9]

But whoever deserves credit for its origin, the arena stage has assumed a position of genuine importance in the modern American Theatre. Since the

[8] Kenneth Macgowan and Robert E. Jones, *Continental Stagecraft,* Harcourt, Brace and Company, Inc., 1922, pp. 198–212.

[9] Norris Houghton, *Moscow Rehearsals,* Harcourt, Brace and Company, Inc., 1936, pp. 148–149.

construction of the Penthouse Theatre at the University of Washington in 1940, arena stages have sprung up all over the country. Perhaps the most famous to date is the Margo Jones theatre, in Dallas, Texas. Another new and very beautiful one has been completed at Miami University. Ohio State has equipped one under its stadium, and in the summer of 1950 arena staging successfully invaded Broadway, with full-scale professional productions in the ballroom of the Hotel Edison.

It seems too early to say for certain whether the arena stage will become the theatre of the future or whether it will prove to be a passing fad. Among its limitations are:

1. The back of an actor's head—both from an auditory and a visual standpoint—is less expressive than the front of it.

2. Scenery, which the arena eliminates, can often add to the actor's ability to move and perform effectively.

3. The illusion of space and freedom (such things as the feeling of open sky) is lacking.

4. The necessity of playing to all sides of the house tends to give a pattern of rotation to the action that can be disturbing.

5. Effective lighting is difficult to achieve.

On the affirmative side is the matter of cost and convenience. Had every producing group had a theatre like the one at the University of Iowa it seems doubtful whether the arena stage would be enjoying such a vogue, but most nonprofessionals are faced with barnlike auditoriums, terrible acoustics, no stage space, and innumerable restrictions upon the use of both the stage and the auditorium. In such cases an arena stage becomes not necessarily the ideal theatre but certainly the lesser of two evils. In most cases a large room can be found somewhere in the school or community and easily converted into an acceptable arena theatre. Even if such a theatre is built from scratch, the cost is only a fraction of the amount required for a playhouse of the proscenium type. There is also the saving, both in labor and expense, that results from the elimination of scenery. And finally there is the inherent quality of intimacy, the sharing of experience between actor and audience that is so essential to good theatre. Here at least is a type of theatre that movies and television cannot duplicate. Here is a legitimate theatre, a theatre returned to the actor and the playwright, and a theatre where everyone can see and hear.

If it has done nothing else, the arena theatre has done great service in puncturing some of the sacred myths and conventions that had grown up around the proscenium. It has shattered some of the more extreme notions about the need for maintaining distance—for keeping everything behind a picture frame. It has destroyed the notions that elaborate, expensive, and cluttering scenery is indispensable, and has reminded us that the only fundamental elements in theatre are play, audience, and players.[10]

Having freed us from the absolute necessity of the proscenium arch, it is to be hoped that crusaders for the arena idea will not carry their own system to an equally rigid and unnecessarily opposite extreme. It might be well to pause and realize that during most of the great historical periods the spectators have viewed the show not from the round but from the semi-round—they have *partially* surrounded the playing area (Plate 24). The trend away from this idea began, of course, with the Farnese Theatre and its pictorial proscenium. However, it was not until the late nineteenth and early twentieth century that architects, influenced first by a craving for peephole realism and next by the necessity of avoiding side-seat distortion when watching a movie, began carrying the proscenium idea to an extreme by overemphasizing the importance of sight lines. The result tended toward long narrow auditoriums, which if small, reduced seating capacity to a few hundred, or if large, placed the rear seats so far from the stage that effectiveness and intimacy disappeared. Then came the complete revolt, the opposite extreme, the complete encirclement of the actor, the arena.

Common sense and compromise should eventually prevail. We should remind ourselves of the fundamentals: we must have the play; we must have the actor. The audience should be able to see and hear them, clearly, easily, and comfortably. Finally, the actor should move in an environment that reinforces, or at least does not distract from the play. The University of Minnesota has successfully produced plays in three proscenium-type theatres, in one semi-arena theatre, in two student lounges, a lobby, a fine arts room, on the lawn behind the theatre, on the steps in front of the auditorium, in the football stadium, and at one time made plans to produce *The Frogs* in the women's swimming pool. We should remember that Gilmor Brown's original Playbox was as revolutionary in its flexibility as in its intimacy. In other words, neither a proscenium nor a complete arena is indispensable. In fact there is an encouraging tendency in some of the newer theatres, such as the one at Sarah Lawrence College, to try to combine the best features of each type by returning to auditoriums that partially, but not entirely, surround the actor. Such a compromise has tremendous advantages over either of the extremes.

[10] Recent evidence may force us to revise many of our standard ideas about the Elizabethan stage. Leslie Hotson, in an article entitled "Shakespeare's Arena," *Atlantic Monthly*, Feb. 1954, p. 62, argues with considerable conviction that Shakespeare used an essentially arena type theatre.

CHAPTER X

Scenic Design

NTIL THE RENAISSANCE, THEATRE ARCHITECTURE AND THE ART OF scenic design were essentially inseparable. In other words, there was a strong tendency for the visual background of the play to be a permanent part of the theatre itself: the architectural façade in the Greek, Roman, and Elizabethan theatres, the platform or station in the medieval. True, there was some consciousness of "scenery": Aristotle credits Sophocles with its introduction; Vitruvius speaks of the *periaktoi* and other devices, and craftsmen of the medieval mystery plays must have lavished great imaginative skill on their "stations," especially upon the hell mouth, but is was not until the Renaissance with its picture-perspective settings that the art of scenic design really assumed a place of its own.

It has already been mentioned that this idea of preparing a pictorial illusion of place was a natural outgrowth of the fifteenth century interest in linear perspective, which had quite literally opened new horizons for Renaissance painters. In fact, some of these Renaissance painters, including the great Raphael himself, were among the first to design scenery. Thus there was a strong tendency to transfer to the stage the same techniques of painting and perspective that had already been developed on canvas.

In general the earliest pictorial backgrounds for the stage, like early backgrounds in painting, show an almost scientific and mechanical preoccupation with perspective, almost as if the designer's primary objective had been to create the visual illusion of the longest possible street. This can be seen to some extent in the famous designs by Serlio (Fig. 14), which resemble architectural drawings. They have been called classic, in contrast to the more romantic style that followed, for they tend to be intellectual and mechanically accurate rather than emotional or inspirational. There is an architectural hardness about these early settings, which in practice was heightened by the fact that they were not simply painted on a flat surface but, whenever possible, built up in relief, using real, three-dimensional moldings and other solid features.

The Italian monopoly of picture-perspective was of short duration. Early in the seventeenth century the English developed a passion of their own for scenic spectacle in their lavish court masques. As already mentioned, the man responsible for most of this scenic embellishment was Inigo Jones. He traveled a great deal, saw much, and learned much. To the English he introduced the Italian scenic perspectives, the proscenium arch, and the contemporary continental systems of building and shifting scenery. But Jones was more than a borrower; he was an artist and innovator in his own right. His designs show a much freer and more florid style than those by Serlio. Most of his work has an imaginative and elaborate touch that is entirely individual. Perhaps his greatest innovation was the development of a system of changing scenes by sliding flats in grooves as illustrated in Fig. 18, a system that remained standard in most theatres for almost three centuries.

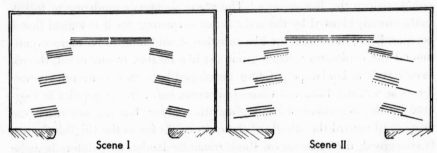

Scene I   Scene II

FIG. 18.   The Inigo Jones System of Shifting Scenes. Bottoms and tops of all flats fit into grooves permitting them to slide on or off stage as desired. In Scene I, above, all sets of flats are in place on stage. The shift to Act II is accomplished by simply sliding the first flat of each set off stage.

Any leadership that Inigo Jones or the English Court may have assumed in the matter of scenic design was cut short by the rise of the Commonwealth in the 1640's. At a time when the Puritans had destroyed every trace of the theatre in England, Italian scenic designers were carrying the art of scenery to extravagant heights. In Venice, Giacomo Torelli is reported to have so overwhelmed his fellow citizens with some of his scenic effects that, believing him to be in league with the devil, they tried to kill him. He fled to Paris, where his beautiful scenes and elaborate effects might be less dangerously appreciated. Although Torelli left Italy, many other designers did not; in fact the country fairly blossomed with scenic and operatic wonders. A study of the lavish baroque designs contributed by these Italian scenic artists during the late seventeenth, eighteenth, and nineteenth centuries is enough for a book in itself. The beginner should probably concentrate on remembering one name, Bibiena, a family name that stretched through four generations. From Giovanni Bibiena, the founder, to Alessandro and Carlo, the great-grandsons, the Bibienas created some of the most overwhelming visual effects the theatrical and operatic world has ever seen (Plate 25). And while such scenery may be regarded today as old-fashioned and outmoded, we must at least pay tribute to the skill, the patience, and the craftsmanship shown by the Bibienas and others like them. In their way these baroque settings achieved marvels of proportion, beauty, and scenic splendor.

Although painted scenery held the stage for three centuries, not all of it followed the lavish style of the Bibienas. Just as there was a close relationship between the designer and the painter during the Renaissance, so James Thompson has found a similar relationship between designers and painters since the Renaissance.[1] The scene designer's tendency to follow paths already charted by the artist is not surprising, for it is logical that a comparatively individual art like painting should tend to be more experimental and exploratory than a group art like theatre. In any event, the romantic style of landscape painting, developed by such seventeenth-century artists as Salvator Rosa and Claude Lorraine, had become popular in England by the beginning of the eighteenth century, but did not reach the stage until toward the middle of the century. As far as the English theatre is concerned, the influence of these romantic landscape painters may be seen at its best in the work of Philip Loutherbourg (c. 1740–1812). His settings, painted mostly for David Garrick at Drury Lane, had qualities of their own. He was especially skillful in scenes featuring mist and wild mountain crags. To achieve these effects he developed the technique of combining translucent drops with built-up foregrounds in a manner that excited the wonder and admiration of all who saw them. On a lower level the designer's tendency to follow the painter resulted in skillfully executed settings that were little more than out-and-out copies of paintings (Plate 26), while on the lowest level the copies were not even skillful. By the end of the nineteenth century most scenery was "manufactured" on a business basis by workers who used stencils, patterns, formulas, and the barest minimum of creativity.

[1] James R. Thompson, *Influences of Modern Painting on the New Stagecraft*, M.A. thesis, University of Minnesota, 1951.

Scenic Design

THE REVOLT AGAINST PAINTED SCENERY

This tendency for painted scenery to be manufactured, not created, to imitate good art or bad art, may well have been an important factor in causing the scenic revolt that developed toward the end of the nineteenth century against the picture-painted scenery that had held the stage for almost three hundred years, a revolt that for a while almost drove the painter from the theatre.

The growing tendency to manufacture scenery was not the only cause of this revolt. The factors behind it are numerous and complex. Perhaps the theatre was once again merely following in the footsteps of the painter, who as early as 1830 moved toward realism, and then, by the time of Ibsen, away from realism and toward modernism. Perhaps the camera, with its ability to hold the mirror up to nature, was responsible for the general dissatisfaction with the scene painter, or perhaps the new flat glare from gas or electric footlights and borderlights tended to highlight the false perspectives, painted shadows, waving pillars, and incongruous proportions that resulted when an actor moving too far upstage loomed higher than the painted mountains. But whatever the reasons, by the beginning of the twentieth century there was widespread revolt against painted scenery.

Yet while critics agreed in their antagonism toward painted scenery, they were not agreed as to an alternative. From the first there were two major schools of thought: the realists, who sought to remedy unconvincing painted scenery by making it "real"; and the antirealists, who sought to remedy the same unconvincing scenery by making it frankly theatrical, an art in and of itself rather than an imitation of nature.

THE REALISTS AND NATURALISTS

In general the realists have been the more practical, businesslike, and financially successful. In England as early as the 1850's Tom Robertson and the Bancrofts began using "box settings" (settings with a ceiling, back wall, and side walls) instead of the usual painted wings and drops. This led to the use of practical doors, practical windows, and such items as three-dimensional fireplaces. In America, toward the end of the century, David Belasco established his reputation as the most painstaking realist of them all, sparing neither time nor money in his quest for the real and the lifelike.

In producing *The Easiest Way* (such a delightfully ironic title) Belasco went to a dilapidated rooming house, found the exact room he wanted, bought the entire interior, including doors, windows, and wallpaper, and transported these to the theatre, where they were reassembled with diligent care.[2] In other plays he even sent agents abroad to find exact and authentic props.

In theory at least, Stanislavski, Antoine, and other European naturalists carried scenery beyond the realism of Belasco. Actors often began rehearsing in naturally furnished surroundings, not knowing which wall would eventually be removed, allowing the audience to peer in on their private lives.

But such extreme attempts only served to focus attention on the inherent limitations of realism and naturalism, limitations which many critics had realized from the beginning. For one thing, complete realism is impossible. Belasco could set up a real house, but was defeated by such problems as lakes, mountains, and sky. Stanislavski could set up a real room, but eventually had to remove one wall. Much more important, complete realism is undesirable. How far would music have gone had it limited itself to a reproduction of sounds heard in nature? Imagine a great symphony orchestra rehearsing for weeks to produce a lifelike imitation of the song of the blackbirds, the babbling brook, or even the wind in the pines! Music has obviously moved ahead into the realm of pure art, using rhythm and tone independent of nature. The visual arts must likewise free themselves and move beyond nature if they are to have a future worth bothering about.

There are other charges against realism: it is expensive, cumbersome, time-consuming; it can easily become distracting rather than helpful; and finally, stage realism could never hope to compete with motion picture realism even if it wanted to.

But while modern designers agree that extreme realism for its own sake is bad, there are many who still argue that modified realism can be very effective. The illustrations (Plate 27) suggest some of the possible modifications and simplifications.

THE ANTIREALISTS

As John Dolman points out,[3] the antirealists were in revolt against both the old painted scenery and the realists. In general, while antirealistic theories have been sound and stimulating, their realization has been muddled and impractical. Adolphe Appia, whose influence on the art of directing has already been considered, is a notable exception. This quiet, scholarly Ger-

---

[2] David Belasco, *The Theatre Through Its Stage Door*, Harper & Brothers, 1919, p. 77.

[3] John Dolman, Jr., *The Art of Play Production*, Harper & Brothers, 1946, pp. 299 ff.

man-Swiss gave us a clear view of the functions and limitations of scenery. His settings were designed to harmonize with and assist the three-dimensional actor who played in them. He emphasized steps, levels, columns, and rhythm of line—the things stage art could do within the confines of the theatre (Plate 28). He also insisted that good lighting could fuse the actor and his environment into an organic whole. Both in theory and design he showed the way to a sound solution of the problem of modern scenery.

Gordon Craig, who has also been considered in relation to directing, held theories of design similar to those of Appia, though he verged toward the impractical, the radical, and the extreme. In his passion for design he frequently forgot both the actor and the limitations of the theatre. Still it must be admitted that his scenes are stimulating and often beautiful. His influence on other designers and on the twentieth-century theatre in general has been enormous.

Most college classes in scenic design spend some time studying various movements in modern art: expressionism, stylization, symbolism, surrealism, constructivism. While such study has obvious value, it can easily be overemphasized. The best designers from Serlio to Jo Mielziner have shown slight disposition to follow slavishly any given style.

Of all antirealists, the expressionists are the most extreme. In theory they turn to music as the purest of the arts, and attempt to do with light what the composer does with sound. Suppose that a naturalist, an impressionist, and an expressionist should decide to paint the same view of an old willow down in the meadow. The naturalist's job would be clear and definite. He would strive to give us a photographic reproduction of the old tree in full color. The impressionist might say, "My impression of the tree is what counts, and my impression is one of vague, nostalgic gloom." In his painting the tree might be softened in mist; hazy blues, quiet greens, and soft violets might replace the more positive hues of life; the droop of the limbs might be heavily exaggerated. Still, the finished work would bear some resemblance to the tree itself. But the expressionist might say, "I want to paint not a tree at all, but the very essence of gloom and loneliness, a painting of the complex mood and depression that the view of the old tree has stirred in my soul." Consequently, he would use color, mass, rhythm, and form with no more concern about whether the final result looked like the tree than a composer would have about whether his mood music sounded like the rustling of wind in its limbs or the chirp of a lonely sparrow on one of its dead branches. His painting would probably turn out to be an abstraction with no resemblance to the tree itself, but it could look like a tree or an octopus or anything else so long as it conveyed his idea of the essence of gloom and loneliness.

On the stage, expressionism has generally relied upon distortion rather than abstraction, though both elements are usually present to some degree. There has also been a tendency to associate expressionism with moods that are somber—the tragic, the bitter, the pathological—although nothing inherent in expressionism completely rules out the comic or other moods. Perhaps the expressionist will one day realize his dream of pure visual expression if color organs ever become common enough so that he can begin creating visual melodies of moving, fluid light. As it is, the essentially static quality of a single stage setting or a single painting is a serious limitation. Perhaps this is why some of the most successful excursions into expressionism on the stage have relied heavily on lighting, which can give a fluid projection of color and form that is dynamic and moving, patterns that can change to fit varying rhythms of dance and drama just as music does. Perhaps if man ever learns to apply some of his electronic genius to the problem, the visual artist may someday find a medium to express his dreams.

Many other trends in modern art have found their way to the stage, particularly through ballet, which has attracted the talents of such famous modern artists as Pablo Picasso and Salvador Dali. On the legitimate stage, however, there has been little purity of style. The layman tends to label distortion of the tragic, the pathological, and the dramatic, "expressionism." He dubs distortion of the delightful, the comic, and the fantastic, "stylization." He classifies the ironic, the bitter, and the incongruous as surrealism or dadaism. All have this much in common: all want to express something visually, and for the most part seek to realize this objective through some form of abstraction or distortion. In other words all try to be expressive and nonrealistic.

OTHER STYLES OF SCENERY

Two styles that may have more meaning on stage than in painting are constructivism and formalism. As a visual background, constructivism (Plate 29) makes little sense. It becomes meaningful in the theatre only when we consider what the actor can *do* in such a setting, for the platforms, spiral chutes, springboards, and towers are there to be used by the actors. A circus tent, with its animal cages, tight wires, nets, and trapezes makes little sense either until the performers take over. Constructivism exists as something to be used rather than as something to be seen.

Formalism is also a recognized style of scenic design, though it is hardly

The Greek Theatre at Epidauros

The Roman Theatre at Orange

PLATE 17. Ruins of Ancient Theatres

Heaven   Jerusalem   House of Bishops   Sea   Hell

Stage for Valenciennes Mystery Play, 1547.

Sea   Temple of Delphi   Palace of Epirus   Prison

Pandoste at the *Hotel de Bergogne,* 17th Century.

Friar Lawrence's Cell   Inn   Church   Capulet's Home   Balcony
Tomb   Street
                                    Apothecary

Romeo and Juliet at the University of Minnesota, 1939.

PLATE 18. Simultaneous Settings

The Greek Theatre at Delphi with modern
scene building

Early Renaissance stage for productions of
Terence

The Olympic Theatre (Teatro Olympico)

PLATE 19. Forestage Theatres

Reconstruction of an Elizabethan theatre, The Fortune

Jacques Copeau's stage at the *Vieux Colombier,* Paris

PLATE 19 (Continued)

Farnese Theatre at Parma, 1618 or 1619

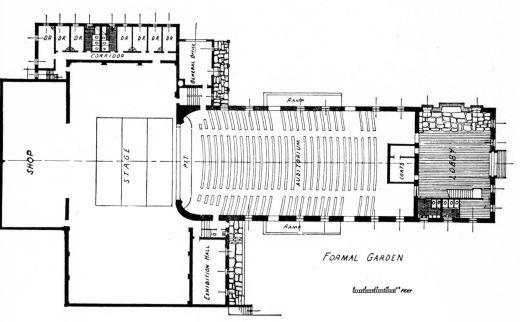

Ground plan of the Paper Mill Playhouse. Note the long, narrow auditorium.

PLATE 20. Proscenium Theatres

Henry Miller Theatre, New York. Typical of the Broadway playhouses of the late 19th and early 20th centuries.

Plate 20 (Continued)

Dorset Garden, English Restoration playhouse

The second Park Theatre, New York, 1834

The Theatre at Malmö, Sweden, 1944

PLATE 21. Compromise Between the Proscenium and Forestage Theatres

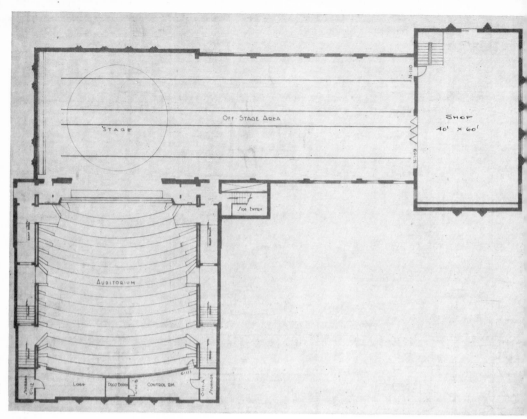

University of Iowa Theatre, 1936. Ground plan.

University of Iowa Theatre, 1936. Interior.

PLATE 22. Three Modern University Theatres of the Standard Proscenium Type

University of Wisconsin Theatre, 1939. Interior.

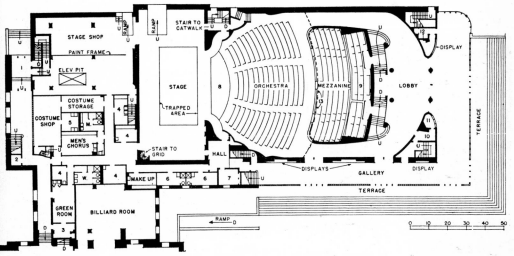

University of Wisconsin Theatre, 1939. Ground plan.

PLATE 22 (Continued)

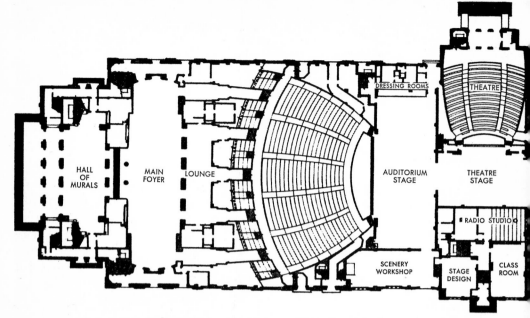

Indiana University Theatre, 1941. Ground plan.

Indiana University Theatre, 1941. Interior.

PLATE 22 (Continued)

Primitive Arena

Gilmor Brown's Playbox, Pasadena

PLATE 23. Arena Theatres

Penthouse Theatre, University of Washington

Ring Theatre, Miami University

PLATE 23 (Continued)

Margo Jones' Theatre, Dallas. Exterior.

Performance of *The Learned Young Ladies,* Molière, at Margo Jones' Theatre

PLATE 23 (Continued)

Grosses Schauspielhaus, Berlin, 1920

Sketch of performance in proposed theatre, University of Minnesota. Plans call for a flexible forestage mounted on four elevators.

PLATE 24. Semi-Arena Theatres

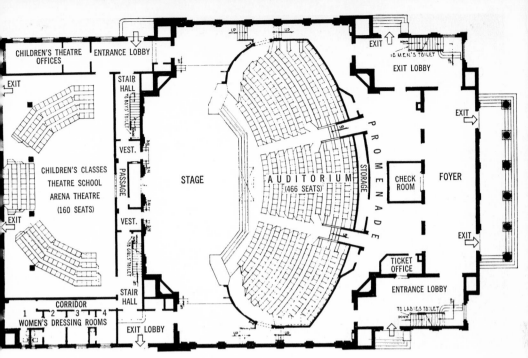

The Euclid–77th Street Cleveland Playhouse, 1953. Ground plan.

The Euclid–77th Street Cleveland Playhouse, 1953. Interior.

PLATE 24 (Continued)

Theatre and Student Art Center, Sarah Lawrence College, 1953. Interior.

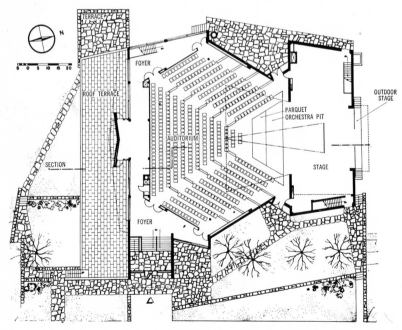

Theatre and Student Art Center, Sarah Lawrence College, 1953. Ground
plan.

PLATE 24 (Continued)

related to those already discussed. We can think of formalism almost as an "ism" to end all "isms." It arose as a reaction against all the fuss about styles and scenery. Someone shrewdly observed that during the world's two greatest periods of theatre, the Greek and the Elizabethan, there was no scenery, at least not in the conventional sense. These periods had used the forestage-façade type of theatre. Actors simply played against an accepted background that varied little from scene to scene, from play to play, or from season to season. It was a background essentially pleasing but at the same time formal and permanent—a stage on which and before which almost any play might be presented. Perhaps the best example of a comparatively modern theatre that has tried to return to the formalism of the days of Sophocles and Shakespeare is the *Théâtre du Vieux Colombier* that Jacques Copeau built in Paris in 1913. Some steps, some units, and the furnishings could be changed, but the idea of scenery in its popular sense was taboo. It is not necessary, however, to go to Paris to find a formal theatre. Outdoor and arena stages, which can be found in almost every state of the union, are also essentially formal. Even the conventional stage may use formal settings, the most common example being the cyclorama or arras setting used in most high schools. These curtained stages employ the same background not only for various plays but also for speakers, musicians, cheer leaders, and tumblers. A variation of the cyclorama setting is the space stage, which usually surrounds the playing area with black velour instead of the usual tan or grey, then sharply manipulates the lights so that only the actors, the properties, and occasional fragments of scenery stand out in a black void. Finally there is architectural formalism, which may consist of an expensive and elaborate arrangement of steps, levels, pillars, and screens, yet these are never so elaborate or so specific that they could not be used for more than one play. The one common element in all types of formalism is that the background could become an accepted environment for many plays.

THE FUNCTIONS OF SCENERY

Out of such theories and countertheories can anyone hope to arrive at a rational understanding of the place and function of scenery? Perhaps not entirely, yet some of the confusion can surely be eliminated. We can begin where we just left off by considering the formalist's challenge and asking, "Is scenery necessary? What if anything does scenery really add to the sum total of the theatrical experience?" These questions are not purely academic. The success of *Our Town* and of a few other plays on essentially bare Broadway stages, as well as the present-day popularity of arena and modified-arena productions, makes the challenge a practical and serious one.

Obviously if we limit "scenery" to its picture-proscenium style; if we think of it as painted flats, painted drops, columns, and levels, then scenery is not necessary, or at least not indispensable. But if we think of scenery in its larger sense, as the background against which, upon which, and in which a play is produced, there is no escape. In this larger sense all the nonscenery plays did have scenery. Actors cannot act in a vacuum. An environment of some sort is inevitable. In *Our Town* there was the back wall of the stage with its dirty radiators; in *Julius Caesar* there were levels and shafts of light; in the arena theatre there is the propertied acting area and the dim faces beyond; even in the space stage the black void itself is something. Consequently, in this larger sense the problem of whether or not there should be scenery vanishes. A background or environment of some kind is inevitable. The only question of importance becomes: Is the environment appropriate or inappropriate, effective or ineffective, an asset or a source of distraction? A designer who remembers this may save himself much senseless confusion.

But while in the final analysis scenery is a matter of effectiveness, this does not answer the question of what constitutes effectiveness. For obvious reasons such a question has never been, and never will be completely answered. Nevertheless we can eliminate some of the vagueness by considering a few of the theatrical functions that a good setting can perform.

Scenery Can Aid the Actor

John Dolman lists the functions of scenery as: (1) concealment, (2) decoration, (3) suggestion of mood, (4) suggestion of place, and (5) portrayal of place.[4] He says nothing, however, regarding the relationship of scenery to the actor's stage movement and stage business. Scenery's relationship to the actor is no new idea. It was clearly recognized by Appia and others, yet many still think of scenery primarily as something to be "looked at," not acted in or upon. As Robert Edmond Jones has implied, the questions is not what the set will look like, but what it will make the actor do. The first time we produced *Peter Pan* at the University of Minnesota we went to the trouble of making a real rope ladder for the pirate ship. Shortly before the play opened two art students confronted the technical director with the question, "Why go to the trouble and expense of making a real rope ladder when a more fantastic and interesting one could be painted on

[4] John Dolman, *op. cit.*, pp. 292–293.

a backdrop?" The question was answered when they saw what the actors did on the rope ladder. It was used as a lookout post; Lost Boys hung on it to save themselves from falling overboard, and finally at the grand climax it served as a battle ground. One of the most exciting moments of the entire production came as a six-foot-six pirate, knife in teeth, pursued little Michael up the ladder until both disappeared from sight. The melee below was forgotten; pirates and Lost Boys stopped their sword play to gaze aloft in horrified silence; even Captain Hook paused in his mortal combat with Peter. Then came a blood-curdling scream. Actors covered their faces in horror, and the body of Smee (a dummy of course) came plunging through space to land in the ocean beyond the ship with a mighty splash. Try this with a ladder painted on a backdrop!

Even Russian constructivism, which has failed to make sense to most Americans, begins to take on meaning as we consider what the actors *do* in these settings. Take, for example, the following description by Norris Houghton of the lover's entrance in Meyerhold's production of *The Magnificent Cuckold:*

At another theatre there would be a knock at the door, the man would enter, see the object of his affection, move toward her with eager steps, smile and take her in his arms. They would both "register" joy at the meeting. Meierhold places the lady at the foot of a tin slide, the lover climbs up a ladder to the top of the slide, zooms down it, feet first, knocks the lady off onto the floor, and shouts something that sounds like Russian for "Whee!" . . . Of course, Meierhold knows that lovers don't enter down slides in real life, but he believes . . . that the emotion of abandonment and joy with which the man is filled can much more accurately be revealed if he slides down a ten-foot S curve to meet his lady than if he follows the dictates of natural movement. When this is understood, there is some meaning to Meierhold's work.[5]

The designer is under constant temptation to design a set that will "look well," one that will bring a burst of applause from the audience as the curtain rises, for it is by the "looks" of the set that the average audience will judge his work. As will be explained later it is important and legitimate for the set to be attractive, but never at the expense of the actors' action. Scenery is essentially the environment in which the actors live and move (Plates 30 and 31).

Scenery Can Conceal What Would Otherwise Be Distracting

We have already seen that there must be some sort of background, and that this background, if inappropriate, may become a source of distraction.

[5] Norris Houghton, *Moscow Rehearsals,* Harcourt, Brace and Company, Inc., 1936, pp. 20, 21.

Even in "no scenery" productions some provision is usually made to get characters out of view when they are not supposed to be on stage. Moreover, in the conventional modern theatre the back wall of the average stage with its radiators, service doors, and piles of scenery, provides neither an attractive nor appropriate background. *Our Town* got by largely because of the novelty of the idea and because of the fact that the play was presentational and frankly theatrical in nature. It is highly significant that other plays have not followed its example. Of course, it is perfectly possible to design and build a theatre with a neutral and attractive background against which almost any play might be presented. The Greeks did it, the Elizabethans did it, Copeau did it; but until architects in general decide to make the undecorated stage more attractive, curtains, cycloramas, or some kind of scenery must ordinarily be used to cover its ugly nakedness.

In modern proscenium productions the requirement of concealment sometimes forces severe limitations upon the designer's freedom by introducing problems of masking. Exterior settings offer more difficulty in this respect than interiors. Unless the theatre is fortunate enough to have a sky dome or a full sky cyclorama, the necessity of designing masking pieces that will mask both sides and top of a setting becomes an annoying problem, one that beginning designers habitually neglect. There are several possible solutions. One is to mask the setting with curtains, preferably black velour. A second is to view the exterior through a huge archway or some other appropriate form that serves as a false proscenium. A third is to mask with trees, rocks, or some other integral part of the design. In any event something must be used; otherwise bricks, radiators, old scenery, and wandering stagehands will become the background.

Scenery Can Add an Element of Decoration

Few would be satisfied with concealment alone, for decoration is one of the oldest and most fundamental urges. The child and the savage no sooner think of a celebration than they begin to think of embellishment, of making the principal objects of the occasion colorful and exciting. Kept within sensible bounds there is nothing wrong with this urge. However, opinion as to what constitutes a well-decorated or attractive setting changes from generation to generation. Our grandfathers took delight in elaborately painted palaces and woodland glens, our parents in the minuteness and multiplicity of naturalistic detail; moderns may be devoted to expressionism, surrealism, or constructivism. As far as mere visual appearance is concerned, the most practical solution seems to be to consider both the needs of the individual play and current taste. If elaborate realism is out of style, there is little sense in trying to revive it.

Of course, attractiveness is not entirely a matter of style. There are principles of composition (unity, balance, rhythm, proportion, etc.) that are fairly constant, and with which every designer should be thoroughly familiar, but on the whole the matter of taste in decoration is a highly individual and elusive matter, one that is not likely to be acquired in a few easy lessons.

The Setting Can Create Atmosphere and Suggest Mood

It matters little whether one claims to be an expressionist or a realist, all agree that mood and atmosphere are of great importance. These can easily be defended as a genuine contribution to the final success of a play.

The realist tries to create his atmosphere by means of association. If, for example, he were trying to convey the terrifying atmosphere of the witches' cavern in *Macbeth,* he might design a cave with bats, spider webs, skeletons, and other objects commonly associated with terror. The expressionist, on the other hand, might depend upon abstraction, the inherent values of light, form, rhythm, and color. He would probably prefer it if the design conveyed the proper atmosphere of horror without the aid of anything recognizable as a "real" cavern. In actual practice, however, the realist and the expressionist tend to merge. The realist usually finds it necessary to select, to arrange, and to exaggerate, while the expressionist may despair of the intangibility of pure abstraction. His splotches of green may assume the form of grotesque mossy skeletons, his reds may become scarlet, spiderlike horrors. Such blending of styles is nothing to be alarmed about. As far as the stage is concerned realism is most dangerous when it stifles imagination by admitting nothing that cannot be found in nature, while expressionism is most dangerous when it stifles creativeness by insisting on complete abstraction, by fearing to bring in anything, no matter how effective it might be, if it looks too real. The scene designer's job is a practical one and he probably worries little about all this. As Robert Edmond Jones once said, "The problem is not one of expressionism but of expression."

One final comment on the subject of atmosphere: the designer must realize that lighting is his trump card. The most gruesome cavern scene will lose its effect under a brilliant flood of general illumination that reveals every seam and scratch on the scenery; while the gay colors of a lovely, springtime garden may become ominous when lights grow dim and shadows heavy. Sound effects also play their part: rain, wind, and thunder are as old as the theatre itself, not because they are either "real" or "abstract" but because they create atmosphere. For the lowliest groundling to the loftiest critic they fulfill the requirement of "expression."

Scenery Can Suggest Time and Place

Compared with the other functions of scenery, the contribution made by its indication of time and place is of minor significance. Realism as an end in itself is a thing of the past, though as a means to an end it may still serve a worthy function. There are times when storms, for example, may become a part of the action, as in *The Tempest*. Generally, however, such effects are used to create atmosphere, in which case the storm that creates the most atmosphere with the least distraction must be considered best. This does not necessarily mean that it must seem most "real."

There are obviously times when it clarifies the meaning of the play to see clearly that the actors are in a hovel, a palace, a prison, a forest; or it may be a genuine help to see clearly that it is evening or morning, June or December. But on the whole, such things are apparent to almost everyone, and the danger is not so much that such factual details will be slighted as that they will be overemphasized and utilized for their own sake. Hours of work in perfecting the suggestion of moonlight because moonlight happens to convey exactly the atmosphere and romantic beauty that a scene requires may be well spent, but the same devotion to perfecting the suggestion of moonlight just because you want it to look like real moonlight is another matter, one that belongs in the lighting laboratory, not in the play itself.

THE DESIGNER AND HIS LIMITATIONS

Compared with the painter the scene designer faces many limitations. First there are the physical limitations of the stage. Through a 15- by 25-foot proscenium opening he may be required to suggest castles, mountains, deserts, and the rolling sea. His two-dimensional paintings may fight with three-dimensional actors. His painted shadows may contrast with real shadows. His expressionistic set may fail to harmonize with the obvious "realness" of the actor. His setting might appear to be solidly convincing were it not necessary to shift it in 30 seconds. He might do wonders with plastic, chrome, and silk were they not so expensive.

Some limitations have, of course, been reduced by modern styles and by better theatres. Elevator, wagon, and revolving stages can eliminate most shifting and handling problems. Better lighting, better cycloramas, and better flying systems can always help. However, the total contribution of such modern improvements to the final effect can be easily overestimated. Excellent scenery has the most amazing habit of making its appearance in barns, old mills, and cracker-box stages.

It almost seems safe to say that an outstanding designer will turn out excellent sets whether he works in an ideal theatre or in one where facilities are meager. Many of the best professional designs could be set up on all but the most limited stages. Equipment can help, but the chief bottleneck is still human—still the designer and his imagination or absence of it.

As to simplification of scenery for nonprofessional use, such things as selective realism, formalism, and unit sets have already been mentioned. It should be emphasized that unit sets can be employed with almost any style, as can the idea behind selective realism; but for the most part those who would turn out effective scenery for the amateur stage must rely heavily upon ingenuity, flexibility, and especially upon the judicious use of materials at hand. In Florida, for example, the easiest way to suggest a tropical forest might be to decorate the stage with palms or other tropical foliage that might be found almost at the stage door. If skillfully selected, arranged, and well lighted, results might be satisfying, expense and effort negligible. On the other hand, if a Canadian theatre were to import real palm trees, the practice might suggest Belasco realism in its most expensive and unnecessary form. In other words, the good designer is seldom a slave to a particular style. Some achieve better results through a knack for selecting and arranging ordinary things they find about them than do others who squander time, effort, and money. There is no substitute for good taste and ingenuity. (Plate 32).

ORGANIZATION AND PROCEDURE

There is obviously no set technique by which designers work. Jo Mielziner likes to begin by painting figures of the actors at important moments in the script and then fill in the scenic background about them. Lee Simonson, on the other hand, usually begins with ground plans and follows with elevations and working drawings. He may never bother to work out a colored sketch at all. Yet while methods vary, the following procedure is standard, at least for the beginning designer.

The designer submits either a model of the setting, done in color and to scale, or a water-color sketch, ground plan, and elevation (Plate 33). The last two are mechanical drawings and should be drawn to scale. In commercial and large noncommercial theatres the actual work of constructing and painting the scenery is usually entrusted to other craftsmen, though the designer usually maintains a constant check on the work. In smaller organizations the designer may be responsible for both the creation and the execution of the design. This may be exhausting, but there are times when it has resulted in beautifully integrated productions. In fact, it does not seem to matter much what particular system is followed, provided there is an organized system of some kind.

CHAPTER XI

The Crafts

IDEAS AND DREAMS WITHOUT THE SKILL AND CRAFTSMANSHIP TO EXPRESS them can be quite as futile as skill and craftsmanship without ideas or dreams. Yet in spite of this obvious truth many students shy away from craft courses in theatre, many educators still oppose the inclusion of such courses in a college curriculum, and many American institutions of higher learning still refuse to allow the teaching of such skills. Some colleges permit the production of plays provided that only the literary values are emphasized, or as a student of one large university recently expressed it, "We can do plays provided that we do not do them very well."

A sincere desire on the part of some educators to deëmphasize "skill" and to avoid any tendency to permit a liberal education to become a trade school education is understandable; but surely the truly educated man should be able to *do* as well as know what to do. Like the public speaker and the writer, the student in theatre should strive for a balance between something to say and skill in saying it; both qualities are necessary. To do a production of *Hamlet* that will excite discussion, stimulate ideas, and fulfill its function either as art or education, demands that the production be done with skill and craftsmanship. While the crafts and techniques that go into such a production should be regarded as a means to an end and not as the end, this does not mean that they should be ignored.

The foregoing discussion is not intended to give the impression that creation and craftsmanship, or if you prefer, art and technique, are somehow antagonistic, and that development of one is likely to inhibit the other. There is no evidence that skill in the use of even such homely and practical objects as a saw and hammer will cripple the mind or blight the soul. Yet one of the most persistent false assumptions made by so many with a taste for the literary is that good playwriting is somehow antagonistic to good production. Actually the reasoning of such purists goes through not one but two steps, for they begin by asking for an actor who will "just say the lines," then ask that he be placed in the simplest possible setting, fearing that the acting will detract from the play and the scenery from the actor. Actually, the reverse is nearer the truth. Time after time imaginative lights, sound, and scenery have stirred life into unimaginative actors, after which actors, lights, sound, and scenery together have stirred life into the play. True, bad productions can be beautifully and skillfully staged, but to one such, hundreds are miserably staged. A high degree of correlation usually exists between the quality of the acting, the quality of the staging, and the degree of success with which the playwright's intention is conveyed to the audience. Excellence in any one element of theatre is likely to start a chain reaction that will affect the others. They are more likely to function as partners than as competitors. To repeat, something to say plus skill in saying it is the desirable balance, and this seems to require that the vision of the playwright, the director, and the designer be augmented by the skill and craftsmanship of the technicians.

For both the student and the teacher of theatre, technical courses also provide a kind of educational balance, in that after dealing with such intangible and subjective matters as acting and directing, it is refreshing to turn to such a tangible and objective subject as stagecraft, which is comparatively easy to standardize, even though ingenuity and imagination are frequently indispensable. On the whole the crafts provide an opportunity to be both objective and definite, to distinguish the right way from the wrong way, and to make use of formulas and techniques that stick. They give the theatre student some training in the exact methods of science to balance his training in the more intuitive and creative methods of art. Such a balance is highly desirable.

As to the history of the crafts there is little to relate. The technical developments in stage carpentry, painting, and shifting are of minor importance. A few notes, however, about the men responsible for these crafts may be significant. For example, the elaborate technical effects achieved by some of the medieval mystery and miracle plays were undoubtedly related to the fact that the trade guilds were responsible for these productions. This meant that some of the best technical skill and knowledge of the day was available to provide the hell mouth with its smoke, fireworks, dragons, and other spectacular elements that contributed no small share to the entertainment.

Those working behind the scenes after the English Restoration also left their mark. Terms like "belaying pin" and "pin rail" are nautical in origin, and their transfer to the theatre is easily explained by the fact that in England much of the backstage work was done by sailors, who were either on leave or retired. These men knew how to handle ropes and rigging. They seem to have enjoyed working backstage, probably because feminine glamour provided an even greater incentive than did the ropes and rigging.

In America the most significant item in the group history of those who have labored behind the scenes concerns the development of the stagehands' union, which was organized as a defense against intolerable abuses of the old system. Of all those the theatre has exploited and neglected, none compare with the men who worked behind the wings, in the flies, or in the ill-equipped shops and storage crannies under the stage. These were often either sensitive and skillful workers who were genuinely devoted to backstage work, or else unsuccessful actors clinging to anything that gave them some foothold in the theatre. They were therefore easy prey for greedy managers. Finally, in self-defense, these stagehands organized, fought for power, and won. Unfortunately their victory has not been an unqualified blessing as far as the general good of the theatre is concerned. All too often the stagehands' union has countered the selfishness of management with a limited and narrow selfishness of its own, until along with commercialism and competition of movies, the shortsighted policy of the union must bear a share of responsibility for the decline of the legitimate professional theatre in America. Many a small company could have survived the depression had the stagehands been willing to share with actors and managers in the necessary curtailment of income. Many a traveling company has collapsed under the burden of paying a full crew of local stand-ins to do nothing, while the company's own crews shifted the scenes. Many a show has suffered intense damage to morale because of the demoralizing attitude of stagehands who could see nothing more in the production than a temporary job for themselves.

The gravest charge against the stagehands' union, however, is not that it has often forced companies to pay more than its services were worth, but that it has denied its own members the joy and satisfaction of a job well done. It seems doubtful that the legitimate theatre can survive without the loyalty, devotion, and enthusiasm of all who work in it, and yet any union member guilty of such enthusiasm is likely to find himself labeled a "scab." A few years ago two famous actors were appearing in a Shakespearean production at a large state university. The second change of scenery ran far overtime. Finally the local manager went backstage to determine the cause of the delay. He was told that a small table used in the preceding scene had not been moved. In reply to his query, "Why doesn't some one move it?" he was informed that the property crew could not move it because there was a lamp on it and only the electrical crew could disconnect the lamp. In reply to his query, "Where are the electricians?" no one knew. The manager finally found them smoking in the basement. According to them they thought the lamp had been disconnected and that the shift was long since completed.

While an incident such as this is extreme, and in this case may have been influenced by ill will between the university and the union, it nevertheless illustrates the narrow, shortsighted attitude of all too many union members. The legitimate theatre has survived and can survive only when there is a general *esprit de corps,* when there is enthusiasm, work, and effort far beyond the call of duty on the part of actors, director, designers, and stagehands. Hours mean very little to the true craftsman or artist.

Nonprofessional groups should think twice before they try to become professional, for to do so is to abandon that blissful state where stagehands, actors, directors, and ushers all have a stake in the show, where lights help props and actors double as members of the shifting crew, where hard work and extra work reflect honor and credit, where one can contribute to the limit of his abilities without being labeled "scab."

The ultimate solution to the union problem is difficult to predict. The root of the difficulty in the first place, and still the barrier to any ideal solution, lies in the fact that too many producers (professional and nonprofessional) will exploit labor if they possibly can. In the face of this, labor cannot be blamed for setting up rigid rules for self-protection. Fortunately most unions are liberal about making exceptions to these rules when dealing with nonprofessionals and semiprofessionals. If the union wants to be unreasonable, however, it has the power to put the theatre out of business and its members out of jobs.

THE CONSTRUCTION OF SCENERY

Although a thorough study of scene construction can be very technical and exacting, the majority of a theatre's construction problems can be solved by a few basic techniques. It should be obvious that, unlike the work of the cabinetmaker, that of the stage carpenter is not ordinarily scrutinized from close range, not ordinarily permanent, and not ordinarily viewed from more than one side. These considerations greatly simplify his task, and a moderately gifted individual can soon learn to build good scenery. On the other hand, let no one imagine that skill, know-how, and good judgment are unimportant. In fact in certain respects the construction of scenery is more difficult than cabinetmaking. Speed is almost always a factor. In the time it takes the cabinetmaker to finish a single unit of furniture the scene carpenter may be expected to turn out a palace, a city street, or the Forest of Arden. Scenery must also be tough and rigidly joined, for the stress of rapid shifting leaves no time for delicate handling. At the same time it should be light, portable, inexpensive, and capable of being easily remodeled for future productions.

We have already seen that the scene designer is normally expected to provide either (1) a model or (2) a ground plan, elevation, and sketch of the setting. From these the working drawings (Fig. 19) are prepared.

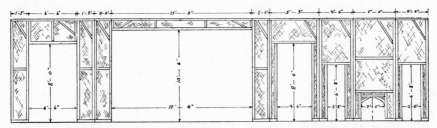

Fig. 19. Working Drawings. A rear elevation (simplified) of the setting for *Blithe Spirit*, Plate 34. Large rear elevations, drawn mechanically and to scale, plus detail drawings and ground plans provide the basic blueprints which guide the technicians in building the set.

Working drawings resemble elevation drawings, except that they view the set from the rear and consequently indicate the basic plan of construction. A wall of a realistic interior setting, for example, is almost never made in a single section, but consists of smaller units known as flats and jogs.

In order to dispel any notion that no brains or skill are required to construct scenery, let us consider in moderate detail the construction of one of these basic units. At first glance the building of such a unit seems obvious and foolproof, since a flat is nothing but a light wooden framework covered with muslin or canvas (Fig. 20). But although a good technician can build one in less than an hour there are many pitfalls into which beginners habitually plunge. Let us consider a few of the more common errors.

To begin with, take such a simple matter as the size of the flat. In our case the plans call for one 5 feet wide and 12 feet high, yet it is amazing how many beginners will cut the stiles (the side members of the frame) a full 12 feet in length. Then when the flat is assembled they are aston-

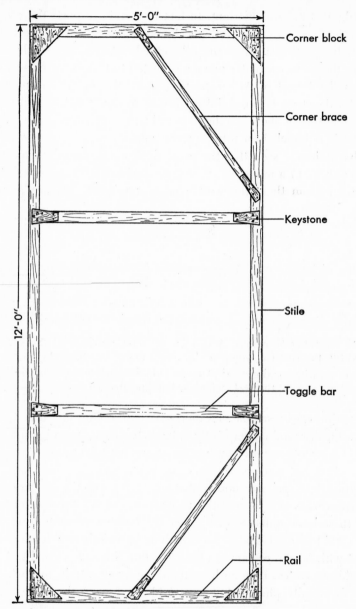

FIG. 20. The frame of the standard flat.

ished to find it approximately 12 feet 6 inches high, because a 3-inch board, the rail, has been added at each end (Fig. 21).[1]

[1] The 1 by 3-inch piece from which the frame of the average flat is made is not ordinarily a full 3 inches in width nor is it a full inch in thickness. These measurements were reduced when the lumber passed through the planing mill.

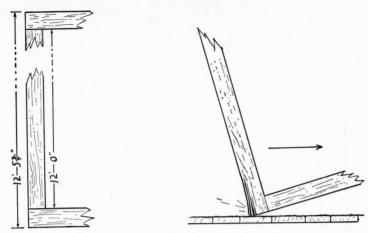

Fig. 21. Common Errors: stiles and rails.

Another common error is to extend the stiles past the rails rather than the rails past the stiles when joining these with the usual butt joint. If the flat is small and need never be shifted by dragging the bottom across a rough floor the mistake is not serious, but otherwise the ends of the stiles are almost certain to splinter, and the accompanying vibrations will be heard to the back of the house.

Several errors are commonly made in joining members of the frame together. Many kinds of joints are possible, but, as already mentioned, the most common type is a butt joint reinforced by a corner block and fastened with wedge-shaped nails known as clout nails.

If the outside grain of the corner block, which is cut from ¼-inch 3-ply, runs parallel to the crack between the rail and stile, the result will be a very weak joint that can be broken with the bare hands (Fig. 22).

If one forgets to leave a space the thickness of a 1-inch board between

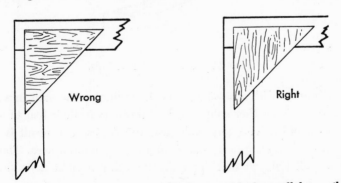

Wrong   Right

Fig. 22. Common Error: grain of corner block parallel to rail.

the edge of the corner block and the edge of the stile there will be trouble should the flat ever need to be joined to a second flat with the backs at right angles to one another. The edge of the second flat will rest on the corner blocks, leaving a ¼-inch crack that can be eliminated only by much awkward extra labor (Fig. 23).

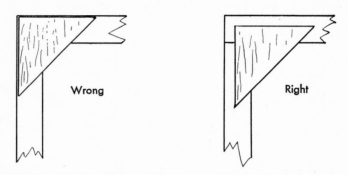

FIG. 23. Common Error: corner block extends to edge of stile.

The placement and arrangement of clout nails is important. Even such a small matter as the relationship between a single clout nail and the grain of the wood can mean the difference between a solid joint and a weak one, for if the wedge-shaped nail is driven so that it spreads the grain of the wood the board is likely to split (Fig. 24).

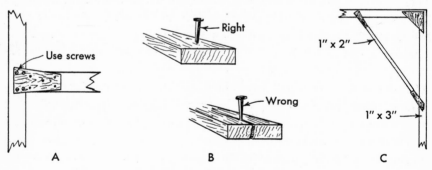

FIG. 24. Construction details.

Some beginners with a passion for neatness line up the nails in a straight row. The result is another split board. Still others in their fear of splitting the lumber avoid driving any nails near the edges. The result is a weak joint because all the support comes from a very limited area. Those who know best will tell you that approximately eleven clout nails should be used as indicated in the sketch marked "right" (Fig. 25). The seven nails marked with x are the crucial ones.

If you will return to the drawing of the entire flat (Fig. 20) you will notice that there are horizontal members between the rails. These are known as toggle bars and are usually placed 5 feet or less apart. They are joined to the stiles with butt joints essentially as just described, except that

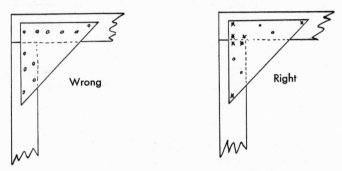

Fig. 25.   Nail placement in corner blocks.

a piece of 3-ply shaped like the keystone instead of like a triangle is used. It is also highly advisable to fasten these to the stile with screws rather than clout nails (Fig. 24), for changes in the position of these toggle bars are frequently necessary. For example, even with reasonably complete planning, one may find after the set is up for dress rehearsal that a toggle bar must be raised or lowered to provide a base for fastening a picture or lighting fixture to the wall. In such a case it is infinitely easier to remove and reinsert a few screws than it is to tear down the set, lay the flat on the floor, pull the old clout nails, and drive new ones. Many technicians prefer to dispense with clout nails altogether and use screws throughout for fastening corner blocks as well as keystones. In the nonprofessional shop where scenery is frequently reused, the practice has obvious advantages.

There are also tricks of the trade when it comes to covering a flat. Many beginners make the mistake of tacking the covering material along the outside edge of rails and stiles, then find it next to impossible to glue the material to the frame. Others fasten the material to corner braces and toggle bars, which thereafter insist on being visible from the front. The experienced technician proceeds as follows. After placing the frame of the flat on a bench, table, or floor with corner blocks down, he spreads muslin or canvas over the top surface. Next he fastens it to inside edge of the rails and stiles with carpet tacks or wire staples. He then turns back the loose

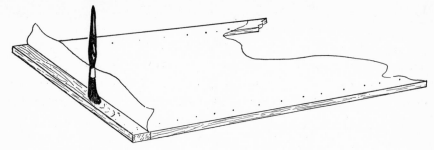

FIG. 26.   Tacking and gluing.

edges as illustrated (Fig. 26) and applies a coat of hot dope. The covering material is then pressed firmly into the dope and the edges are trimmed with a sharp knife. After the dope is thoroughly dry, a size coat and a flame-proofing solution[2] are applied, and the flat is ready to be painted.

Even the preparation of dope can present unexpected problems. Many an amateur has had the painful experience of using pure liquid (fish) glue as dope, only to discover that it is next to impossible to prevent the glue from staining through and discoloring whatever scene paint is afterward applied. The scene carpenter who knows his job begins with either flake glue or furniture glue. He places the desired amount in a container, covers it with water, soaks it overnight, then heats it in a double boiler until it dissolves into a hot liquid known as concentrated glue. If he wants to glue muslin or canvas to the frames of flats he mixes one part of this hot concentrated glue with one or two parts of whiting and adds hot water until it becomes a creamy paste. He calls the mixture dope.[3] If he wants size water he adds one part hot concentrated glue to from eight to sixteen parts of water. The use of a double boiler when heating glue is of extreme importance, since burned glue emits a sickening odor.

Flats are built in a wide variety of sizes, although 5 feet 9 inches is the maximum width used on commercial stages. (Narrow flats are called jogs, short ones are called plugs.) Larger flats are not only difficult to load through a boxcar door if the show tours, but are also hard for one man to handle. Since most scene canvas comes in a 72-inch width, a flat width of 5 feet 9 inches leaves enough material for easy trimming. In the off-Broadway theatre, however, these considerations may not be significant. Especially in building a flat that is to be temporary, it is often wise to exceed

[2] The formula for a good flameproofing solution is one pound of borax plus one pound sal ammoniac plus three quarts of water.

[3] There are many other satisfactory formulas.

the 5 feet 9 inch maximum. Arbitrary standards should never interfere with common sense.

The above account may seem unnecessarily detailed, but actually it is only an introduction to one of the more simple and fundamental processes involved in the building of a setting. The construction of scenery is not so simple as it sometimes appears to those who never see more than the finished product. During the remainder of this section, however, techniques and methods employed in scene construction will of necessity be treated in a much more condensed and general fashion.

Modifications of the Flat

Before leaving the subject of the simple flat, we should note some of the common ways in which it can be varied. If the stage carpenter wishes to construct a flat with an opening for a doorway, he need only place a toggle bar so that the lower edge falls at the desired height, add two uprights to frame the sides of the opening and finally cut out the bottom rail so that actors will not literally come tripping onto the stage (Fig. 27).

Fig. 27.   Flats modified to receive doors and windows.

A window flat is made in the same manner as a door flat, except that a second toggle bar must be added to provide a bottom for the window opening. An archway (Fig. 28) likewise employs the same technique ex-

FIG. 28. Flat for an archway.

cept that curved pieces called sweeps must be added at the top of the opening to form whatever pattern of archway is desired.

Each of the above techniques provides only the opening for a door, a window, or an archway. The construction of the door, window, or arch unit itself, including thicknesses, facings, shutters, and decorations, is beyond the scope of this chapter. Moreover these units ordinarily involve techniques of standard carpentry that are not unique to the theatre. One exception is the manner in which such units are commonly fastened into flat openings by means of strap hinges, as illustrated in Fig. 29.

Joining of Flats

Flats seldom stand alone, of course, but are used in various combinations with other flats; this ordinarily requires hardware for fastening them together. Not so many years ago the standard practice was to lash flats together as indicated in Fig. 30. To do this the technician attaches a lash line of No. 8 cotton sash cord to the right upper corner of each flat and cuts it the same length as the flat. It is then lashed behind cleats provided at intervals along the stiles of each flat and is finally tied off around tie-off cleats placed about 30 inches from the floor.

Since lashing always leaves a visible crack between the flats, the practice

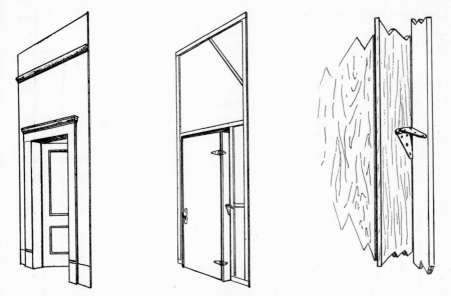

Fig. 29.   Door unit held into flat opening by means of strap hinges.

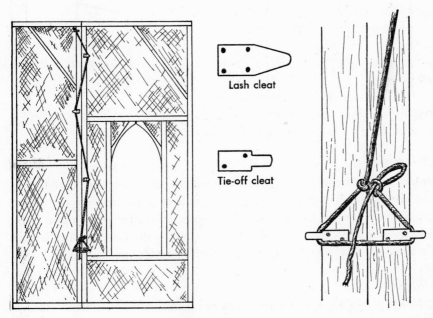

Lash cleat

Tie-off cleat

Fig. 30.   Lashing.

has been generally discarded except at the corners of a setting or where a crack can be covered or disguised in some way. To eliminate cracks in a setting that is to be assembled for the duration of a given show or else moved as a unit, each wall is simply battened together from behind and the cracks between the individual flats covered by pasting a long narrow strip of muslin or canvas (a dutchman) over them.

In cases where a play must go on tour or where flats must be folded in shifting and can no longer be battened together from the back, two and sometimes three flats can be hinged together and combined into two-folds and three-folds (Fig. 31). To do this three back-flap hinges are usu-

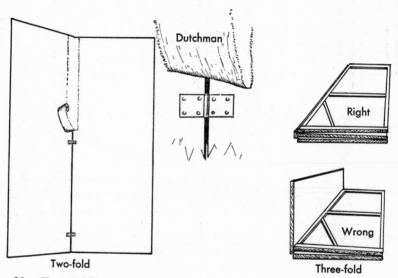

Fig. 31. Two-Folds and Three-Folds. Note that the three-fold must use a tumbler in order to fold.

ally set into the front face of the flats that are to be joined together. A dutchman wide enough to cover not only the crack between the flats but also the hinges is then applied. If three flats of approximately equal size are to be hinged in this manner, it is necessary to insert an extra 1- by 3-inch piece known as a tumbler between two of the flats to avoid having the third flat bind against the edge of the first or vice versa.

Profiles

Many pieces such as two-dimensional trees, columns, foliage clumps, and ground rows representing mountains or city skylines call for units with irregular edges. Such pieces are known as profiles, and all employ the same basic construction technique.

If the unit is small—not over 4 by 8 feet—it is possible simply to outline it on a large piece of either 3-ply or wallboard, saw out the silhouette, and paint it. If a larger unit is necessary the scene technician will probably follow the type of construction shown in Fig. 32. This consists of building

Fig. 32. Profile construction.

a frame, using essentially the same technique as in flat construction except that the outside edge of the frame is lined with 3-ply. If a table saw is available, it is wise to notch the frame as illustrated, so that the face of the 3-ply lies flush with the face of the frame. Units such as large ground rows are usually made in two or more pieces and hinged to provide greater ease in handling.

Cutouts

When the irregular outline lies within the frame as in the case of an ornamental grill, a balustrade, or certain foliage units, the cutout technique may be the answer. Suppose it were necessary to construct the ornamental railing shown in Fig. 33. The stage carpenter begins by building a flat. He then paints on the posts, using plenty of paint and glue to provide stiffness. After the paint has hardened he cuts out and discards the unpainted material between the posts, and finally reinforces the posts by gluing scrim

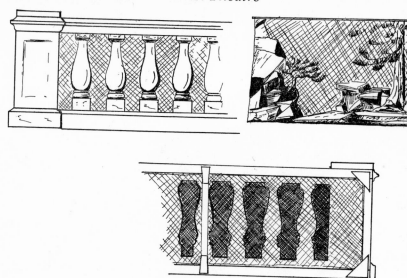

FIG. 33. Cut-out construction.

or netting across the back of them. If the unit is not framed but flexible, as in the case of a foliage border, he substitutes rosine (a type of glue that is flexible) in place of the dope (which will crack) in gluing the cutout to the scrim.

Maché

When irregular three-dimensional objects such as rocks, tree trunks, and capitals of pillars must be constructed, the maché technique (Fig. 34) is employed. First the stage carpenter builds a rough wooden framework of the object. He next nails chicken wire over the framework, and molds it into the desired shape. Finally he covers the wire with old muslin or canvas that has been soaked in a solution of old pigment and dope. The dope and pigment mixture should be hot and of creamy consistency. Old newspapers may be used to build up thickness and body. The last coat, however, should be of cloth, and should be applied in small enough pieces to avoid wrinkles.

A new product, Celastic, is excellent for maché work. It hardens to a tough leatherlike finish, and while too expensive for such large articles as tree trunks and rocks, can be used to excellent advantage in reproducing such objects as armor, statuary, and vases. The final product is light, tough, and comparatively unbreakable.

FIG. 34.   Maché construction.

Parallels

As in the case of doors and windows, the construction of most platforms and stairways belongs in a course of stagecraft. There is, however, one unit that is so useful and unique to the theatre that it should be explained. This is the parallel, a type of platform that can be folded and stored away when not in use. The top, usually cut from a solid piece of 5-ply, is detachable. In most cases the sides and ends are constructed in a manner resembling small flats, as illustrated (Fig. 35). The essential element is the hinging arrangement. Two corners diagonal from one another may be hinged on the inside, but the opposite corners must hinge on the outside. Otherwise the frame will bind and refuse to fold.

Cycloramas and Curtains

Curtains for stage use are ordinarily made in much the same way whether they are to be used as sky cyclorama, scrim, or drapes. Strips of material are sewed together with the seams running vertically. A heavy strip of burlap or canvas webbing is then sewed securely across the top of each section (Fig. 36). Large grommets are inserted along the top, and tie lines are inserted into the grommets. The hem at the bottom of the curtain is usually made large enough to form a pocket that can be weighted with a chain or a pipe batten. Velour curtains and others used for similar purposes usually have fullness sewed in at the time they are made. Scrims

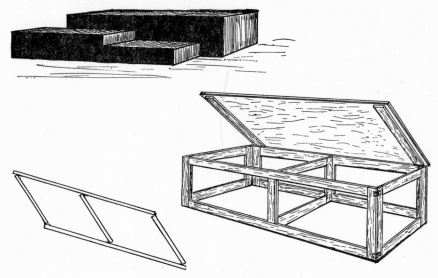

FIG. 35.   Parallels.

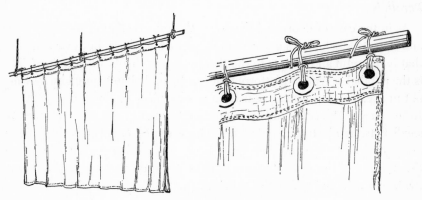

FIG. 36.   Curtains and cyclorama.

and sky cycloramas are, of course, made so that they can be stretched tight.

It is somewhat surprising that the twentieth century has seen so few new developments in techniques of scene construction. Some effective use has been made of aluminum scaffolding. New plastic materials have occasionally been employed, but on the whole methods of construction have changed little. With so many exciting new developments on every side it seems that the imaginative technician should someday find ways of adapting more of these to the stage.

There is no substitute for intelligence, resourcefulness, and ingenuity on the part of the scene technician, especially when faced with a limited budget. Even the most complete textbooks on the subject, including Burris-Meyer and Cole's outstanding *Scenery for the Theatre,* cannot cover all the techniques that one who works in the theatre will need to employ. On the other hand, it is well to remember that scene construction, unlike many elements in theatre, is essentially a craft rather than an art. Many nonprofessionals waste time and money trying to build scenery in original ways when the standard methods developed by technicians who have spent a lifetime in theatre would be much simpler, faster, and more economical.

THE PAINTING OF SCENERY

As noted in the discussion of scenic design, the art of scene painting came into prominence during the Renaissance, and dominated the stage during the seventeenth, eighteenth, and nineteenth centuries. With the coming of realism and modernism, the scene painter with his innumerable stencils and elaborate techniques lost much of his prestige, but even so the art—or perhaps we should say craft—of scene painting is important (Plate 34). Therefore, an introduction to a few fundamentals is included here.

Scene Paints

1. In most scene shops dry colors are standard.[4] The least expensive of all scene paints, they come in powdered form (a few pulp colors come in paste), and are easily prepared, mixed, and stored. There is a wide selection of colors, and they are easy to use. No matter how long they set, they can be removed from brushes, hands, and floors by simply washing with water. They dry to a soft, flat finish, which is generally desirable on stage.

2. In recent years casein paints have challenged the supremacy of dry colors for scene painting.[5] They come in paste form, are prepared by simply adding water, and the colors are generally of excellent quality. They cover unusually well and are easy to handle, although if allowed to dry thoroughly (usually a matter of days) they become insoluble. This is ordinarily an advantage rather than a disadvantage, for sometimes, especially if the show goes on tour, a waterproof paint job is a necessity. As to disadvantages: partly used cans of paste have a tendency to dry and deteriorate; clothing and brushes must be cleaned before the paint has thoroughly set; the cost is greater than for dry colors. Yet, all things considered, the ad-

[4] Dry colors are prepared by mixing them with size water. Size water is prepared by adding one part of hot concentrated glue to approximately ten parts of water. A small amount of carbolic acid is ordinarily included to prevent decay.

[5] Resin and rubber base paints are also being used but are rather expensive.

vantages tend to balance the disadvantages, and many scene shops have switched from dry colors to casein paints.

3. Oil paints and varnishes are almost never employed on stage except in special instances, such as the painting of certain properties. In general they are expensive, inflammable, slow drying, and dirty to handle. Brushes, clothing, and floors when splashed with oil paints should be cleaned immediately with turpentine, a process both expensive and inconvenient.

4. Metallic paints (bronze, aluminum, and many other hues) have some value, especially in the property department. They are ordinarily used sparingly, and primarily for decoration or detail work.

5. Shellac is frequently useful. It dries quickly and is sometimes applied over scene paint to counteract the tendency of that paint to rub off when subjected to heavy wear. It can also be used to give a hard, glossy effect to a surface, or to give a varnished effect to woodwork.

Brushes and Equipment

The most common brush in the scene shop is the four- or five-inch lay-in brush (Fig. 37). Dutch brushes five to eight inches in width are generally

6" dutch   4" lay-in   2" lay-in   Liners

FIG. 37. Paint brushes.

better but are expensive. Many nonprofessionals rely upon inexpensive fiber brushes for their basic work. While good equipment is desirable, it is consoling to know that in most present-day scene shops any kind of brush is usually superior to the technician wielding it. Some scenic artists turn out beautiful work using equipment that most modern university students would shudder to touch.

The brushes mentioned are all large and are used for applying base coats where speed and ease of application are important. In addition, a few smaller brushes 1 to 3 inches in width are useful, while a few long-handled lining brushes are quite indispensable for certain detail work.

The cleaning and care of brushes is extremely important. A $45.00 dutch brush can be ruined during the course of a single show by careless treatment, whereas it will last many years in the loving hands of a real craftsman. The care is simple. Brushes used in oil paints or varnish should be cleaned with turpentine; those used in shellac, with wood alcohol; and those used in scene paints or casein paints, with water. At the end of each day painters with pride in their work clean the brushes thoroughly, smooth the bristles neatly into place, and hang them up to dry.

Techniques of Painting

Even today a gifted scenic artist is a great asset to any producing organization. Though naturalism and romanticism are no longer in vogue, there is still a great need for artists who understand highlight and shadow, color and form, and know how to create the illusion of the third dimension. Such skills, however, are beyond the scope of the present discussion; also they are largely a matter of practice and experience. Therefore only a few of the basic techniques that the layman might employ in painting the average setting will be considered.

The base coat is applied with a large brush.[6] Good scene painters work easily but rapidly, using the ends of the bristles, and wielding the brush in a pattern of large X's. If the job is a good one, an even base color will appear when the flats have dried.

Scenery is almost never used with a base color alone. The painter applies a secondary coat to give it texture (Fig. 38), and especially to cover the defects (dutchmen, patches, nailheads, and bumps) that tend to loom vividly on a perfectly smooth, plain surface. This secondary coat is usually applied by one of the following techniques.

1. Spattering is perhaps the most useful. Some practice is required to develop the necessary skill. A brush with long bristles is ordinarily preferred. It is dipped lightly into the secondary color, dried somewhat by squeezing or shaking the bristles, then tapped across the free hand or wrist in such a way that small dots of pigment are sprayed against the flat surface. If the dots are too large the painter knows that the paint is too thin, the brush too large, or the bristles too wet.

2. Stippling is ordinarily done with a sponge, although burlap and other materials may be employed. The painter simply dips the sponge in the

---

[6] If new, the scenery should be sized and flameproofed before the base coat is applied. See p. 226.

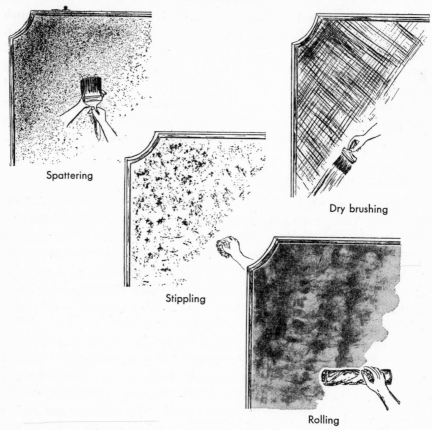

Spattering

Dry brushing

Stippling

Rolling

Fig. 38. Painting techniques.

secondary color, drys it slightly, and applies it to the flat, using a light, sharp, patting motion.

3. Dry brushing includes crosshatching, and is both popular and useful. Secondary coats are simply applied with a partly dry brush. Plaid or tapestrylike textures, as well as wood graining, can be suggested by this method.

4. Rolling is sometimes effective. The common rollers used in modern home decoration may be used to apply base coats as well as secondary colors, though the flexibility of canvas on a flat makes a roller less satisfactory than it is on a solid plaster wall. A practically dry roller can be used to produce interesting effects and textures. Rollers covered with burlap, Turkish toweling, and other coarse materials give the best patterns.

Other common techniques employed by scene painters include the use

The Crafts

of spray guns and stencils.[7] The things that really matter in scene painting, however, are beyond the scope of this chapter; in fact, beyond the scope of an entire book, for these things involve such items as taste, color, and a sense of design; they also include the skill and craftsmanship that commonly comes only from practice and experience.

THE SHIFTING OF SCENERY

Good sceneshifting is a far greater problem today than it once was. Audiences accustomed to an uninterrupted flow of action in movies, radio, and television are no longer content to pause from five to twenty-five minutes between each scene while stagehands laboriously shift the scenery. Modern settings, moreover, are usually much heavier and more complex than the old painted wings and drops that once were standard. More numerous too are multiple-scene plays. Fast shifting has become a necessity.

Today many methods of shifting are employed, but none is perfect; all have advantages and disadvantages. No system can act as a substitute for careful planning, imaginative organization, and effective rehearsal. Shifts that would normally take four to five minutes can be cut to as little as twenty seconds by the split-second coördination of an excellent shifting crew. Nor is the shifting problem one that can be delayed until dress rehearsal. In a multiple-set show the requirements of shifting should be a major factor in determining the design of the scenery itself. Somewhere in the rehearsal schedule it may be necessary also to arrange for technical rehearsals that concentrate on the movement of scenery alone, and finally it will almost certainly be necessary to coördinate this with lights, sound, movement of properties, and movement of actors. Nowhere in theatre is coördination and high morale at a greater premium.

As to the basic methods employed in the handling of scene shifts, we have already considered the simultaneous setting, where all the scenes are set up at once; the Elizabethan system, where scenes alternated between the forestage and inner stage; and the Inigo Jones system, where the scenes were shifted by sliding flats in grooves. Following Jones, the craze for spectacular scenery soon led to the development of elaborate flying systems, which, although employed primarily to achieve such effects as the illusion of drifting clouds, were also used in the shifting of scenes. With the coming of the box set and realism, the flying of scenery was partially replaced by the hinging and lashing of flats. Finally, as sets became

[7] Real wallpaper is sometimes used for realistic interior settings.

heavier, more plastic, and more dependent upon steps and levels, it became increasingly necessary to resort to the use of heavy mechanical devices, such as wagons, revolving stages, and elevator stages, in order to meet the demands of quick and efficient shifting.

Running of Scenery

Of all the systems of shifting still in use today the most common is probably the lashing and running of flats. Many stages are so limited in floor space, so lacking in flying space, and so poorly equipped in general that no other system of shifting is practical. The procedure in shifting a typical box setting by this method might be about as follows. The ceiling of the first set is raised; lights and backings are cleared; props are moved away from the walls and toward the front of the acting area; then the flats and jogs composing the set are unlashed one by one, run to a backstage area and stacked in order. Properties from the first set are then struck and properties for the coming scene moved to the front and center of the acting area; flats and jogs composing the second set are now run into place and lashed; properties are moved into place; backing lights are set in; the ceiling is lowered; actors are called, and the show is ready to resume its action. While a well-trained crew can become highly efficient in this method of shifting, they obviously can never hope to reduce shifting time enough to avoid a distinct break in the action of the play. If such breaks are repeated too often during the course of an evening they may well prove fatal to the play's success.

Flying

On stages equipped with a gridiron, the flying of scenery can often assist in shifting. It is possible, in fact, to fly an entire set, though this is seldom done, since it practically eliminates the possibility of using the flying space for anything else. Exterior units such as trees and foliage drops are especially adaptable to flying. Moreover, a good flying system will prove to be useful in handling such things as draperies, cycloramas, and front curtains. Two basic systems are employed. The ordinary system consists of a set of three lines: center, short, and long (Fig. 39). Each goes from the top of the unit to be flown, over a loft block on the grid, over a head block above the fly gallery, and down to the pin rail where the flyman, after raising the drop, ties off the lines on a belaying pin. For flying light weights this system is foolproof and satisfactory, but if heavy weights are involved trouble ensues. Sandbags can be temporarily clamped

Design for an opera by Guiseppe Galli Bibiena, 1719

Design for a stage setting by Guiseppe Galli Bibiena, 1740

Exterior scene for a New York production in 1914. Wings, borders, and backdrops such as these had become standard in almost all theatres. They were a contributing factor in the revolt against painted scenery.

PLATE 25. Painted Scenery

"St. Jerome," a 17th century painting by Salvator Rosa

Drop, probably by W. Telbin, on the Covent Garden paint frame about 1889. In this case the designer has not directly copied the painter, but he does reveal the same romantic style.

PLATE 26. Influences of the Painter upon the Scene Designer

"The Golden Bough," painting by J. M. W. Turner

Designs by W. Gordon for *A Midsummer Night's Dream.* In this case the designer frankly and honestly copied the famous painting. Unfortunately many designers were neither so skillful nor so honest.

PLATE 26 (Continued)

David Belasco's production of *The Girl of the Golden West*. Realism in every detail.

The Myrmidons by Irene Yalman, with setting by James Riley, at Yale University, 1950. Realistic but less detailed than the Belasco setting.

PLATE 27. Degrees of Realism

Vandamm

The Affairs of Anatol, setting by Jo Mielziner. Here the realism has become much more selective. Both sides and top disappear into darkness.

No More Frontier, University of Minnesota. An example of cut-down scenery using a bare minimum of realistic background.

All the King's Men, University of Minnesota. The background disappears in the black void of the space stage.

PLATE 27 (Continued)

Setting for an ideal theatr
1907. Gordon Craig.

Model of a setting for *Th
Valkyrie* by Adolphe Appia.

PLATE 28. Craig and Appia

Stylization. *The Bourgeois Gentleman*, Civic University Theatre, Syracuse University.

PLATE 29. Stylization and Expressionism

Stylization. *Cosi Fan Tutti,* State University of Iowa. Designer, Arnold Gillette.

Expressionism in light. *Captive at Large,* University of Illinois. Designer, George McKinney. Projections designed by Daniel Krempel.

PLATE 29 (Continued)

Expressionism. *L'Histoir du Soldat* (Stravinsky), University of Minnesota. Designer, Paul Frazier.

PLATE 29 (Continued)

Prelude

Act I, Scene 4

Act V, Scene 1

PLATE 30. Lee Simonson Designs for *Hamlet*. The Prologue is in pantomime with the court carousing and Hamlet brooding at one side. When the King, Queen, and their retinue exit, the first scene of the play on the parapet begins. The castle structure revolves on a turn-table. Smaller screen units for the more intimate scenes are brought on from the central arches while the lights are momentarily dimmed.

Billy Budd, University of Minnesota. Designer, Lyle Hendricks.

PLATE 31. Scenery as an Aid to Action

Billy Budd, University of California, Los Angeles. Designer, Oren Stein.

PLATE 31 (Continued)

The Birds (Aristophanes), University of Michigan. An example of constructivism. Designer, Jack Bender.

PLATE 31 (Continued)

Macbeth. Designer, Robert E. Jones.

The Marriage of Figaro, University of Michigan. Note the excellent use of screen. Designer, Robert Mellencamp.

PLATE 32. Excellent Settings Need Not Be Expensive

Dr. Faustus, Northwestern University. Note the excellent use of curtains. Designer, Herbert Philippi.

The Importance of Being Earnest, University of Minnesota. Freshman production in a studio theatre with an 8 x 15 foot proscenium opening. Total budget including properties, costumes, and scenery was $15.00.

PLATE 32 (Continued)

Affairs of State, University of Utah. Designer, Vern Adix.

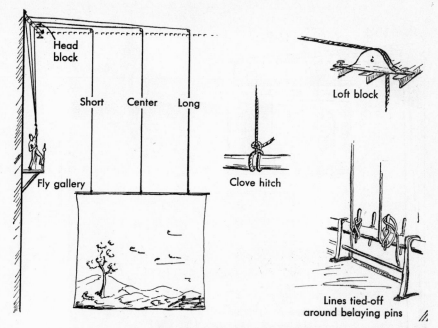

Head
block

Short   Center   Long

Loft block

Fly gallery

Clove hitch

Lines tied-off
around belaying pins

Fig. 39. Ordinary flying system.

to the lines to help counterbalance the excess weight of the scenery, but
the best solution, if available, especially for permanent equipment such as
light borders and drop curtains, is to employ a counterweight system. As
in the ordinary system, ropes or cables extend from the unit to be flown,
over their loft blocks and over their head block, but instead of tying
off on the pin rail they are clamped to a counterweight unit, which can be
weighted to balance the weight of the scenery. The trick then is to raise
and lower the counterweight, which will of course lower and raise the
scenery. This is accomplished by an endless line as shown in the diagram
(Fig. 40). Pull one side and the scenery goes up, pull the other and the
scenery comes down.

Sometimes as a part of the play's action a character like Peter Pan must
fly. There are many ways of achieving this, but perhaps the best is to employ a single well-tested line, with a well-coördinated and muscular stagehand at one end and a well-coördinated and fearless actor at the other
(Fig. 41). A piano wire painted dull black to cut down visibility stretches
from a steel ring at the rope's end to a steel harness snap that snaps into
the actor's flying belt. A good actor aided by a good stagehand can soon
learn to fly almost anywhere by employing the natural swing of the rope

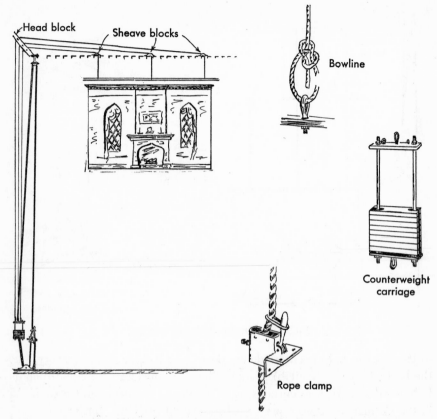

FIG. 40.   Counterweight system.

plus the momentum of the actor's take-off. Needless to say danger is involved. Equipment must be thoroughly tested to make certain the margin of safety is more than ample.

Wagon Stages

For multiple-set plays using heavy, three-dimensional elements such as properties, step units, and levels, none of the systems of shifting described thus far is very satisfactory. Either a revolving or a wagon stage is needed in such cases. The least expensive and most common are the wagons. There is no standard size; they vary from small "dollies" to huge stages the size of the entire acting area, on which complete sets, including properties and even the actors, can be rolled into place in a single action. Construction of these is not difficult. A low, sturdy platform is built and equipped with

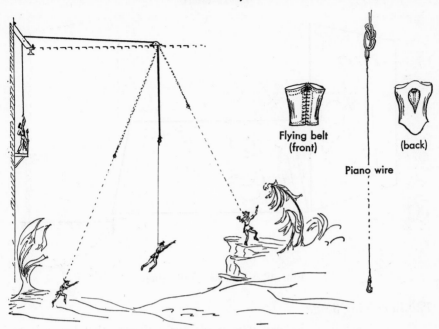

Fig. 41.   Rig for flying Peter Pan.

rugged, rubber-tired casters. One of the most reliable forms is the jackknife stage (Fig. 42), in which one corner pivots on a shaft securely anchored to the stage floor. Since this forces the wagon to travel always in the same arc, it makes possible the use of nonswivel casters that do not twist and bind against one another as do the swivel castors of the ordinary wagon. The result is that the jackknife can swing in and out both easily and accurately. Obviously its use requires moderate wing space. Jackknives can shift two large and complete sets. If additional scenes are necessary, these are handled in numerous ways. Flying is possible if there is a grid; a third wagon can be moved in from up center if the stage is deep; and sometimes changes are made on one jackknife while a scene is playing on the other.

For many plays the jackknife stage provides reliable solution to shifting problems. It is however, only one of many types of wagon stages, which, as already mentioned, come in all shapes and sizes. These wagons, together with their companions, lift jacks and tip jacks, provide the answers to many a stage problem. The modern theatre owes much to the rubber-tired, ball-bearing or roller-bearing casters that are the essential elements in all such devices.

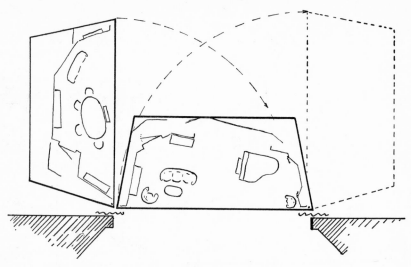

FIG. 42.   The Jack-knife stage.

The Revolving Stage

The designer or technician who works for a theatre that has a large, permanent, motor-driven revolving stage is fortunate indeed, for there are times when no other method of shifting can equal it in speed and effectiveness. With its use, it is frequently possible to design two, three, and even more sets that when properly mounted can be shifted in the space of a few seconds simply by pressing a button. On the other hand, the revolving stage has its limitations. The problem of designing sets so that the back of one becomes the front of another can become a headache. Also there is a problem of filling in down-stage corners that are missed by the arc of the revolver; and finally, there is some tendency for a revolving stage to force interior settings into angular sections that resemble pieces of pie. Fortunately, a revolving stage works well in conjunction with a flying system, with wagons, and with most other systems. In spite of its inherent limitations, it does give the designer and the technician a powerful weapon with which to attack the problem of shifting.

Many directors do not realize that it is possible to build a temporary revolving stage, especially a small one or a combination of small ones (Fig. 43) that rides on the regular stage floor. Such a stage is constructed something like a wagon except that it is round, is anchored to the stage floor by a shaft at its center, and is equipped with rigid rather than swivel

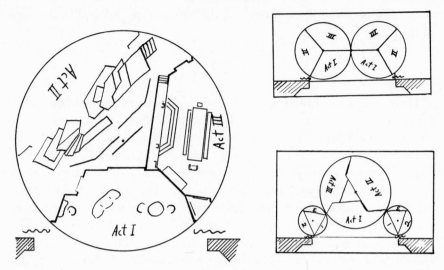

FIG. 43. Revolving stages.

casters. Such temporary stages are usually turned by hand, and since they project six inches or more above the stage floor, interfere with the use of wagons. Still, in certain instances they have rendered valuable service to the modern theatre.

Projection of Scenery

Projected scenery perhaps belongs in the discussion of lighting rather than shifting. Its use is of course limited, since it tends to work best in poetic, nonrealistic plays. There are times, however, when no other solution to the problem of changing scenery can approach the use of light. The accompanying scenes from *The Dream Play* by Strindberg should be self-explanatory (Plate 35). Two angular-shaped walls and a gray sky drop were the only tangible pieces of construction, except for the simple levels on the stage floor. Four ordinary 500-watt slide projectors were used. These were equipped with extremely short focal-length objective lenses that greatly enlarged the images. One projector was focused on the left wall, one on the right, and two on the back. The slides were made from designs that had been painted by hand and then photographed in color. With this system there was no break whatever, as one scene merged into another without even the necessity of a blackout. Such elements as mood, rhythm, and transition were sustained without the usual distraction of curtains, or noise. Actors stayed in character and the audience stayed rapt in the spell of the play.

There are many shifting methods and devices that have not been mentioned. Elevator stages, which range from Steele MacKaye's famous invention for the old Madison Square Theatre to the various platform lifts such as those employed at the Philadelphia Convention Hall, can be very useful. Certain types of scenery—unit sets, selective realism, and drapery settings —owe much of their use to the ease with which they can be shifted. All in all, enough systems have been devised so that the well-informed technician with a reasonably adequate stage should be able to find some combination that will solve his problems. Usually when shifting is slow, chaotic, and confused, the difficulty lies not so much in lack of equipment as in lack of imagination and organization. In shifting, the limitations of the human mind are the chief bottleneck.

STAGE PROPERTIES

Plays can be and frequently have been staged without lighting, make-up, scenery, or costumes, but they have almost never been staged without properties. In fact most plays cannot even be rehearsed without something to represent such items as chairs, tables, and benches, for these things are usually indispensable to the action of the actors. Wherever one finds theatre he will find props. Moreover, methods of securing them, their tendency to be realistic in style, and the techniques of handling them show slight variation down through the ages. One striking exception to this generalization is the case of the Oriental theatre, where highly symbolic properties are common. A few other exceptions may be found in certain religious and ritualistic forms of drama, but for the most part property men ever since Thespis seem to have gone their way borrowing, building, and improvising in much the same ageless pattern. Thus the passion play at Mons, 1501,[8] used "apples old and new and also cherries to hang on the trees of the earthly paradise." Also required were rabbits, lambs, fishes, birds, boats, real water, and other naturalistic items tending to outdo even Belasco's craving for authenticity. As is true today, however, not all properties could be borrowed, for the list included dragons, serpents, devils, an artificial

[8] Lee Simonson, *The Stage Is Set,* Harcourt, Brace and Company, Inc., 1932, pp. 172–193.

donkey, and other props or prop-costumes that must indeed have taxed the construction skill and ingenuity of the prop crew. Thus the story goes, even to the modern arena theatre which, managing nicely without conventional scenery, would be at a loss without properties. Even *Our Town,* while dispensing with most of the properties, could not ask the actors to sit on imaginary chairs.

In its most general sense the term "properties" is a catch-all classification. During the eighteenth and most of the nineteenth centuries it referred to just about everything on stage except scenery, actors, and costumes. Later, with the advent of electricity, lights were removed to a category of their own. Today there is a tendency for sound and musical effects likewise to break away from the property classification and either join lighting or become a division of their own, but even so the old attitude still prevails: "If it isn't anything else it's a prop."

Four general classes may be distinguished.

1. Set props (chairs, tables, rugs, etc.)—furnishings that stand on the floor.

2. Hand props (letters, guns, food, etc.)—articles used by or carried on stage by actors.

3. Trim props (paintings, tapestries, draperies, etc.)—articles used to decorate the walls of the set.

4. Effects (snow, rain, wind, thunder, breaking glass, etc.)—anything not claimed by lighting or some other department.

The above divisions are mentioned primarily to show the wide scope covered by the term properties. Such divisions should not be taken too seriously or as absolute. Extended and ridiculous arguments can develop as to whether a given article is a hand prop or a set prop. Even more common is the argument as to whether the bookshelves in Act I are scenery or properties, or whether the hat and coat in Act II are properties or costumes. The standard rule in such cases has it that if the bookcase is built into the scenery it is scenery, if not, it is a property, while the hat and coat are costumes if worn, properties if not. Even so, such divisions are frequently more academic than useful. Actually it matters not a whit to the performance whether props or scenery provide the bookshelves, or whether costumes or props provide the hat and coat, just so someone provides them. In a good noncommercial organization the stage carpenter may build both scenery and furniture, while the property man may lend a hand in painting the scenery.[9] Although such reshuffling of duties may be

[9] Such reshuffling is of course seldom possible in a union shop.

advantageous, it must be clearly understood in advance. Nothing is more amateurish than the last-minute confusion that occurs when Jones insists that the large rocks for Act III are scenery while Smith maintains that he considers them props. At the first general meeting all such questions of responsibility should be pleasantly but firmly fixed, even if it means flipping a coin.

In the process of rehearsal, set props—or rather their substitutes—come first, for chairs, table, tree stumps, and benches are necessary as soon as blocking rehearsals begin. Hand props come next, usually being introduced as soon as the actors free themselves from their scripts. Trim props and effects ordinarily make their appearance at the time of the first dress rehearsal.

Needless to say, the selection, gathering, construction, care, and return of properties are of great importance to any theatre organization. The good prop man usually prides himself that there is nothing he cannot find or build, and if he stays in the theatre long he is apt to find his boast challenged. Everything from bloody heads to real steamboats have at one time or another found their way into prop lists.

In the nonprofessional theatre most properties are borrowed. This means that a prop man should know his town thoroughly, especially second-hand shops, florist shops, and antique shops. In this respect a large city has its advantages. Next he should take such good care of borrowed items, and return them so promptly and in such good condition that he will always be welcome to borrow again. Such courtesies as program notes and passes can also go a long way toward promoting good will. Some theatres can borrow practically anything in town, including expensive new furniture, while others can borrow practically nothing. It all depends upon the conscientiousness of the organization, especially the prop man.

If storage facilities are available, permanent organizations like community and university theatres can simplify their problem by accumulating a permanent supply of properties. Some of the more expensive pieces of furniture may be made to serve double duty by adorning offices and lobbies when not in use on stage. Wise purchase and repair of second-hand items, plus the practice of encouraging patrons to donate to the theatre antiques from their attics, can build up a gold mine for the theatre. Add to this the more permanent and useful of the gadgets that are constantly having to be constructed, and a large proportion of prop problems can be solved within the organization's own storage rooms.

In the construction of properties, the techniques employed are practically limitless. Skill as a cabinetmaker, as an upholsterer, and as an interior decorator are wonderful talents if one has them, but these barely scratch the surface. Knowledge of physics and chemistry, of zoology and botany, of almost every branch of human learning, will sooner or later prove an asset. One technique especially useful in constructing such things as statuary is the papier-maché or, better still, the Celastic process already described in the discussion of scenery. Maché patterns may be made of almost anything by first taking a plaster cast of the object, then pressing maché pulp into the greased cast and allowing it to dry there before removing. If you can afford Celastic, just follow the directions and the results will be even more satisfying.

One final word in regard to organization is necessary. Since the job is usually too much for one person, a crew is ordinarily assigned to work under the property manager. The best division of labor for a given crew will depend on the play. If shifts are complicated, one crew may be assigned to gather the props while another crew shifts and cares for them during rehearsals and performances. A cupboard or table containing hand props is usually placed backstage, and actors are required to assume responsibility for selecting and returning whatever they use. Further rules are either obvious or invalid, for each play differs, and properties differ most of all. Interest, conscientiousness, and ingenuity are the basic ingredients for success in this difficult but fascinating division.

SOUND AND MUSIC

Sound and music are frequently considered a subdivision of the property department. On the other hand, since modern sound equipment is electronic, its care and repair usually falls upon the man who is responsible for lights. Moreover, lights and sound are drawn together by the necessity of careful syncronization between the two. In other words, sound may be classified under properties, lights, or in a department of its own, according to the organizational design of the particular group.

Sound effects and mood music are as old as the theatre. From the drums of savage ritual to the sound track of a modern movie, these auditory elements have lent powerful reinforcement to the creation of atmosphere. The historical record, while far from complete, is nevertheless substantial. Thus if we once again turn to the expense account of the passion play at Mons in 1501 we find items for two large sheets of bronze and two big copper tubs that were used to make thunder. Included in the script is also the delightful production note: "Remind those who work the secrets [machinery] of the thunder barrels to do what is assigned to them by following their instruction slips and let them not forget to stop when God says: 'Cease and let tranquillity reign'. . ."[10]

Anyone who has read Shakespeare must be aware of the importance of sound and music in the Elizabethan theatre, for notes on sound make up a large percentage of the stage directions. Among them we find: "solemn music within," "soft music," "solemn and strange music," "trumpets within," "alarms, drums and trumpets," "alarms afar off, as at a sea-fight," "thunder," "a storm, thunder and lightning," and many others. Indeed, as far as sound effects and mood music are concerned, there seems to have been no radical change from the time of Shakespeare to the twentieth century. An extreme was reached in the case of melodrama, for as the name itself implies this form of drama threw great stress on music as an atmospheric element, particularly in scenes of love, pathos, or villainous and violent conflict. Such music eventually became so overused that when Antoine, Stanislavski, and other theatrical reformers appeared, they abolished it along with other elements of cheap and trashy theatrical showmanship.

Today, attitudes on the subject seem hopelessly muddled. Some theatres try to avoid musical embellishment of any kind; some accept it only when definitely called for by the script; some make greater use of it than ever before in history. The last practice is particularly true in radio, television, and motion pictures, for which elaborate scores are often composed, and where a dramatic scene played cold (without music) is the exception rather than the rule.

Some argue that good mood music helps not only the audience but also the actor. Answering those who believe that music destroys the purity of drama, they maintain that good theatre is, and always has been, a blending of numerous arts and crafts—that its effect should be judged by the integration of these arts and crafts into an effective and unified whole rather than by ruling out any one element.

On the other hand, those who object to mood music point out that it is an unnecessary embellishment, that it arouses the emotions at the expense of the intellect, and that it lowers the legitimate theatre to the level of movies, television, and radio. Still others point out that it is difficult and expensive to compose, render, and synchronize original music with each script, while if well-known standard recordings are used, the themes often

[10] Simonson, *op. cit.*, p. 177.

do not fit and are consequently distracting, or will be recognized as old familiar tunes and again prove distracting.

Enough arguments can be found on both sides to justify either use or nonuse of background music. Perhaps it is best to keep an open mind toward the controversy and be guided by the particular needs of the particular play. Certainly romantic melodrama and poetic tragedy offer more opportunity and justification for mood music than do Shaw or Ibsen.

Without becoming further involved in the controversy of mood music versus no music, we may recognize that modern electronic equipment, especially tape recorders, plus the wide selection of available recordings, of both sound effects and music, has made it possible for even a small amateur group to reinforce its plays with a reasonably effective sound background if it chooses to do so. Even if the director disapproves of mood music he cannot escape the problem of sound effects, for rain, wind, thunder, airplanes, explosions, battle noises, barking dogs, and literally hundreds of other effects are frequently called for by playwrights.

Since radio came of age, recorded sound effects have gradually improved in quality and range until they have almost pushed the old manually operated devices from both the studio and the stage. Skill in operation and split-second timing, so necessary if the sound is to reinforce mood and not distract from it, are more difficult to achieve on records and even on tape than they were when manually produced. Yet an operator with a sense of rhythm, steady nerves, and an alert awareness of the show, can soon master complicated cues. Rehearsal, skill, and timing are essential, for good sound must reinforce and not compete with the show. Both sound and music are probably best when the average member of the audience is not even consciously aware of them.

CHAPTER XII

Stage Lighting

THE GREATEST TECHNICAL ADVANTAGE THAT THE TWENTIETH-CEN-
tury theatre enjoys over those of past ages lies in its comparative
mastery of the art of stage lighting. Of all the technical crafts
that a director can employ to reinforce the work of his actors, good lighting is the most unobtrusive, flexible, and in many ways the most expressive
of the lot. With it the director not only can illuminate the stage and the
actors; he can select what he illuminates. In other words, lighting can focus
audience attention on the significant and the attractive, while quietly
ignoring the nonsignificant and the distracting. Thus on the well-lighted
stage, the actors, generally the most important element of the visual design,
tend to work in a pool of light, while the scenic background retires into
the softer shadow. Nor should the scenery itself be evenly and equally
illuminated. Even when lighting an ordinary realistic interior the more
significant elements—perhaps furnishings, fireplace, large window, and
stairway—will be highlighted, while the ceiling and upper portions of
each wall will blend into shadow. Furthermore, good lighting is not static.
It changes its focus to suit the varying action pattern of the play. In a
poetic, nonrealistic drama, such as *The Dream Play*, this change of focus
may be noticeably swift, provided that it is in harmony with the rhythm
and mood of the action. Even in the realistic play a very subtle ebb and
flow of intensity among the acting areas can be effective, although it should
never be obvious enough to call attention to itself. Thus if Grandma and
Grandpa play a scene by the fireplace down right, anyone taking the
trouble to check would discover that they are playing in the brightest area
on the stage. Then as the old folks leave, and the young lovers settle themselves on the sofa down left, a further check would discover that the focus
of the lighting had quietly shifted until the brightest area on the stage had
become the one surrounding the sofa.

But focus of attention, or selective illumination, is not the only function that lighting can perform. It can enhance if not create beauty. The golden hair of the leading lady may get the credit, although no small portion of its lustre may come from just the right touch of back lighting. A romantic setting recently brought a shower of compliments to its designer, when the element responsible was the lighting, which turned a dirty grey wall behind a huge Indian archway into an evening sky that was a transparent blend from turquoise to midnight blue. The effect in this case was completed by cross beams from two baby spots, which transformed a flat cardboard urn filled with plain dried weeds into a gorgeous display of lacy gold and green foliage. Many a setting that seems entirely satisfying and attractive under stage lights looks cheap and shabby under work lights. A group limited in funds, yet still wishing to build a reputation for attractive and high quality staging, will do well to look to its lighting. In capable hands it can work wonders.

The third and most vital contribution of lighting lies in its power to create atmosphere. In *Macbeth* our fears and anxieties for Banquo and Fleance grow deeper as the lights grow dim, leaving the murderers barely visible in heavy black shadows. The Never Never Land in *Peter Pan* lies ominous and gloomy when we first see it, for the nervous Lost Boys are without their leader, and pirates are on the prowl. Then as Tootles shoots the great white bird, The Wendy, there is a moment of rejoicing, and the sunshine obligingly sparkles forth only to fade a few seconds later as the realization grows on them that The Wendy may have been a lady. The gloom of a cloudy evening lies across the island as Peter arrives to confirm their worst fears: Wendy is dead. But the sun obligingly bursts forth again as they discover that by a miracle "She lives, The Wendy lady lives!"

The brilliance of Wilde's wit in *The Importance of Being Earnest* can be reinforced by brilliance of illumination. The Daughter's cry of anguish in *The Dream Play* can be accentuated by a stab of light from the darkness. Then, as her anguish dies into a tired sob, the light shaft disintegrates, leaving only a cold, diffused glow. Lights are the mood music of vision, and if skillfully done can achieve maximum results with a minimum of distraction.

Thus light has the power to focus attention, enhance beauty, and reinforce atmosphere. Authors of texts on the subject also point out its value in revealing form, suggesting time, suggesting place, and reproducing such naturalistic effects as clouds and sky. In the case of projected scenery, such as that used for *The Dream Play*, light provides practically the entire visual background. It is unfortunate that the tremendous potentials of good lighting are so seldom realized, for in skilled hands it becomes a sort of twentieth-century genie—dependable, responsive, willing—a servant content to enhance the work of actor, costumer, designer, and property man without demanding a spotlight for itself.

THE HISTORY OF LIGHTING

The functions and services mentioned above have been available only during the late nineteenth and twentieth centuries. Prior to this, stage lighting was almost entirely concerned with one problem: the search for sufficient illumination. Greeks, Romans, and Elizabethans generally conceded defeat as far as artificial illumination was concerned, and staged their productions under the open sky. Though some purists have accordingly argued that daylight is therefore superior to artificial light for theatrical work, there is no basis for such an assumption. On the contrary, even primitive men generally recognized the emotional effectiveness of ritual by firelight. Shadowy objects that terrify the child at night surrender their power under the full light of day. It was undoubtedly necessity rather than choice that kept the classic and the Elizabethan public theatres outdoors.

Shakespeare's plays contain numerous references to the use of light. Such directions as "Enter with torches," have led some to the assumption that artificial illumination was highly developed in his day. Recent research,[1] however, points to the conclusion that torches, tapers, and lanterns were used not for illumination but as a convention to designate time of day. Thus the entrance of servants with lighted torches was a cue that night had fallen rather than an attempt to illuminate the stage. This symbolic use of light does not necessarily hold true for indoor theatres like the Blackfriars, where artificial illumination was probably a necessity.

Wicks floating in oil and tallow candles were the principal sources of illumination during the Elizabethan period (Fig. 44), and with the addition of wax candles, continued to be standard until almost the close of the eighteenth century. They were grouped into chandeliers and later into footlights and border lights, in an effort to solve the constant need for brighter and brighter illumination. About the time of the American Revolution, oil lamps with wicks and chimneys began to replace candles (Fig. 45). A few years later, in 1803, the Lyceum Theatre in London installed gas lights.

[1] Lee Mitchell, "Shakespeare's Lighting Effects," *Speech Monographs*, Vol. XV, No. 1, 1948.

FIG. 44. Torch, floating oil wicks, tallow candle, from *Theatre Lighting, Past and Present*, through courtesy of the Ward Leonard Electric Co.

FIG. 45. Camphine burner, oil lamp with chimney, gas (open-flame), gas with incandescent mantle, from *Theatre Lighting, Past and Present*, through courtesy of the Ward Leonard Electric Co.

With this latter development the problem of illumination finally approached a solution. During the last half of the nineteenth century, long rows of gas jets in borders and foots flooded stages with light, but they also flooded both stage and auditorium with heat and fumes. Above all there was the constant fire hazard, for gas lighting was the cause of some of the worst disasters in theatre history.

Nor was gas lighting the only development of the period. The calcium or limelight (Fig. 46) made possible the first spotlights. A piece of lime was simply heated to brilliant incandescence by an oxyhydrogen flame. It emitted a clear white light of excellent quality and brilliance, but was expensive and needed constant attention.

As early as 1808 Sir Humphrey Davey had demonstrated the electric arc, but it was almost half a century before this powerful source of light began to find use in theatres. Even then it flickered, was noisy, could not be dimmed, and required much attention; but in spite of all its defects the

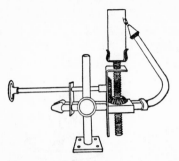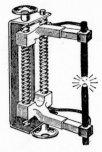

FIG. 46. Limelight, carbon electric arc, early incandescent electric lamp, from *Theatre Lighting, Past and Present,* through courtesy of the Ward Leonard Electric Co.

electric arc, especially in spotlights, made an enormous contribution. Then in 1879, the year Ibsen wrote *The Doll's House,* Thomas Edison invented the incandescent lamp. Theatres were among the first to recognize this new source of illumination. The Paris Opera led the way by installing the new system in 1880. Within a few years incandescent lights found their way into theatres all over the world. By the turn of the century they were in general use except in spotlights, where lamps with a sufficiently powerful concentrated filament were not available until shortly before World War I. Today new light sources such as neon lights are competing with incandescent lamps in homes, on streets, and in factories, but on the stage incandescents still rule supreme. Though somewhat inefficient they are safe, inexpensive, foolproof, and can be dimmed. Whether they will continue their monopoly indefinitely, however, seems at the moment to be doubtful. Fluorescent tubes can now be dimmed by both electronic dimmers and autotransformers. A new carbon arc spotlight has also appeared which is a vast improvement over its ancestors. It can be plugged into an ordinary household circuit to provide a quality of light and an efficiency that for many uses cannot be matched by any other present day instrument. Perhaps we stand at the beginning of a new era in stage illumination.

Although until the twentieth century the primary search in stage lighting was simply for brighter illumination, there have been scattered attempts to achieve other values. Both Serlio and Sabbatini experimented with lighting effects. Inigo Jones is said to have brought continental lighting to England and may have invented reflectors. In Germany Joseph Furtenbach invented footlights; David Garrick introduced them into England almost a century later. But for the most part inadequate illuminants held lighting in check until the last of the nineteenth century, when gas and electricity opened the way for stage lighting to become an art.

Among the first to sense the new possibilities were: Sir Henry Irving, whose well-lighted plays awakened much interest; Steele MacKaye, whose lighting plans and inventions were far ahead of his time; and David Belasco, MacKaye's one-time partner, whose practical business sense and executive ability enabled him to demonstrate in actual production many of the naturalistic lighting effects that MacKaye had left on paper or in the dream stage.

Belasco also developed the baby spotlight, a spotlight employing an incandescent lamp rather than a carbon arc or limelight as its larger predecessors had done. It was called a "baby" because only small wattage incandescent lamps were available at that time. It was Belasco who brought stage lighting into the consciousness of the theatrical world with scenes like his naturalistic sunset over the Sierra Nevadas in *The Girl of the Golden West*, and especially with his reproduction of a Japanese night, sunset to sunrise, in *Madame Butterfly*, where actors stood motionless while music and light held the stage. "Lights are to drama what music is to the lyrics of a song," he wrote. "No other factor that enters into a play is so effective in conveying its moods and feeling."[2]

But in spite of Belasco's great contributions, he is overshadowed in the history of lighting by Adolphe Appia, who by the close of the nineteenth century wrote about the potential contributions of light with an insight and vision that were half a century ahead of his time. He was the first to protest in clear terms against the flat, even illumination that comes from the overuse of footlights and borderlights. Appia named this diffused, uninteresting light "general illumination," but pointed out that artistic stage lighting could be achieved only through "specific illumination," the type of light produced by spotlights and hence subject to control—light that could be localized, emotional, form-revealing (Plate 36). Lee Simonson, in writing about Appia, vividly describes the difference between these two kinds of light.

Diffused light produces blank visibility, in which we recognize objects without emotion. But the light that is blocked by an object and casts shadows has a sculpturesque quality that by the vehemence of its definition, by the balance of light and shade, can carve an object before our eyes. It is capable of arousing us

[2] David Belasco, *The Theatre Through Its Stage Door*, Harper & Brothers, 1919, p. 56.

emotionally because it can so emphasize and accent forms as to give them new force and meaning. In Appia's theories, as well as in his drawings, the light that in paintings had already been called dramatic was for the first time brought into the theatre, where its dramatic values could be utilized.[3]

But Appia's awareness of the psychological potentials of light may perhaps best be realized by quoting at length from his description of the staging of a scene from *Tristan and Isolda.*

Act II: As Isolda enters she sees only two things: the burning torch set as a signal for Tristan and enveloping darkness. She does not see the castle park, the luminous distance of the night. For her it is only horrible emptiness that separates her from Tristan. Only the torch remains irrefutably just what it is: a signal separating her from the man she loves. Finally she extinguishes it. Time stands still. Time, space, the echoes of the natural world, the threatening torch—everything is wiped out. Nothing exists, for Tristan is in her arms.

How is this to be scenically realized so that the spectator, without resorting to logical reasoning, without conscious mental effort, identifies himself unreservedly with the inner meaning of these events?

At the rise of the curtain a large torch, stage center. The stage is bright enough so that one can recognize the actors clearly but not bright enough to dim the torch's flare. The forms that bound the stage are barely visible. A few barely perceptible lines indicate trees.

By degrees the eye grows accustomed to the scene. Gradually it becomes aware of the more or less distinct mass of a building adjoining the terrace. During the entire first scene Isolda and Brangane remain on this terrace, and between them and the foreground one senses a declivity but one cannot determine its precise character. When Isolda extinguishes the torch the setting is shrouded in a half-light in which the eye loses itself.

Isolda is submerged in this whispering darkness as she rushes to Tristan. During the first ecstasy of their meeting they remain on the terrace. At its climax they approach [the audience]. By almost imperceptible degrees they leave the terrace and by a barely visible flight of steps reach a sort of platform near the foreground. Then, as their desire appeases itself somewhat and only one idea unites them, as we grow more and more aware of the Death of Time, they finally reach the extreme foreground, where—we notice it for the first time—a bench awaits them. The tone of the whole secret, shadowy space surrounding them grows even more uniform; the forms of the terrace and the castle are submerged, even the different levels of the stage floor are hardly perceptible.

Whether because of the contrast of deepened darkness induced by extinguishing the torch, or perhaps because our eye has followed the path that Tristan and Isolda have just trod—however that may be, in any case we feel how softly they are cradled by every object about them. During Brangane's song the light grows still dimmer; the bodily forms of the people themselves no longer have a distinct

[3] Lee Simonson, *The Stage Is Set*, Harcourt, Brace and Company, Inc., 1932, p. 358.

Fig. 47. Old standard lighting system consisting of footlights and borderlights
and unfortunately still in general use. The one above, from *L'Illustration*, June 18,
1887, shows the then modern system at the Paris Opera.

outline. Then (page 162, first ff, of the orchestra) suddenly a pale glimmer of light strikes the right side of stage rear: King Mark and his men-at-arms break in. Slowly the cold colourless light of day increases. The eye begins to recognize the main outlines of the stage setting and its colour begins to register in all its harshness. Then as Tristan with the greatest effort at self-mastery realizes that he is after all among the living, he challenges Melot to a duel.

In the setting, cold in colour, hard as bone, only one spot is shaded from the dawning day and remains soft and shadowy, the bench at the foot of the terrace.[4]

A BASIC PLAN FOR LIGHTING THE STAGE

Any attempt to set up a standard plan for lighting the present-day stage is hazardous and difficult, for the art is still young; moreover, no two plays are entirely alike. Even the playhouses themselves show variations in architecture that force variations in lighting, particularly if we include such radical innovations as the arena stage. In fact, flexibility and adaptability are major characteristics of any good modern lighting system. This is a marked contrast to the old standard system that with but few exceptions held sway on the professional stage from before the time of Ibsen until somewhere in the twenties, and still dominates most school stages today. This old standard system (Fig. 47) is an unimaginative carry-over from the day when, in order to illuminate the acting area to a satisfactory degree of brilliance it was necessary to employ long strips of footlights and borderlights, even though these covered everything with an unselective and undramatic flood of general illumination. To make matters worse, these footlights and borderlights were ordinarily wired to an old standard switchboard, which though expensive was as inflexible and inadequate as the instruments it was meant to control. Practically every authority on lighting since Appia has condemned this old layout as obsolete, and yet unscrupulous manufacturers and salesmen still manage to install such systems in new schools and civic auditoriums. Because of this it is not unusual to see amateur craftsmen in poverty-stricken summer theatres turn out a quality of lighting that puts to shame the new local high school with its $30,000 worth of obsolete equipment.

In the better theatres of today the most essential lights are the beam spotlights. These, usually ellipsoidal in type, shine through a slot in the auditorium ceiling, their beams of light striking the downstage areas of the stage at about a 40-degree angle from the horizontal.

---

[4] *Ibid.*, pp. 362–363. Simonson is quoting from Appia's *Die Musik und die Inscenierung*, 1899, translation his own. Passage quoted by permission of Harcourt, Brace and Company, Inc.

Consider the problem of illuminating an actor or public speaker who stands downstage center. Light him from the foots; the result will be distracting distortion, for the light shoots up from below and spills on the set. Light him from the borders; only the top of the head and shoulders will be illuminated. Light him from the tormentors; only his sides will be illuminated. Light him from the balcony front; sharp shadows will appear on the set. There is only one solution: light him from above and in front, in other words, from the auditorium ceiling or "the beams." At least two spots rather than one should be used. This causes less glare, provides two-tone possibilities, and insures protection should a lamp burn out during performance. Beam lights provide the only satisfactory solution to the problem of lighting not only plays, but especially speakers and singers. Nevertheless expensive auditoriums are still being built without them. Taxpayers and students are victims of incompetence, ignorance, or a plain swindle.

As soon as one understands this basic plan for lighting a single area, it is easy to understand the following standard setup for lighting the entire stage (Fig. 48). The three downstage areas (right, center, and left) are each covered by two spots from the beams. The system is repeated for the three upstage areas except that the light for these areas comes from six spots placed immediately behind the front curtain and mounted either on a teaser batten or a light bridge. If the lights are well focused and controlled, the actor now plays in a flexible pool of light capable of becoming brighter or dimmer in any area or combination of areas desired. Action can now be followed, not by distracting follow spots, but by subtly varying the intensities of the various areas as the actor moves from one to another.

The above plan is not intended to be rigid. Many settings require less, while others employ more than the six conventional areas. Moreover, only one basic function of lighting, selective illumination, has been considered. Many of the most interesting effects depend on such items as windows, sky, firelight, shadows. Others depend on highlighting: shafts of sunlight, moonlight, or frankly theatrical backlighting and crosslighting, that cut form and sparkle into the objects on stage. These vary to suit each play and each theatre. A relative mastery of them requires study and experience, plus good taste and a keen sense of aesthetic values.

LIGHTING INSTRUMENTS

Having completed a general view of the functions, the history, and the general plan employed in lighting the stage, we may now take a closer view of the various lighting instruments commonly employed. The following

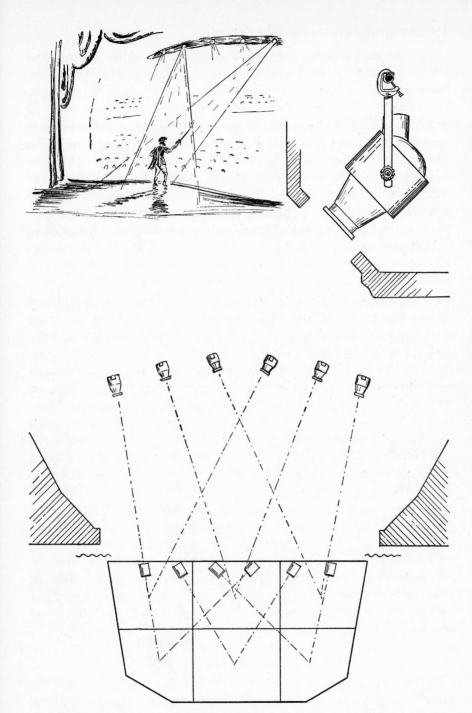

Fig. 48.   The Core of a Modern System of Lighting: beam spotlights and bridge spotlights.

discussion avoids technical language and physical principles, but this does not mean that these are unimportant. A knowledge of elementary electricity should be an absolute prerequisite before one actually begins lighting the stage. We may have too many trained engineers who know all about wiring, electrical codes, and physical theory, but are completely ignorant of the aesthetic needs of the theatre, but they are not so dangerous as the self-appointed "artists" whose aesthetic dreams literally blow fuses and sometimes create genuine fire hazards. Obviously the really qualified artist-technician will present a balance of both: the know-how, reliability, and safety of the technician, plus the aesthetic sensitivity of the artist. With this in mind let us proceed with our relatively untechnical discussion of lighting instruments.

Striplights

Footlights, borderlights, and cyclorama lights all belong to the general classification known as striplights (Fig. 49). As already mentioned, these are instruments producing what Appia called general illumination. They were the basic instruments of the old theatre, and still are overemphasized in badly designed modern theatres. Though their importance in good modern lighting has greatly diminished, striplights can still perform such

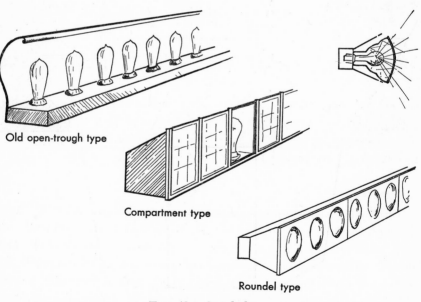

Old open-trough type

Compartment type

Roundel type

FIG. 49. Striplights.

functions as blending and toning the acting area, and are especially valuable in lighting sky cycloramas. Footlights are also useful in lighting a revival of an old-fashioned melodrama or in lighting the front curtain before an act begins. But unless the theatre has ample funds, it is folly to equip modern stages with long rows of footlights and borderlights. A few portable six-foot sections of the roundel type striplights, capable of being used wherever needed, will meet lighting requirements quite adequately and will release thousands of dollars for much more essential equipment, such as spotlights and dimmers.

Floodlights

A floodlight (Fig. 50) is simply a ventilated hood equipped with a socket for a large incandescent lamp, a frame for holding color media, and some means of mounting the instrument on the floor, the walls, or a pipe

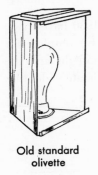

Old standard
olivette

Home-made from
5 gal. can

Modern
floodlight

FIG. 50.   Floodlights.

batten. Homemade floodlights often serve quite as well as those of the most expensive modern design. Floodlights are generally used to light backings and cycloramas, and for crosslighting. They are generally quite rugged and comparatively inexpensive.

Spotlights

The most basic instrument in the present-day theatre is the spotlight. The ordinary or standard spot (Fig. 51) dates back to the nineteenth century, when either limelight or a carbon arc provided the source of illumination. Its present form usually consists of a condensing lens mounted in a long hood, which houses an incandescent lamp with an especially concentrated filament. This lamp rides in a movable base. The hood is equipped

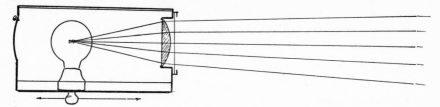

Fig. 51. The old standard plano-convex spotlight.

with a yoke for mounting, and grooves to receive color media; it is well-ventilated and is blackened inside to kill undesirable reflection. The lens serves no magic purpose; it simply condenses the light into a brighter and narrower beam. The size of the beam is controlled by sliding the lamp back and forth in the housing. Ordinary spots are inefficient, transmitting to the acting area but a small percentage of the total light emitted inside the hood by the filament. Their efficiency may be increased by placing a small spherical reflector behind the lamp.

Two spotlights that have come into general use since 1930 have made ordinary spotlights (except for the inexpensive baby spots) obsolete for most purposes. These are the Fresnel or stepped-lens spotlight and the ellipsoidal spotlight. The Fresnel spot (Fig. 52) approximately doubles

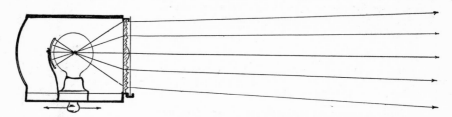

Fig. 52. The Fresnel spotlight.

the efficiency of the ordinary spot by using a stepped lens, which although of comparatively wide diameter and short focal length, still emits a good quality of light, a feat that the lens of the standard spot cannot accomplish. Optically the Fresnel lens is crude, but in a spotlight this very crudeness gives a soft edge to the beam which is usually desirable. The diagrams (Fig. 53) should assist one in understanding the increased efficiency of the Fresnel spotlight.

The ellipsoidal spotlight (Fig. 54) increases efficiency above that of either the Fresnel or the ordinary spot by reflecting rays that the others waste. An ellipsoidal reflector gathers the rays coming from the filament,

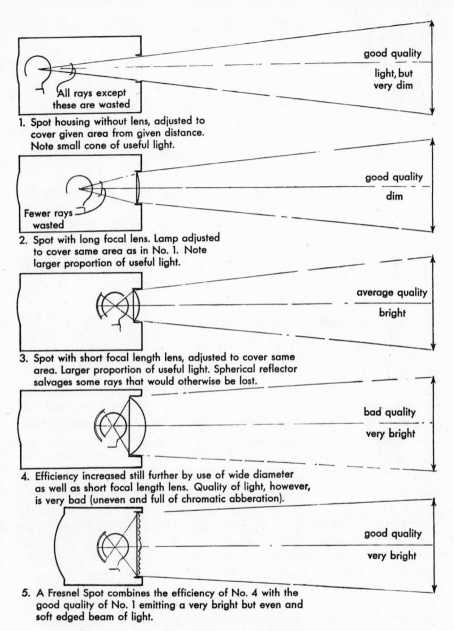

1. Spot housing without lens, adjusted to cover given area from given distance. Note small cone of useful light.

2. Spot with long focal lens. Lamp adjusted to cover same area as in No. 1. Note larger proportion of useful light.

3. Spot with short focal length lens, adjusted to cover same area. Larger proportion of useful light. Spherical reflector salvages some rays that would otherwise be lost.

4. Efficiency increased still further by use of wide diameter as well as short focal length lens. Quality of light, however, is very bad (uneven and full of chromatic abberation).

5. A Fresnel Spot combines the efficiency of No. 4 with the good quality of No. 1 emitting a very bright but even and soft edged beam of light.

FIG. 53.   Study in lens efficiency.

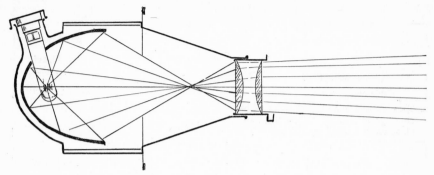

FIG. 54.   The ellipsoidal spotlight.

located at focal point 1, and returns them to focal point 2, with the important difference that as they leave focal point 2 they are all traveling *toward*
the lens. The result is as though we had a filament capable of emitting its
rays toward the lens, where they are useful rather than in all directions
where most of them are wasted.

The size and shape of the beam emitted by an ellipsoidal spotlight may
be varied by the use of an iris and/or framing shutters. Both devices de-
crease efficiency, and if used to any extent may render the ellipsoidal spot
no more efficient than its competitors.

Other developments in spotlight design are reaching the market. For
example, one new type, the Strong Trouperette Incandescent Spotlight uses
features of the Fresnel spot to collect the light from the lamp filament and
direct it through a variable focal length lens system. The result is a spot
producing a sharp-edged beam of light that can be focused into a narrow
beam without sacrificing its efficiency. The optical system of this spotlight
is similar to that of the new high intensity carbon arc spotlight described
earlier, which, although it draws only 10 amperes when plugged into the
ordinary household circuit, produces a beam of light comparable in power
to the old-style 150 ampere instrument.

Reflector and Projector Lamps

In these lights the lamp alone serves the function of a fixed-focus
spotlight. They are commonly called Birdseyes after Clarence Birdseye,
who developed the first successful model during the 1930's. They are now
manufactured by a number of companies and are available in a wide
variety of types and sizes. In general they are light, efficient, and inexpensive. The quality of their light is good, but they lack flexibility, for

the focus of a given lamp is fixed. This limitation is overcome to some extent by the wide variety of lamps available. Thus one cannot change from a wide to a narrow beam, using the same lamp, but it is possible to make the shift to a narrow beam by changing lamps. Hoods of various types are available that contain a socket to receive the lamp and a yoke or bracket of some sort to facilitate mounting. The better ones also provide for the use of color media, and a few include spill rings, which cut down the objectionable spill or light close to the lamp. These lamps have recently become available with colors fused into the glass itself.

While reflector lamps cannot duplicate stage spotlights, they are nevertheless of great value in the modern theatre, especially where economy, efficiency, and compactness are important. Even on the completely equipped stage there are functions that they can perform more effectively than any other light.

Effect Machines

Modern productions often require the projection of clouds, skylines, and other scenic forms. Two types of projectors are used. A Linnebach lantern is merely a shadow box, and a home-made one can be quite satisfactory. It projects a crude but large image from a short throw. Where detail and sharpness are required the lens projector (Fig. 55) is superior. With ordi-

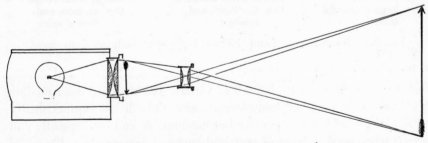

Fig. 55.   Lens projector (stereopticon).

nary lenses a long throw is necessary in order to secure a large image. However, if distortion does not matter much, an objective lens of extremely short focal length[5] can be used to increase the size of the image. Not only stationary images but also moving effects, such as drifting clouds, driving rain, rolling waves, and raging fires, can be projected in this manner. A motion picture machine can also be used to produce moving backgrounds,

[5] If a standard short focal-length objective lens is not readily available, simply add a condensing lens from a baby spotlight to the objective lens already in use.

but noise of the projector, expense of the film, and danger of a breakdown are some of its limitations.

Lamps and Accessories

As already mentioned, the source of illumination in all the above instruments is the incandescent lamp. Lamps used in stage lighting are commonly designated according to (1) type of bulb, (2) kind of base, and (3) size of base (Fig. 56). They are, of course, also rated as to wattage and voltage.

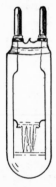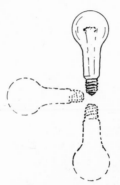

Bulb: T. (tubular)
Type of base: prong
    or bi-post
Use: large ellipsoidal
    spots

Bulb: P.S. (pear-shaped)
Type of base: screw
Size of base: standard
Use: floodlights and
    striplights

Bulb: G. (globular)
Type of base: pre-focus
Size of base: mogul
Use: ordinary and
    Fresnel spots

FIG. 56. Incandescent Lamps. Three types commonly used on stage.

Plugs, cables, and sockets used on stage are much heavier and sturdier than those of the ordinary household variety. The standard color medium is gelatine. Transpara and transolene are more durable but more expensive, while cellophane is less expensive but inflammable and consequently dangerous when used in front of powerful lamps. A new product, Cinemoid, developed in England and now available in America, appears to be of such superior quality that it is well worth the high initial cost of over a dollar per sheet. It is thick enough and stiff enough so that frames are not necessary when using it in spotlights. It is comparatively fadeproof and practically indestructible.

LIGHTING CONTROL

When one thinks of lighting control for the stage he seldom thinks of just "off" or "on" but rather in terms of graduations of intensity requiring the use of dimmers. The following are the more common types employed in dimming lights on the stage.

1. *Salt-water dimmers.* The oldest and easiest dimmer to construct in an emergency is the salt-water dimmer (Fig. 57). These are still used commercially to some extent in England and on the continent, but are seldom seen in America except in lighting laboratories or in situations of a temporary or emergency nature.

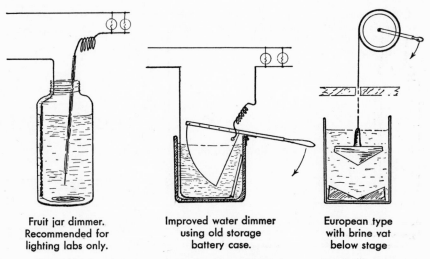

Fruit jar dimmer. Recommended for lighting labs only.

Improved water dimmer using old storage battery case.

European type with brine vat below stage

FIG. 57.   Salt water dimmers.

2. *Rheostats* (*resistance dimmers*). The most commonly used dimmer in the American theatre is the rheostat. The simple slide-bar type is easiest to understand. Resistance wire is wound around insulation (a transite bar is satisfactory), and a sliding contact varies the amount of resistance, thus dimming the light (Fig. 58). Good rheostats have many mechanical refinements, but the electrical principle remains the same in all. They are sturdy and reliable, but waste electricity and above all are limited in capacity. If a load heavier than the rated capacity of the dimmer is applied, they will overheat and burn out. If the load is too small the dimmer will not dim it to blackout; if very small it will not dim at all so far as human eyes can tell.

3. *Autotransformers.* Since about 1930 dimmers of the autotransformer type (Fig. 59) have been finding more and more use in the theatre. Not quite so rugged as rheostats, they are nonetheless smoother in operation, do not waste so much current, and have complete variable capacity. In other words a 5000-watt autotransformer will operate equally well in dimming a

1. With contact in this position all the resistance is in the circuit and the lamp is out.

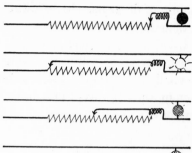

2. With contact in this position no resistance is in the circuit and lamp is bright.

3. With contact in this position half the resistance is in the circuit and lamp is dim.

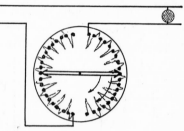

4. Round plate dimmer. Most commercial dimmers are of this type. The electrical principal is the same as in the simplified type above.

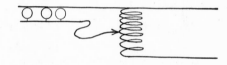

FIG. 58. Resistance dimmers (rheostats).

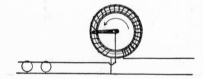

FIG. 59. Autotransformers.

load anywhere from 5 to 5000 watts. This is an enormous advantage, and autotransformers are rapidly replacing the older rheostats.

4. *Davis Dimmers.* Shortly after the close of the Second World War, Ariel Davis, working in a small shop in Provo, Utah, developed a method of operating six slide-type dimmers on a single autotransformer coil. The result was a small, portable, and relatively inexpensive controlboard. Mr. Davis is now working on models that will allow him to operate as many as forty circuits on a single core.

The advantage of all this lies not only in the promise of better control but also in the promise of economy. There is reason to hope that multiple circuit autotransformers may someday bring effective lighting control within the budgetary range of almost all theatre groups.

5. *Electronic controls.* Electronic control boards are the newest major development in the field of stage lighting. The essential element is a thyratron tube that acts as an electric valve. This valve, which regulates a

very large flow of current, is remotely controlled by regulating a very small flow of current.

CONTROL BOARDS

There are almost as many different designs in control boards as there are different theatres. They tend to be hand-made, custom-built mechanisms that cost ridiculous sums. Only a few general types will be considered here.

1. *The old standard system.* Average schools throughout the country tend to employ what is probably the worst control system of all, for the old standard type (Fig. 60) is expensive but not very useful. This system

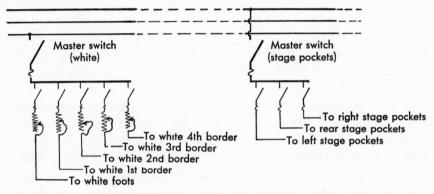

Master switch
(white)

Master switch
(stage pockets)

To right stage pockets
To rear stage pockets
To left stage pockets

To white 4th border
To white 3rd border
To white 2nd border
To white 1st border
To white foots

FIG. 60.   Permanent control.

usually contains twelve or more rheostats, but connects them permanently, one to each red, white, and blue circuit in the footlights, first border, second border, and third border, leaving no dimming control whatever for the spotlights and floodlights that should actually light most of the show! When questioned about such practices, electrical engineers responsible for the installation usually reply, with the lordly superiority that only a lighting engineer can assume, that since the control board is for a school the system must be 100% safe and foolproof. Such reasoning implies that a more modern and flexible type of board is not safe. This is simply not true. If dimmers can be provided for all the circuits, this old permanent-control system may be reasonably satisfactory, but even at best it is bulky, awkward, and expensive.

2. *The by-pass system.* For small or temporary installations that can afford only one or two dimmers, the best solution is probably to employ a by-pass system (Fig. 61), where the dimmer is plugged into any circuit that

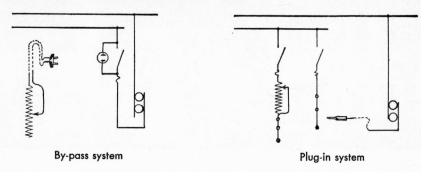

By-pass system   Plug-in system

Fig. 61.   Two simple types of flexible control.

one wishes to dim. The basic difficulty with this system is that when a dimmer is not plugged into the circuit lights can only be on at full brilliance or out. In spite of such obvious limitations, a home-made by-pass board in the hands of a gifted artist-technician can turn out lighting that would shame some of the standard systems found in American high schools.

3. *The plug-in system.* One of the simplest ways to achieve flexibility, especially in a small theatre, is to use plugs instead of permanent connections between the line and the load circuits. Each lighting instrument that needs to be dimmed can be plugged into a dimmer circuit, into an off-on circuit if it does not have to dim, or not plugged into any circuit if it is not needed for the particular play. Thus if footlights are not needed, they are simply unplugged and the dimmers released for the control of other instruments. Each circuit usually has several outlets, permitting several loads to be grouped together on a given dimmer. This is not so foolproof as permanent control, since if too many instruments are plugged into a given circuit the resulting overload may burn out the dimmer. Even students, however, can usually add. Moreover, if properly fused, the fuse should burn out before the dimmer does.

4. *Interconnecting panels, patch cords, and multiple selectors.* From an electrical standpoint these devices accomplish essentially the same thing as does the plug-in system. In other words, each permits the electrician to place a given load (spotlight, floodlight, etc.) on whichever circuit of the switchboard he chooses. They are simply mechanical improvements over the plug-in system, permitting somewhat greater flexibility in the grouping of circuits, with less clutter and confusion. The multiple-selector system that is manufactured under the trade name of Rotolector is especially neat and convenient.

Water color sketch of a setting for *Blithe Spirit*.

Ground plan of sketch for *Blithe Spirit*.

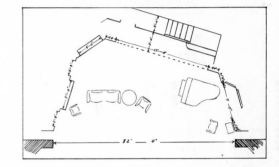

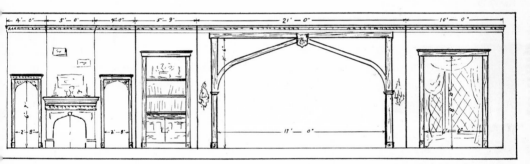

Elevation of sketch for *Blithe Spirit*.

Model of setting for *A Cry of Players*.

PLATE 33. The Designer's Plans

Vandamm

Oklahoma! 1953 production. Designs by Lemuel Ayres.

PLATE 84. The Art of Scene Painting. Still Lives

Design for *Bacchanale* by Salvador Dali.

PLATE 34 (Continued)

The Dream Play (Strindberg), University of Minnesota. The castle.

The Dream Play (Strindberg), University of Minnesota. The street.

PLATE 35. One Solution to Shifting: Projected Scenery

The Dream Play (Strindberg), University of Minnesota. The organ.

The Dream Play (Strindberg), University of Minnesota. Foulstrand.

PLATE 35 (Continued)

The Dream Play (Strindberg), University of Minnesota. The cave.

The Snows of Kilimanjaro, Yale University. Setting by Robert Thayer.

PLATE 35 (Continued)

General illumination.

Specific illumination. *Peter Pan*, Banff School of Fine Arts. Setting by John Russell.

Beam lights—basic in modern stage lighting—in action.

PLATE 36. Specific versus General Illumination

The Hasty Heart, Hopkins High School. An excellent group, but plagued by the usual high school problem—only footlights and border lights.

She Stoops to Conquer, University of Minnesota. Specific illumination by spotlights.

PLATE 36 (Continued)

Spot

Fresnel

Ellipsoidal

PLATE 37. Spotlights

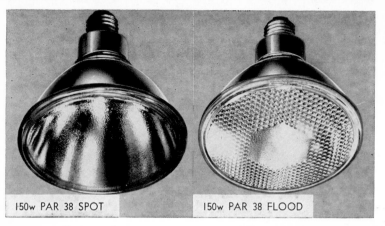

Projector lamps

Reflector lamps

Modern high intensity arc spotlight

PLATE 37 (Continued)

Lens projector for moving effects (Sciopticon).

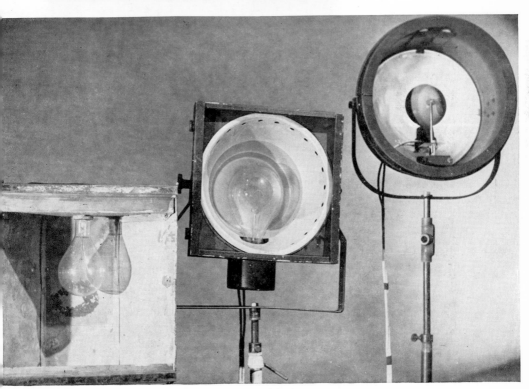

Olivette. Modern floodlight. Spot flood.

PLATE 38. Lighting Instruments and Accessories

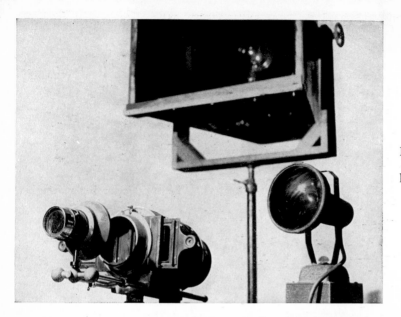

Lens projector for slide
(Steriopticon). Linneback
lantern. Ultra violet lamp

Household plug.
Slip   connector.
Stage plug.

HOUSEHOLD PLUG   SLIP CONNECTOR   STAGE PLUG

Pipe clamps.

PLATE 38 (Continued)

Preset panel at left. Operating
console at right.

THE IZENOUR ELECTRONIC
CONTROLBOARD AT YALE
UNIVERSITY

Tube bank.

PLATE 39. Autotransformers and Controlboards

Variac and Autrastat.

500w VARIAC   2000w VARIAC   5000w AUTRASTAT

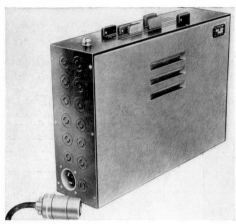

Davis dimmer.

AUTOTRANSFORMEF

The controlboard at the State Universi
of Iowa. Large reactance dimmers are r
motely controlled by the neat, compact o
erating console shown below.

One of the Davis controlboards offering
flexible, autotransformer control at a reasonable price.

PLATE 39 (Continued)

Design for *King Lear* by Norman Bel Geddes. Note the tremendously effective use of light.

Of Thee I Sing, University of Michigan.

Papa Is All, University of Minnesota.

PLATE 40. Well-Lighted Scenes

Children of the Ladybug, Yale University.

Dark of the Moon, University of Minnesota.

PLATE 40 (Continued)

5. *Remote control.* Motor-driven remote control is fairly common but is expensive and tends to limit the speed with which lights can be dimmed. As already mentioned, the ultimate in control boards is the electronic system recently developed by George Izenour at Yale University. The cost is high but the board according to present-day standards is practically perfect. The control panel itself is small and easy to operate, and the possibilities for group-fading, proportional dimming, and presetting of scenes (including dimmer readings) far exceed such features on any other type of control board.

Location of the Control Board

Today the general tendency in the better theatres is to place the control board where the stage can be seen by the operator. The back of the balcony, the front of the balcony, the back of the main floor, the orchestra pit, and the prompter's box have all been used. All these locations have advantages and disadvantages, but in general all are superior to the traditional backstage location that required the operator to run the show blindly from behind the scenery. A location anywhere except backstage requires a telephone intercommunication system, but any inconvenience that this may entail to the operator is more than offset by his freedom from backstage confusion. Moreover, if the lighting artist knows his play as he should, he will need but few cues from backstage.

COLOR

Color should be demonstrated, not written about. Its aesthetic and psychological values are second in importance only to those of light and shade. One or two constantly recurring misconceptions can be corrected by a little more understanding of the physical properties of light. To begin with, many theatre workers become overly concerned and confused through having heard that colored lights do not mix in the same way as colored pigments; the former mix by what is known as the "additive" method, the latter by the "subtractive." The idea behind these has been overemphasized, for as far as hue is concerned the two systems produce similar results. Blue pigment plus green pigment equals blue-green; blue light plus green light will likewise equal blue-green. The only difference lies in the value of the blue-green; in the case of pigment it is darker than either the blue or the green, while in the case of light it will be lighter. Thus, when a brightness of 5 foot-candles of blue is added to a surface already illuminated by 5 foot-candles of green, the result will be about

10 foot-candles of blue-green. If we work by subtraction, on the other hand (and we can use color media instead of the usual pigment) then a green gelatine (that transmits but part of the light) when placed in front of a blue gelatine (that is already transmitting but part of the light) will result in a blue-green that transmits less than either the blue or the green would transmit alone. Thus red light plus green light equals yellow, while the same hues in pigment equal brown. But brown and yellow are really the same hue; brown is simply a very dark yellow. Again, complementaries in light tend toward white (light gray), while complementaries in pigment tend toward black (dark gray). To repeat, the hues remain the same in both additive and subtractive mixtures, only the values differ.

A more practical problem grows from the fact that contrast is extremely important in color vision: a dancer in a flaming red costume might logically expect the vividness of her gown to be accented by a beam of pure red light. If she tries it she will find that the result strains the eyes, while the red of the dress will wash out to what seems to be a dirty reddish-yellow. If the stage electrician is an old-timer he will probably explain that "red kills red." As far as the human eye is concerned he is right, for when everything is red nothing seems to be very red. To catch the full brilliance of any hue, back it by contrast.

LIGHTING PRACTICE

As a practical illustration of some methods employed in actually lighting a play, let us assume that we are to light a simple realistic interior for *Papa Is All* (Plate 40). We would probably begin by setting up our six basic areas as illustrated in Fig. 48, being sure that the lights were focused high enough to catch the faces, not the feet, of the actors. We might next adjust the up right area so that at least one spotlight catches the face of anyone standing on the stairway. We might then adjust the up center area so that faces are visible as characters stand in the doorway. Our next step would be to add crosslighting and highlights, for without these the effect is flat and uninteresting. In a realistic play these highlights should be motivated by some natural source; in *Papa Is All*, moonlight, morning sunlight, afternoon sunlight, and lamplight can all be used for the purpose. As the play begins it is late afternoon. In the plan suggested in Fig. 62 a 1000-watt Fresnel spot from up left pours amber light through the translucent back window and highlights the cupboard; a 500-watt Fresnel shines through the doorway and highlights the stairway, while a third Fresnel seems to

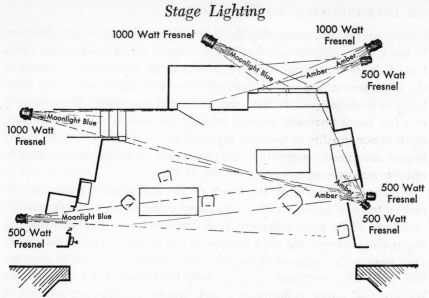

FIG. 62. Plot for side and back lighting for *Papa Is All*.

come from a window below the stove highlighting Jake, who sits at the table.

By the end of the act it is late evening. The area lights have faded except those lighting the faces of Mama and Papa. Highlights in pale green-blue, as if from a full moon, now come from up right in much the same pattern as the amber of late afternoon came from up left when the act began. As Mama slips back to the door and unbars it, the stage is dark except for the up center area, the moonlight through the back window, and a glimmer of moonlight from the window at the head of the stairway.

In Act II, scene 2, the effect of early morning is achieved by leaving the beam and bridge lights quite low and the stage in shadow except for the brilliant rays of clear morning sunlight, which now strike across the stage from up right. The same instruments as those used for moonlight in Act I can be employed by simply removing the moonlight-blue color media. The highlights should catch significant areas: perhaps the window, Mama at the stove, and Emma by the table. One trick of the trade is to set the lights for a rather striking and atmospheric picture as the curtain rises. Then, as the action begins and the actors take over, increase the general intensity of the acting areas and minimize the pictorial effect of the highlights.

Basic plans for lighting an exterior differ but little from the basic plan for lighting an interior, except that the arrangement of stage areas is likely to be much more irregular and the sky a problem of major concern. The problem of sky is not difficult to solve, provided the theatre has an excellent sky cyclorama with permanent striplights[6] at the bottom and either striplights or floodlights above. But even with such equipment, the projection of a few clouds may add interest, while if the material used to represent sky is of poor quality (a wrinkled sky drop, or a battered back wall) it may become an absolute necessity to use clouds or a projection of some kind in order to achieve any suggestion of sky at all.

In summary, lighting in the hands of the skilled artist technician can make a tremendous and aesthetically sound contribution to the theatre. To make use of its great potentials does not necessarily require expensive equipment, although the right equipment can certainly help. It does, however, require the guidance of someone who combines the artist's imagination, sensitivity, and good judgment with the technician's knowledge, reliability, and safety. Unfortunately such artist-technicians are not easy to find.

[6] Such striplights should contain circuits of red, green, and blue. By mixing these primaries in various proportions any hue is theoretically possible.

PART FOUR

Professional·Work in the Theatre

CHAPTER XIII

The Theatre as a Profession

ANY INTELLIGENT AND TALENTED STUDENTS WHO WOULD LIKE TO major in theatre resist the temptation to do so because they see in it no future. Others plunge into the program, finding it stimulating and worth-while for four years of college, only to face the eventual disillusionment of graduating into a world that has no place for them. Unemployment, always chronic in theatre, has reached proportions today that may well cause the intelligent student to consider carefully before burning his bridges and dedicating his life to the stage. Professor Hubert Heffner in an excellent article on the subject[1] points out that in 1900 the United States had over 5000 legitimate professional theatres, not counting innumerable opera houses and music halls; by 1946 he could find less than 200. On Broadway 80 theatres were in operation in 1927–28; by 1950[2] the number was 28. In 1927–28, 302 plays were produced in New York; in 1949–50 there were 60. The 1946–47 season offered jobs to fewer than 500 professional actors, yet Actor's Equity had a paid up membership of 6300 in good standing!

Costs of production have skyrocketed. In 1927–28 a popular Broadway play could be produced for about $5000; today the simplest legitimate comedy seldom costs less than $50,000, while musicals range from about $200,000 to $350,000. When one considers that approximately three-fourths of the Broadway productions fail, it is easy to understand why men with money are reluctant to invest in show business. "Any program," concludes Professor Heffner, "in theatre and drama in a college or university that is based primarily upon training for the legitimate professional theatre— professional education, that is—is unworthy of academic recognition. Stu-

[1] Hubert C. Heffner, "The Decline of the Professional Theatre In America," *The Quarterly Journal of Speech,* April, 1949, pp. 170–177.
[2] The 1949–50 figures are from Margo Jones, *Theatre-in-the-round,* Rinehart & Company, Inc., 1951, pp. 8–13.

dents enrolled in such a program are being trained for a profession that is virtually non-existant."[3]

In spite of these facts each new season finds many students quietly ignoring all advice and heading for Broadway. If one is financially independent this is not an alarming decision. A few years in New York can be a valuable and interesting experience if one does not have to worry much about living costs; besides, there is always the outside chance that one might be struck by the lightning of success. But to arrive in New York penniless is a vastly different matter. Some artists may thrive on hardship and suffering, at least in romantic novels, but hardship and suffering are more likely to be disastrous. Most good actors caught in the stress of poverty lose self-confidence, give way to desperation, and begin begging for parts. In the theatre nothing succeeds like success, and nothing fails like failure. Fear, anxiety, and shabby clothing are poison to most actors. Still, if one can afford it, it may be worth-while to spend a year in the big town making the rounds of the casting offices, seeing the plays, and meeting as many stage people as possible. While chances are hazardous, a few do manage to break in by this method.

Many try to reach Broadway by way of summer stock. A few of these summer theatres offer young actors a chance to meet established Broadway personalities; a few offer chances to work under professional directors, and to be seen by professional producers; but for the most part, summer theatre as a stepping stone to Broadway is a case of the blind leading the blind. The "professionals" with whom the apprentice is privileged to appear are frequently unemployed actors who are searching for jobs themselves. While some newcomers have managed to get a professional break through summer stock, thousands of others have spent good money for the privilege of being flunkies to actors with no more professional standing than the flunkies themselves.

The best prospect of employment for the legitimate professional actor lies in the often-expressed but seldom-realized hope for the decentralization of Broadway. One can understand why the automobile industry centers in Detroit, why the movies center in Hollywood, but there is no good reason why theatre should be limited to New York. True, a few community theatres are scattered across the land. Both Pasadena and Cleveland have playhouses with traditions of quality, success, and stability. The Barter Theatre of Virginia has a unique and enviable record as a state theatre and touring group. Hedgerow has proved that America can support at least

[3] Hubert C. Heffner, *op. cit.*, p. 175.

one permanent repertory company. The Erie Playhouse manages to maintain a company of paid actors. Perhaps the most inspiring example of all is
the success of Margo Jones and her theatre-in-the-round, at Dallas, Texas.
But in spite of these and other patterns of success,[4] the process of decentralization has been slow and the path littered with failures. Nevertheless,
if and when the best actors no longer look upon local groups as stepping
stones to Broadway or Hollywood, if and when they become content and
proud to work in Minneapolis, Memphis, Seattle, or Salt Lake City, then
legitimate theatre may again offer a reasonable future to those who are
genuinely gifted. Until that time, however, professional acting must be regarded as an utterly mad profession, one that should not be trusted unless
the actor has money, knows someone, or is at least gifted with an unquenchable sense of humor, unlimited resourcefulness, and a talent for
withstanding abuse.

The student's chances of an acting career in radio, motion picture, and
television, are not much more promising than for an acting career on the
stage. At the moment no one knows what to expect from television. Like
radio, it offers many more small jobs than does theatre, but really top acting
jobs are scarce, and a large percentage of these go to "names" from Broadway or Hollywood. As for the movies, the best way to get in through acting
ability is first to prove oneself on Broadway. Otherwise the best advice
seems to be to stay home and work with your own community or university
group. A letter from your director will probably bring a talent scout to see
you if you really have what it takes. Generally it is type, physical appeal, or
personality that Hollywood seeks rather than acting ability.

What is needed at the professional level is not the stage-struck actor
who wants to act and act and act if only someone else will provide the
theatre, the audience, the director, the technical necessities, and the salary;
what is needed is the young director-producer—the imaginative, pioneer-
ing, artist-executive who can organize and build an exciting theatre from
the materials at hand; someone with a touch of Columbus, Thespis,
Molière, or Stanislavski; someone with the courage and dreams that created
the Abbey Playhouse, the Provincetown Playhouse, and the Group Theatre.
Such a rare spirit need not be of the male sex. In fact, some of the most

---

[4] The community theatre movement, although it employs but few actors at a living
wage, has made impressive strides since World War II. For example, Mary Eva Duthie,
"The Community Theatre at Mid-Century," *Educational Theatre Journal*, March, 1951,
p. 54, reports 135 community theatres in New York State as of 1951, while Barnard
Hewitt, "Theatre U.S.A.: Actual and Potential," *Quarterly Journal of Speech*, December, 1952, p. 386, found over 80 community theatres in Illinois in 1952.

inspiring present day examples are women. It is probable that Margo Jones, Hallie Flannigan Davis, or Margaret Webster could, if they wished, move into any one of a hundred American cities and soon have the town alive with theatre consciousness. Opportunities still exist for those with the courage and ability to create them.

THE TEACHING PROFESSION

For those both talented in theatre and at the same time genuinely interested in teaching, for those who love theatre, not themselves in theatre, the prospect is excellent for finding a financially modest but nevertheless reliable and rewarding profession as a teacher. Norris Houghton warns against the danger of "teaching teachers to teach teachers to teach,"[5] but if the things taught by these teachers are sound enough, if the teachers who go into our high schools and colleges are gifted, well-trained, and thoroughly equipped to handle their jobs, they may yet succeed where professionals have failed.[6]

The American theatre might learn much by studying the pattern evolved by its rich and successful rival, American athletics. Citizens of Hibbing, Minnesota, for example, do not have to go to the University of Minnesota to see a basketball game. Their local high school plays the game well enough to catch the interest and enthusiasm of half the community. In turn, it is not necessary for students at the University of Minnesota to go to New York to see the New York Giants play football. In a good year they grow sufficiently hysterical over their own Golden Gophers.

Other arts, too, are far more decentralized than theatre. Music, for example, boasts many metropolitan centers with fine symphonies, while even our smaller towns take pride in their high school bands and orchestras. Why then must theatre, the most democratic of all the arts, be localized to a few blocks on Manhattan Island? There are some answers, of course; America's Puritan tradition has kept theatre from becoming fundamental to the life of many communities, and the competition of radio, motion pictures, and television has been too much for the legitimate theatre of poor

[5] Norris Houghton, *Advance from Broadway*, Harcourt, Brace, and Company, Inc., 1941, p. 216.

[6] *Ibid.*, p. 216. Houghton cites the hypothetical example of an English teacher who becomes head of a college department after directing two one-act plays and taking a few classes. While this may occasionally have happened, it is hardly typical. Many college directors have directed more than a hundred full-length plays for runs of a week or more to large and discriminating audiences—plays that range from Greek tragedy to modern experimental scripts. Where else would one find directors better qualified by the hard school of practical experience?

to mediocre quality. But this need not be. If high school actors will perform to their capacity as well as high school basketball players perform to theirs, they need have no fear of competition. If university theatres will produce plays with the professional skill characteristic of university football, they need no more fear being hopelessly overshadowed by Broadway than Notre Dame need worry about being overshadowed by the New York Giants. In fact, the difference between the good high school, college, and professional theatrical production should resemble in both type and degree the differences between amateurs and professionals on the athletic field. The former should excel in sincerity, enthusiasm, and originality, the latter in poise, maturity, and technical skill. From the standpoint of an audience it is hard to say which is the more enjoyable.

One exception to the analogy between theatre and athletics should be admitted. Many roles call for actors with more maturity than can ordinarily be found among high school students or even college undergraduates. While this is not such a problem in universities having a large enrollment of mature graduate students, there is a growing tendency on all levels to make limited use of alumni, faculty, community actors, and in some cases to employ professionals as guest stars. A few schools, notably Stanford, have adopted the plan of having several young professionals on campus as "artists in residence." How far such professionalization of the college theatre can go and still maintain its primary function as an educational institution is a difficult question, depending for its answer on numerous factors; but at least a limited use of mature actors, especially if they come from the staff, the community, or alumni, is not difficult to justify. The use of a few mature actors might well open the way for a host of fine plays that could hardly be done by a strictly student cast. The total educational value of a play using a cast of two mature actors and eighteen student actors, playing effectively to an audience of 2000, is certainly far greater than the educational value of a production using a cast of no mature actors and twenty students playing ineffectively to an audience of 500. School bands and orchestras that often employ a few community musicians when faced with a public concert have established a precedent that may well be cited in support of such a move. It is a wholesome development for schools to become more than classrooms, to take their places as recreational and cultural centers for community life.

Good theatre, especially if it promotes coöperation between school and community, has excellent possibilities. In fact a few progressive high school systems in towns too small to support a full-time community theatre director are experimenting with the idea of employing an outstanding teacher of theatre to teach one or two classes in dramatics, direct the high school plays, and also direct two or three plays for the community. Should enough programs of this type prove practical and successful, the American theatre might suddenly find itself developing some healthy and permanent roots, and the much-talked-of decentralization of the American theatre might be realized, to the benefit of Broadway and everyone else.

THE THEATRE IN EDUCATION

Values of theatre in an educational system have been variously analyzed, and the following summary is not intended to be absolute or complete. After all, there is but slight agreement as to the ultimate values of education or even of life itself.

Recreational Values

The sheer fun of make-believe accounts for much dramatic activity, especially at its beginning levels. Neighborhood youngsters, church groups, high school players, and college dramatic clubs find play-acting a fascinating and worthy use of leisure time. A major objective neither in life nor theatre, such play activity is healthy, harmless, and may lead to greater and more lasting values.

Cultural Values

Most of this book has been directly or indirectly concerned with the cultural values of the theatre. If the reader is not already aware that the stage can offer more than mere entertainment, there is little hope of convincing him now. We might simply remind ourselves that an impressive number of the world's greatest thinkers have expressed themselves in the dramatic form. We might also remember that the theatre appeals not only to intellectual but also to emotional and aesthetic needs of man. Life can be richer, wiser, and better because of it.

Sociological Values

In spite of agitation for rugged individualism and freedom, man does not live alone. In the modern world teamwork and coöperation are indispensable. Theatre, being a group art rather than an individual art, offers excellent training for group living. Promptness, self-control, consideration of others are essential to success. Teamwork among all concerned with the production of a play is of vital importance. In the school such teamwork should extend to other departments. No finer way has been found to breathe life into literature than through skillful and imaginative productions on the stage. But appreciation of literature is not the only value that play production may promote. Good theatre in the school can support and motivate work in music, art, history, physics, shop, business—in fact, practically every subject in the curriculum. The possibilities for coördination and coöperation between theatre and other departments of the school are limitless.

Personality Values

Though there is little objective evidence to support either claims or counterclaims regarding the effect of theatre on personality, most teachers can cite numerous instances of phenomenal personality changes in students as a result of success in a play. Success in anything may be effective, yet success on the stage seems particularly potent, probably because it involves the successful use of speech in a public and trying situation. It involves imagination and make-believe, not in the escapist realm of daydreams and reveries, but in the practical purposeful realm of art.

One common assumption that needs careful study is the belief that the personality of the character played will carry over into the life of the actor. Much of the work in creative dramatics and many exercises in the acting classroom are based on this assumption, and yet as far as memorized public performances are concerned there is some evidence to indicate that the reverse is more likely to be true. A generalization of the old stock theatre had it that the villain was always the most agreeable member of the company, the hero the biggest heel. In any event the practice of miscasting—of placing the timid boy in the rugged part, or the homely girl in the romantic lead—is almost certain to result not only in a bad play, but also in miserable failure and increased maladjustment for the players concerned. If psychiatrists agree on anything it is the desirability of facing one's defects honestly and objectively. A much better procedure than miscasting might be to cast the timid boy in the timid role. Teach him to control, exaggerate, and acknowledge his timidity. Defects thus brought under voluntary control lose most of their terror, while success before an audience may both clear the air and give confidence. This is essentially the theory and technique behind psychodrama, which has achieved striking results with certain psychiatric cases. Patients act out their most intimate fears and troubles, thus bringing these fears into the light where they can be examined, understood, and eventually controlled through objective insight.

Many other values of theatre are frequently eulogized, among them its creative nature, its promotion of tolerance, and its achievements in some of life's homely but practical skills such as painting, wiring, and broom-pushing. Its possible values are almost unlimited, provided always that it is good theatre under good direction.

It would be difficult to overemphasize the last statement, for the values of educational theatre depend largely upon those in charge. Potentials for both good and evil tend toward the extremes. The difference between the good and the bad teacher in theatre is much greater than between the good and bad teacher in most other subjects. For example, the outstanding teacher of algebra may teach most of the facts, the mediocre teacher may teach many of the facts, while even the poor teacher will teach a few of the facts. In theatre, on the other hand, an outstanding teacher may teach infinitely more than the facts, the mediocre teacher may score about zero (the good balances the harm), while the poor teacher becomes an out-and-out liability. Instead of achieving the objectives of good theatre, the poor teacher tends to destroy them; he destroys potential interest in literature, butchers personalities, and becomes a thorn in the path of coöperation and teamwork. Both the opportunities and the dangers are great. Yet in spite of this, practically no attempt has been made to safeguard the teaching of theatre. Speech clinicians and school nurses, since they hold positions where ignorance can do great harm, have long been carefully certified. Teachers of mathematics, English, and other well-established disciplines must pass a required course of study, but the general attitude, especially among high school executives, is that anyone can teach dramatics. Consequently, anyone does, and with such wretched results that all values are lost.

One serious stumbling block in the path of legitimate theatre is its tendency toward group independence and rivalry. All too often the commercial theatre is antagonistic toward the noncommercial and vice versa; colleges jibe at the high schools, and high schools berate one another. This inclination to knife rival groups is not due entirely to malice. It seems next to impossible for a cast of a given play to see another group perform the same play without coming away thoroughly and sincerely convinced that their own interpretation was superior. A different interpretation almost invariably seems, on first encounter, like the wrong interpretation. Group loyalty then steps in to magnify the delusion of superiority, and what began as a friendly exchange between groups too often ends in bitter animosity and serious damage to both.

Coupled with this misleading tendency to regard our own interpretation as the only correct one, we occasionally see a more vicious motive—a motive based on a delusion that a group can increase its own prestige by destroying the prestige of its rivals. Were the market overcrowded with outstanding legitimate theatres there might be brutal wisdom in such tactics, but the fallacy of such action lies in the fact that the rivals of almost any given theatre are not other theatres but movies, television, radio, athletics, dancing. Every legitimate theatre in the nation could be filled tonight to capacity, and yet a huge potential audience would still remain outside, waiting for other groups with sufficient enterprise and skill to enter the field. An excellent drama program in a neighboring school makes it not harder but easier to build a program in one's own. An excellent production anywhere helps legitimate theatre everywhere; while by the same token a bad production or neurotic behavior anywhere hurts legitimate theatre everywhere. Perhaps the American medical profession has carried to an extreme its policy of professional ethics, which permits no criticism of a fellow member, but a judicious application of some such ethics on the part of those in the theatrical profession might have practical and far-reaching effects. Whether we like it or not we live in a world of unions, associations, and pressure groups. In self-defense the theatre must organize or perish.

Three national organizations are now trying to do something about all this. These are The National Theatre Conference (NTC), The American Educational Theatre Association (AETA) and The American National Theatre and Academy (ANTA). Until recently the scope of NTC was the most limited. It was essentially an organization made up of eighty leaders from outstanding noncommercial (university and community) theatres. For many years it drew liberal support from the Rockefeller Foundation and was therefore able to make some significant contributions. Whether it can survive without these funds, which have now been withdrawn, remains to be seen. Its membership includes some of the best minds in the American theatre, and its officers have recently proposed a membership policy that is designed to include almost all active community groups. This seems to be a step in the right direction, for it opens the way for NTC to become the organization that speaks for community theatre in America.

In contrast to NTC, the AETA has always operated with limited funds and upon an essentially unrestricted basis as far as its membership policy is concerned. Although its Advisory Council does have the power to reject undesirable applicants, such power is seldom invoked. In general anyone sufficiently interested in educational theatre to pay the membership fee is welcome to join. From humble beginnings AETA has grown steadily in both size and power. It has an atmosphere of stability and permanence that the theatre desperately needs. It publishes the *Educational Theatre Journal* and is constantly engaged in the promotion of worth-while and vital projects: theatre architecture, children's theatre, placement service, manuscript plays, and many others. Finally, its annual convention brings together hundreds of theatre workers from all sections of the country. It is thoroughly democratic and seems likely to grow in importance.

Operating as a division of AETA is the Children's Theatre Conference, which holds its own annual convention each summer, usually on a college or university campus. From the standpoint of ideals and service this organization is outstanding. By and large its membership is made up not of individuals seeking self-advancement, but of individuals genuinely and honestly concerned with the health and welfare of two things: children and theatre. Some of the quality of this group may stem from the character of those who were instrumental in founding the organization: among them Winifred Ward, whose books and teaching have been an inspiration to thousands; Charlotte Chorpenning, America's best-known author and director of children's plays; and Sara Spencer Campbell, whose devotion to children's theatre and untiring work in play publication has done much to raise the standard of dramatic literature for young people.

Workers in children's theatre are often handicapped by insufficient training and inadequate production facilities, but from the standpoint of attitude, intelligence, and integrity they are one of the most worthy groups in the American theatre.

ANTA is the only national organization designed to include everybody: professional theatre, educational theatre, community theatre, children's theatre, and other branches that make up the complex pattern of theatre in America. It was chartered by Act of Congress in 1935, and thus enjoys a rare status that is shared only by such organizations as the Red Cross and the Boy Scouts of America. For several years ANTA's charter lay dormant. Then, following the second world war, Robert Breen and Robert Porterfield led the struggle to make it an active organization. Its ideals and principles as stated in its charter are inspiring. It recognizes that an American national theatre cannot be a single building, a single company, or a single academy, but that it must be built on a foundation that includes all geographic areas and all levels of theatrical activity. The problem of ANTA lies in the realization of these ideals. So far its activities have largely centered in New York City. One of its most notable projects to date was the purchase and operation of the ANTA Playhouse. Many hailed this project as proof that ANTA was more than a dream and a New York office. Others joined critic George Jean Nathan in wondering just what the real motives of ANTA were. Was it a national cultural force, or just another commercial producer? No matter what ANTA does, it seems to meet criticism. Counteracting the criticism that it is only a New York national theatre, ANTA has held two National Theatre Assemblies which included delegates from every region of the nation; it has also indicated a sincere interest in becoming more active outside New York. It has assisted local groups (within reason) whenever called upon to do so. Perhaps its tendency to be a New York national theatre is due to nothing but lack of energy and ideas on the part of the regions beyond Broadway. Still the problem of how to become a truly national theatre must be solved in a more satisfactory manner than at present. The relationship of ANTA to other organizations, especially AETA, is also puzzling. It will be a disaster if the two organizations end up competing for membership. If ANTA is wise it will find some way to encourage and incorporate the energy of the young and vital educational group.

But in spite of all its problems and shortcomings, ANTA does represent a much needed movement in the American theatre. It represents the most tangible chance of bringing all phases of the American theatre together in friendship and coöperation—and coöperation is something that the legitimate theatre sorely needs if it is to survive.

THEATRE AS LIBERAL EDUCATION

Thus far in this chapter theatre has been considered in its most narrow and practical sense, as a means to an end—the end of earning a living. Even with the most optimistic hopes for teaching, television, decentralization, and the revival of Broadway, justification for theatre training is difficult on the bases discussed above. Its real reason for existing, as far as higher education is concerned, rests on other less tangible but more lasting values. One of the strongest and best university theatres in the country has never turned out a great actor, designer, or playwright in the Broadway-Hollywood sense, yet the state and the university support it with staunch loyalty. The reason for its prestige may easily be surmised when one considers that in 1948 the state's governor, its senior United States senator, the mayor of one leading city, together with an overwhelming list of doctors, lawyers, and community leaders, were all former theatre students. They had not necessarily majored in theatre, but they had been prominent in college plays, had enjoyed the experience, and still testified to the theatre's value.

After concluding that training for a "professional" career in theatre is unjustifiable, Professor Heffner continues:

In differentiating himself from other animals man has invented three great instruments for giving meaning to life—religion, art, and philosophy. Religion is basically a faith held in the face of the great and fearful unknown, and its exercise involves an emotional identification. Philosophy is a deliberative and cognitive act, essentially devoid of emotion. Art, which lies midway between religion and philosophy in giving meaning to life, partakes of the emotional identification of religion and the rational explanation of philosophy.

The greatest of the arts is drama in all of its forms. Through tragedy man has explored his highest ideals and aspirations as well as his deepest sins and most profound despairs. . . . Through tragedy he had aided our understanding and hence, to a definite extent, our banishment of human fears; and through tragic pity he has widened the possibilities of human compassion, human tolerance, and human unity. Through comedy he has exhibited for our laughter and our ridicule those human deviations from the normal which, were they allowed unhampered and uncensored development, would make us less human and less potentially noble. Through comedy he has taught himself to know the ridiculous and to purge the ridiculous through laughter and satire. . . .

. . . Our academic theatres should be great conservatories of living drama as vital to our campuses and the communities they serve as are our museums and our libraries.[7]

We live in the age of science and material things. Man's rise to control of the physical world about him has been breathtaking. In matters of war and destruction, as Shaw observed, man is colossal, but in the art of living, of extracting a fullness of joy and beauty from the magnificent world about him, or of understanding and appreciating others—especially other races, creeds, or nationalities—man is scarcely as advanced as he was at the time of Aeschylus, Sophocles, and Euripides. His weapons and gadgets reveal the genius of the twentieth century, but his thinking and behavior are fettered by fears, traditions, and superstitions that belong to the Dark Ages. Science has outdistanced philosophy, art, and progressive religion. Razor blades in the hands of babies, automobiles in the hands of morons, and atomic power in the hands of twentieth-century man are instruments of potential disaster. Balance between power on one hand and the wisdom and sense of responsibility that should accompany it on the other must somehow be restored. Narrow nationalism and blind tribal loyalty lie at the core of the present danger, and art can do much to counteract these,

[7] Hubert C. Heffner, *op. cit.*, pp. 175–177.

for it is universal by nature. Men with broad liberal educations, men who among other things know Euripides, Shakespeare, Lessing, and Shaw are likely to develop the wisdom to enjoy safely, the compassion to share, and the responsibility that warrants the great material contributions of science. In short, education must strive for a restoration of the balance between science and material things on one hand and art and philosophy on the other. Good theatre is one of the paths leading toward such a goal.

In summary, the possibilities which a study of theatre offers to a beginning student are about as follows.

If you are primarily interested in a liberal education, interested less in how to make money than in how to be happy with or without it, interested in acquiring a well-balanced personality plus a touch of that rare quality known as wisdom, then you might well consider majoring in theatre. This does not guarantee results, but the opportunities for learning and experience should be second to no other course of study in the curriculum.

If, in addition to the cultural values mentioned above, you must eventually face the prospect of earning a living, the by-products of theatre training should prove valuable in almost any profession you may later choose to follow. If you feel that you must earn a living in the theatre itself the problem becomes more serious. Those who are genuinely interested in teaching and at the same time possess qualities that would make them good teachers face prospects that are favorable. Teaching, however, must not be something disagreeable that one intends to fall back on in case he fails to succeed in the professional theatre. One's interest should spring from a love of theatre and a desire to share it with young people. It should include a certain affection and respect for the whole educational environment.

If you are determined to be a professional actor, either on the stage or in one of its modern offsprings—radio, television, or motion pictures—well, good luck. If in spite of the hazards, you become the Sarah Bernhardt or David Garrick of tomorrow, all will cheer and clamor to claim some share of your glory. Second guessers and fair weather friends will cry, "I knew you could," but the decision to try rests with you alone. Blame only yourself if you gamble and fail.

Finally, if you are the director-executive type, if you have ability, work well with others, have the patience to acquire sound experience and training, have a love for the theatre—not just a secret love of personal fame—

if you have these qualities, the theatre needs you whether you need it or not. There are communities and schools the length and breadth of the country that offer opportunities to those with the initiative and imagination to go out and create opportunities.

While many students who want to go into theatre should be discouraged, others, like Richard Brinsley Sheridan, make the equally unfortunate mistake of forcing themselves to become politicians, lawyers, and doctors, whereas if they had only devoted themselves wholeheartedly to the theatre, they might have found an infinitely more rewarding life both for themselves and others. Even in the theatre there is always room at the top.

Selected Bibliography

SELECTED BIBLIOGRAPHY

SUGGESTIONS FOR FURTHER STUDY

Educational balance in the theatre is never easy to achieve. The student may become so involved in doing—acting, building scenery, directing—that he has little time for reflective thinking or study. On the other hand, he can just as easily become a bookworm, the perpetual student who spends a lifetime studying what others have said and done, or rather what others have said about what others have said and done.

Scholarship ordinarily becomes exciting only when one begins dealing with original ideas and primary source material. It is not unusual for students, after having directed plays of their own, to argue with zest and enthusiasm over a book that had seemed only dull and academic until they had faced the problems of production for themselves. Students in drama classes never fail to show interest in a play they have directed or one in which they have acted. Students of acting are always interested in the history and career of an actor or actress they have known. Crew members always relish most that portion of the setting that they helped to construct.

The next step therefore for students who have read *An Introduction to the Theatre* is probably one of gaining some first-hand experience in theatre: acting, writing, working on crews, or at least seeing some live plays.

But granting that we should learn whenever possible from our own experience, the wise student will also continue to learn from the experiences of others, and much of this is packed away in the hundreds of books that reside on library shelves. The following bibliography lists only a small proportion of the rather staggering number of books that might be included. It is admittedly a highly personal and incomplete list consisting largely of books that for one reason or another have appealed to me. Undoubtedly many excellent books have been omitted simply because in the rush of living I have never had the good fortune to make their acquaintance. Others have been omitted because they failed to impress me, which is probably a reflection on me as a reader and not upon the inherent quality of the books themselves. Still others have been omitted because they failed to fit into the outline I have tried to follow.

Many of the books below contain bibliographies far more comprehensive than the one that follows, and any student who wishes to read books about the theatre should have no difficulty in finding a supply quite sufficient to occupy his leisure time for the rest of his life.

GENERAL REFERENCE BOOKS

In addition to *The Readers Guide to Periodical Literature*, students should be familiar with *The Dramatic Index, Who's Who in the Theatre,* and other reference works, including:

Gilder, Rosamond, *A Theatre Library,* Theatre Arts, 1932. A valuable bibliography of one hundred books related to theatre.

Gilder, Rosamond and Freedley, George, *Theatre Collections in Libraries and Museums,* Theatre Arts, 1936.

Sobel, Bernard (ed.), *The Theatre Handbook and Digest of Plays,* Crown Publishers, 1940. An attempt to compile a cyclopedia of information about the theatre. Rather incomplete due to the theatre's all-inclusive nature. George Freedley's bibliography is excellent. Especially valuable is the listing of plays to be found in various anthologies.

Part One. Plays and Playwrights

A. GENERAL HISTORIES OF THE THEATRE

Cheney, Sheldon, *The Theatre: Three Thousand Years of Drama, Acting, and Stagecraft,* Longmans, Green & Co., Inc., 1929. An interesting account of all phases of theatre written in colorful though slightly Victorian manner.

Freedley, George and Reeves, John A., *A History of the Theatre,* Crown Publishers, 1941. An abundance of factual material on all phases of theatre history. Probably the most accurate and reliable of the histories.

Hughes, Glenn, *The Story of the Theatre,* Samuel French, 1928. A history that concentrates on theatre architecture, the crafts, acting, and direction rather than on the plays and playwrights.

Gassner, John, *Masters of the Drama,* Random House, 1940, 1945, 1953. A history of drama (plays and playwrights) from Aeschylus to the present day.

Gorelik, Mordecai, *New Theatres for Old,* Samuel French, 1947. A keen critical analysis of selected portions of theatrical history.

Nicoll, Allardyce, *World Drama,* Harcourt, Brace and Company, Inc. Covers the same general area as Gassner. Quotes at length from hundreds of plays.

B. HISTORIES AND CRITICAL WORKS DEALING WITH MORE SPECIFIC AREAS

Bentley, Eric, *The Playwright as Thinker,* Reynal & Hitchcock, Inc., 1946. One of the most critical and stimulating books in recent years.

Bieber, Margarete, *The History of the Greek and Roman Theatre,* Princeton University Press, 1939.

Clark, Barrett H., and Freedley, George, *A History of Modern Drama,* Appleton-Century-Crofts, Inc., 1947. A history of drama throughout Europe and the Americas from Ibsen to 1945, by twenty-two authorities in the various areas.

Houghton, Norris, *Moscow Rehearsals,* Harcourt, Brace and Company, Inc., 1936. A vivid account of Houghton's visit to theatres of the Soviet Union.

Houghton, Norris, *Advance from Broadway,* Harcourt, Brace and Company, Inc., 1941. An analysis of the American theatre as it existed in 1940 when Houghton spent a year visiting professional and nonprofessional groups from New England to California.

Parrott, Thomas Marc, *William Shakespeare, A Handbook,* C. Scribner's Sons, 1934. A brief but excellent introduction to Shakespeare and his times.

Quinn, Arthur H., *A History of the American Drama, from the Beginning to the Civil War* (Vol. 1); *A History of the American Drama from the Civil War to*

Selected Bibliography

the Present Day (Vol. 2), Harper & Brothers, 1923, 1927. Outstanding books on the history of American plays and playwrights.

Rennert, Hugo Albert, *The Spanish Stage in the Time of Lope de Vega,* Hispanic Society, 1909.

Young, Karl, *The Drama of the Medieval Church* (2 vols.), Oxford University Press, 1933.

C. ANTHOLOGIES

(For a listing of the plays contained in most of the following anthologies see Sobel, *The Theatre Handbook,* pp. 897–900.)

Brooke, C. F. Tucker and Paradise, Nathaniel B., *English Drama, 1580–1642,* D. C. Heath and Company, 1933. A collection of plays by Marlowe, Jonson, and Shakespeare's other contemporaries.

Cerf, Bennett and Cartmell, Van H. (eds.), *Sixteen Famous American Plays,* Garden City Publishing Company, Inc., 1941.

Clark, Barrett H., *World Drama* (2 vols.) D. Appleton & Company, Inc., 1933. From *Prometheus Bound* to *The Doll's House.*

Cordell, Kathryn C. and William H. (eds.), *Pulitzer Prize Plays,* Random House, 1937.

Dickinson, Thomas H., *Chief Contemporary Dramatists* (3 vols.), Houghton Mifflin Company, 1915, 1921, 1930. *Lady Windermere's Fan* to *R. U. R.*

Dickinson, Thomas H. (ed.), *Continental Plays* (2 vols.), Houghton Mifflin Company, 1935. European plays from Strindberg to 1935.

Duckworth, George E., *The Complete Roman Drama* (2 vols.), Random House, 1942.

Fitzgerald, Edward, *Six Dramas of Calderón,* George Routledge & Sons, Ltd., 1904.

Gassner, John, *A Treasury of the Theatre:* Vol. I, *From Aeschylus to Turgenev;* Vol. II, *From Henrik Ibsen to Arthur Miller,* The Dryden Press, Inc., 1950–51. Sixty-five outstanding plays from world drama.

Gassner, John (ed.), *Twenty Best Plays of the Modern American Theatre,* Crown Publishers, 1939, 1945, 1952. First series 1929–1939. Second Series 1939–1945. Third Series 1945–1950.

Landis, Paul, *Six Plays by Corneille and Racine,* Modern Library, Inc., 1931.

MacMillan, Dougald and Jones, Howard Mumford, *Plays of the Restoration and Eighteenth Century,* Henry Holt and Company, Inc., 1931. *The Siege of Rhodes* to *The School for Scandal.*

Mantle, Burns and Gassner, John, *A Treasury of the Theatre,* Simon and Schuster, Inc., 1935. Thirty-four plays, *The Agamemnon* to *Of Thee I Sing.*

Millet, Fred B. and Bentley, Gerald E., *The Play's the Thing,* D. Appleton & Company, Inc., 1936. Twenty-one plays, *Oedipus* to *The Hairy Ape.*

Oates, Whitney J. and O'Neill, Eugene Jr., *The Complete Greek Drama* (2 vols.), Random House, 1938.

Quinn, Arthur Hobson (ed.), *Representative American Plays,* Appleton-Century-Crofts, Inc., 1953. The seventh edition of this popular anthology. Plays from 1767 to the present day.

Tupper, Frederick and James W., *Representative Dramas from Dryden to Sheridan,* rev. ed., Oxford University Press, 1934.

Tucker, S. Marion, *Modern Continental Plays,* Harper & Brothers, 1929. Twenty-two examples of "modern" drama by continental playwrights.

Tucker, S. Marion, *Twenty-Five Modern Plays,* Harper & Brothers, 1931. Outstanding examples of "modern" drama.

Underhill, John Garrett, *Four Plays by Lope de Vega,* Charles Scribner's Sons, 1936.

Part Two. Acting and Directing

A. ACTING

Boleslavsky, Richard, *Acting: The First Six Lessons,* Theatre Arts, 1937. A brief, entertaining, and extremely popular introduction to the Stanislavski method.

Cole, Toby and Chinoy, Helen K., *Actors on Acting,* Crown Publishers, 1949. What the great actors themselves, from ancient Greece to present-day Broadway, have had to say about their art. An excellent contribution.

Dolman, John Jr., *The Art of Acting,* Harper & Brothers, 1949. An excellent text for students interested in understanding the art of acting as well as in the cultivation of a few of its skills.

Lees, C. Lowell, *A Primer of Acting,* Prentice-Hall, Inc., 1940. Contains excellent exercises for those using the creative approach to acting.

Stanislavski, Constantin, *An Actor Prepares,* Theatre Arts, 1936. Probably the most famous book ever written on the subject of acting. Every student of acting should read it whether he agrees with the author or not.

Stanislavski, Constantin, *Building A Character,* Theatre Arts, 1949. The other half (technical or external) of the Stanislavski method.

Stanislavsky, Constantin, *My Life in Art,* Little, Brown & Company, 1924. A fascinating autobiography that throws much light upon Stanislavski's theories of acting.

B. DIRECTING AND PLAY PRODUCTION

Capek, Karel, *How the Play is Produced,* Geoffrey Bles, Ltd., 1928. An amusing account proving that professionals also have their difficulties.

Cole, Toby and Chinoy, Helen K., *Directing the Play,* Bobbs-Merrill Company, 1953. What great directors, from Saxe-Meiningen to Elia Kazan, have had to say on the subject. An excellent contribution.

Dean, Alexander, *Fundamentals of Play Directing,* Farrar & Rinehart, Inc., 1941. A thorough and essentially objective approach to directing.

Dietrich, John E., *Play Direction,* Prentice-Hall, Inc., 1935. One of the newest and most practical books on the much discussed subject of play direction.

Dolman, John, *The Art of Play Production,* rev. ed., Harper & Brothers, 1946. An outstanding text, interestingly written, based on a sound philosophic and aesthetic foundation.

Gassner, John, *Producing the Play,* together with Barber, Philip, *The New Scene Technician's Handbook,* rev. ed., The Dryden Press, Inc., 1953. Contains 915 pages of information about various aspects of modern play production.

Heffner, Hubert C., Selden, Samuel, and Sellman, Hunton D., *Modern Theatre Practice,* F. S. Crofts & Co., 1939. One of the most widely used texts for courses in play production.

Hewitt, Barnard, Foster, J. F., and Wolle, Muriel S., *Play Production, Theory and Practice,* J. B. Lippincott Company, 1952. Another excellent text.

Selden, Samuel, *The Stage in Action,* F. S. Crofts & Co., 1939. Written in an interesting and stimulating style, finds a basis for theatre in song and dance.

Smith, Milton K., *Play Production,* rev. ed., Appleton-Century-Crofts, Inc., 1948. A careful revision of one of the oldest and best books on play production.

C. COSTUMING

Barton, Lucy, *Historic Costumes for the Stage,* Walter H. Baker Co., 1935. A standard text for classes in stage costuming.

Walkup, Fairfax Proudfit, *Dressing the Part,* F. S. Crofts & Co., 1939. A popular and interesting treatment of the subject.

D. MAKE-UP

Corson, Richard, *Stage Make-up,* F. S. Crofts & Co., 1942. A popular modern text.

Strenkovsky, Serge, *The Art of Make-up,* E. P. Dutton & Co., Inc., 1937. Perhaps the most thorough and elaborate text on the subject.

Part Three. Theatres, Artists, and Technicians

A. THEATRE ARCHITECTURE

Burris-Meyer, Harold and Cole, Edward C., *Theatres and Auditoriums,* Reinhold Publishing Corporation, 1949. An analysis of principles and problems involved in present-day theatre construction.

Nicoll, Allardyce, *The Development of the Theatre,* Harcourt, Brace and Company, Inc., 1927; also 3d ed., 1937. Outstanding as far as the general history of the technical side of the theatre is concerned.

Isaacs, Edith J. R., *Architecture for the New Theatre,* Theatre Arts, 1935. Includes articles by Simonson, Geddes, and others.

B. SCENIC DESIGN

Friederich, Willard J. and Fraser, John H., *Scenery Design for the Amateur Stage,* The Macmillan Company, 1950. A comparatively new and widely used text.

Jones, Robert E., *The Dramatic Imagination,* Duell, Sloan & Pearce, Inc., 1941. A brief but inspiring treatment of design in the theatre.

Philippi, Herbert, *Stagecraft and Scene Design,* Houghton Mifflin Company, 1953. Covers a wider area than Friederich and Fraser, including an excellent chapter on properties.

Simonson, Lee, *The Stage Is Set,* Harcourt, Brace and Company, Inc., 1932. More than a book about scenic design. Simonson displays keen critical and philosophical insight into the problems and aesthetics of the theatre as a whole.

C. THE CRAFTS

Burris-Meyer, Harold and Cole, Edward C., *Scenery for the Theatre*, Little, Brown & Company, 1938. The most comprehensive and authoritative book on the subject of scene construction.

Cornberg, S. and Gebauer, E. L., *A Stage Crew Handbook*, Harper & Brothers, 1941. A complete and practical back-stage manual arranged for easy reference.

Selden, S. and Sellman, H., *Stage Scenery and Lighting*, F. S. Crofts & Co., 1941. A standard text in classes dealing with stagecraft and stage lighting.

D. STAGE LIGHTING

Fuchs, Theodore, *Stage Lighting*, Little, Brown & Company, 1929. Needs revision but otherwise the most comprehensive text on the subject of stage lighting.

McCandless, Stanley, *A Method of Lighting the Stage*, Theatre Arts, 1932. A widely used text that describes a basic plan for area lighting in the modern theatre.

See also Selden and Sellman above.

PERIODICALS

Educational Theatre Journal. A quarterly publication of the American Educational Theatre Association, 1949 to the present. An outstanding publication for college students and teachers of theatre.

Dramatics. The official organ of the High School Thespian Society.

Theatre Arts. Published since 1916, beautifully illustrated, and commonly regarded as the outstanding semipopular magazine of the present-day theatre.

Variety. The weekly newspaper about show business.

World Theatre. Published in Paris, distributed by Theatre Arts Books.

PLAY PUBLISHERS

Walter H. Baker, 178 Tremont St., Boston, Mass.
Children's Theatre Press, Cloverlot, Anchorage, Ky.
Dramatic Publishing Company, 59 East Van Buren St., Chicago, Ill.
Dramatists Play Service, Inc., 6 East 39th St., New York, N.Y.
Samuel French, Inc., 25 West 45th St., New York, N.Y.

THEATRICAL SUPPLY HOUSES

Theatre Production Service, 1430 Broadway, New York, N.Y.
J. H. Channon, Inc., 1447–1455 West Hubbard St., Chicago, Ill.
J. R. Clancy, Inc., Syracuse, N.Y.

Lighting

Ariel Davis Mfg. Co., Provo, Utah.
Century Lighting, Inc., 521 West 43rd St., New York, N.Y.
Kliegl Bros., 321 West 50th St., New York, N.Y.

Selected Bibliography

Scene Paint

Gothic Color Company, 90 Ninth Ave., New York, N.Y.
A. Leiser and Company, 48 Horatio St., New York, N.Y.
Aljo Mfg. Company, 130 West 21st St., New York, N.Y.

Sound Effects

Gennet Records, 1600 Broadway, New York, N.Y.
Standard Radio Transcription Service, 360 North Michigan Blvd., Chicago, Ill.

Make-Up

Max Factor's Make-up Studios, Hollywood, Calif.
M. Stein Cosmetic Company, 430 Broome St., New York, N.Y.

Costumes

Brooks Costume Company, Inc., 1150 Sixth Ave., New York, N.Y.
Eaves Costume Company, Inc., 151 West 46th St., New York, N.Y.
Western Costume Company, 5335 Melrose Ave., Hollywood, Calif.

Index

INDEX

Index

Index

Index

Index

Index

Index

Index

Index

Index

Set in Linotype Caledonia
Format by Edwin H. Kaplin
Manufactured by Kingsport Press, Inc.
Published by HARPER & BROTHERS, *New York*

DATE DUE

DATE DUE			
NOV 2 6 1980			
NOV 2 1981			
JAN 1 8 1993			
MAR 3 1 1995			
OCT 1 9 1996			
GAYLORD			PRINTED IN U.S.A.